Heal Traumatic Stress NOW

Complete Recovery with Thought Field Therapy
No Open Wounds

Robert L Bray, Ph.D, LCSW, CTS, TFT-Adv

Heal Traumatic Stress NOW
Complete Recovery with Thought Field Therapy
No Open Wounds

Printed in the United States of America
~ Second Edition ~

To order additional books go to:
www.NoOpenWounds.com

Robertson Publishing
59 N. Santa Cruz Avenue, Suite B
Los Gatos, California 95030 USA
(888) 354-5957 • www.RobertsonPublishing.com

Dedication

This Book is dedicated to the women in my life who have taught me by example the meaning of living a life of integrity: Edna D Bray, my mother, Diane Takvorian, my wife, and Nazeli Cholakian, Diane's grandmother and a survivor of the Armenian genocide.

Acknowledgments

I owe a debt of gratitude, as do all those who benefit from the knowledge and wisdom offered in these pages, to those who helped bring this book into existence. It is my hope that the many people who shared their energy, time, skills, experiences, and intelligence to support this creation will be rewarded in kind.

So many individuals contributed to my learning and growing, and their influence upon me is reflected in this book. However, I unfortunately cannot acknowledge them all by name. I'd like to specially thank the many clients whose trust, patience, and sharing have taught me it is possible to survive and recovery from the worst life has to offer.

Thank you to Roger Callahan, who has been the driving force in creating new ways of healing and a deep source of knowledge and wisdom that greatly enhanced my capacity to help traumatic stress survivors.

I greatly appreciate the following people who assisted in the development of this book: Joanne Callahan, Chris Trautner, Bruce Ramsey, Caroline Sakai, Suzanne Connelly, Walter (Chip) Atkin, Marjorie Helm, Jenny Edwards, Shirley MacInnis, Ron Ringo, Polly Tyler, Neal Rudberg, Holly Colt, and Jayne Crips. I'd also like to thank my business coach, Sabrina Braham; my editor, Nina Amir; my proofreader and indexer, Laura Shelly; my cover designer, Renne Rhae; my publisher, Alicia Robertson, and my photographer, Beatrice Barraza.

Table of Contents

PART TWO: WHAT YOU NEED TO KNOW ABOUT TRAUMATIC STRESS

Chapter Four: Traumatic Stressor Events and Traumatic Stress Responses

Chapter Five: Assessing Your Traumatic Stress Responses

PART FOUR: FREQUENT CONCERNS IN TRAUMATIC STRESS RECOVERY

Basic Steps for Traumatic Stress

Step One.   As you focus on the problem, determine your Subjective Units of Distress (SUD) by rating the upset on a 1 to 10 Scale (1= no upset, 10=worst).

Step Two.   Using your fingertips tap about ten times each:

> Side of Hand,
> Under Nose,
> Beginning of Eyebrow,
> Under Eye,
> Under Arm,
> Under Collarbone,
> Little Finger,
> Under Collarbone,
> Index Finger,
> Under Collarbone.

Step Three.   Do the *9 Gamut Series*. While continuously tapping the gamut spot:

1. Close eyes
2. Open eyes
3. With your eyes look down and left
4. With your eyes look down and right
5. Whirl your eyes in a complete circle in one direction
6. Whirl your eyes in a complete circle in the other direction
7. Hum a couple bars of any tune
8. Count to five
9. Hum again.

Step Four.   Using your fingertips tap about 10 times each:

> Side of Hand,
> Under Nose,
> Beginning of Eyebrow,
> Under Eye,

Under Arm,
Under Collarbone,
Little Finger,
Under Collarbone,
Index Finger,
Under Collarbone.

Step Five.   Think about the problem in the same way again, rate your upset 1-10 as in step one.

Repeat steps Two through Five until:
Your SUD rating is a 1or 2, then go to Step Six.

Or your SUD rating stops changing then go to NEXT STEPS on page 247.

Step Six: The floor to ceiling eye roll.

While continuously tapping the gamut spot and holding your head level, roll your eyes on a vertical line from the floor to the ceiling over 6–7 seconds.

Where to Tap

Location of Tapping Points

Under Arm	On the ribcage about four inches down from the arm pit (at the bra line for women)
Collarbone	One inch down from the V of the neck and 1 inch over, either left or right
Chin	In the cleft between the chin and lower lip
Under Eye	In line with the pupil, just below the rim of the eye socket bone)
Eyebrow	Inside eyebrow (where the eyebrow begins above the bridge of the nose)
Gamut Spot	Between the knuckles of the little and ring fingers, and about 1/2 inch toward the wrist
Index Finger	Between the bed of the fingernail and the first knuckle towards the thumb
Little Finger	Between the bed of the fingernail and the first knuckle towards the thumb
Outside of Eye	About 1/2 inch from the corner of the eye, on the edge of the eye socket bone
Side of Hand	About 1 inch below the little finger
Under Nose	Midway between the bottom of the nose and the upper lip

THE CALLAHAN TECHNIQUES®

Treatment Points
© 1994 by Roger T. Callahan

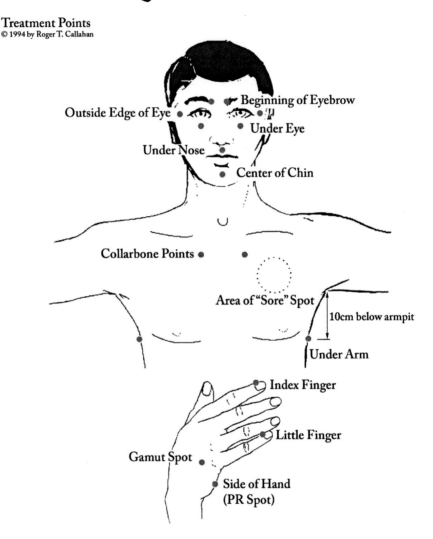

Beginning of Eyebrow

Outside Edge of Eye

Under Eye

Under Nose

Center of Chin

Collarbone Points

Area of "Sore" Spot

10cm below armpit

Under Arm

Index Finger

Little Finger

Gamut Spot

Side of Hand
(PR Spot)

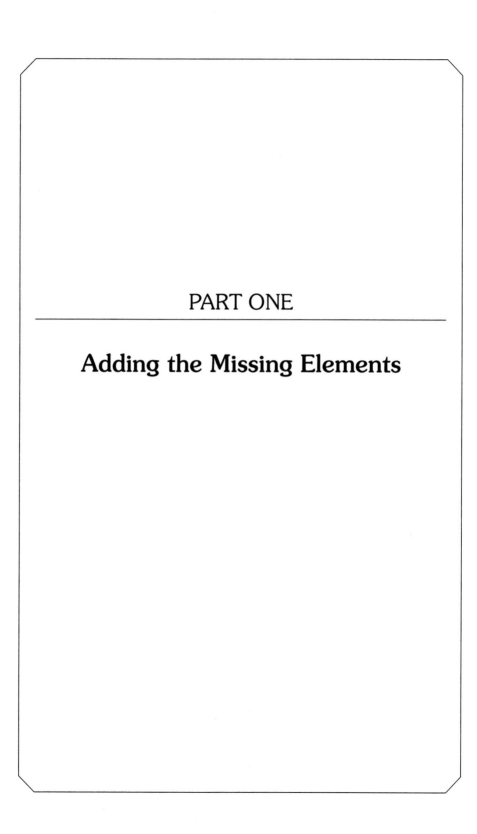

PART ONE

Adding the Missing Elements

Heal Your Wounds.
Live in Health, Love, and Joy. Live Now.

Have you ever felt horrified by something you've personally experienced? Have you ever felt helpless in a situation? Have you ever lost all hope of surviving an event or the conditions of your life? Have your feelings about what you are going through in your life ever overwhelmed your reason and will?

In fact, you may have lived through a onetime event that felt so powerful it stuck in your mind's eye as if burned there permanently. Or, you may have suffered a lifetime of violence and pain that continues to seem endless. As a result you may now find yourself dealing with a single problem like getting to sleep or overreacting to loud noises. Maybe you find yourself dealing with multiple issues, such as outbursts of anger, an inability to be in relationship, compulsive overeating or drinking, dangerous driving, picking fights, or unwanted memories that create pictures in your mind that refuse to fade. And these things make you feel you have lost control, direction, and connection in various parts of your life.

These issues, or symptoms of the trauma you've experienced, can be likened to open wounds. As with most open wounds, they require a large amount of your energy and attention until they heal. They also require energy and attention to help them heal.

Despite your open wounds and the scars you bear, you can rid yourself of the emotional suffering and overwhelming distress that has resulted from past traumatic events you have endured. By using the approaches to traumatic stress recovery presented in this book, you will discover No Open Wounds (NOW) and Thought Field Therapy (TFT). You will find this is a new way to end the pain you feel from your past and the fears you have about your future.

Picking up this book likely represents one of many times you have confronted whatever problem has arisen from your past trauma. You have probably done your homework and read more than one book on how to help resolve whatever issue currently makes your life more difficult. You may have talked to trusted friends or to total strangers as you searched for answers and solutions to why you have suffered and how to stop that suffering. You also may have spent thousands of dollars paying for professional help, which may or may not have offered you some relief. If it had offered you enough of a solution or long lasting help, however, you wouldn't be reading this book.

The biggest problems that psychotherapists, other mental health professionals, and other helpers deal with *have nothing to do with us as human beings knowing what is right or healthy.* Rather these impasses for which we seek help involve our inability to act in accordance with commonsense and that deeper inner guidance we all possess. Most of us know the right thing to do from the wrong thing. Most of us recognize the healthy desires that live within us. Many of us can't, however, prevent the overwhelming emotional upset and loss of strength that can arise in the present making it difficult for us to make good, healthy choices.

The reason for this is simple: The past traumatic events we have suffered can affect us in the present moment. In other words, most of our current emotional upset comes not from what is happening now but what has happened in the past. The memory of that upset or the fear of that upset returning sometimes can be just as powerful in the current moment as it was when it actually occurred; thus, it can stop us in our tracks as we try to make positive change. The anxiety or depression that takes our strength and leaves us unable to do what we know needs to be done prevents us from moving forward. Thought Field Therapy will eliminate that overwhelming emotional upset and restore your strength so you can do what you know is right for you. The NOW recovery processes lead you to feel safe in this moment, understand what happened to you, and move forward into the future with more choices.

I am by professional training a social worker, family therapist, traumatic stress recovery specialist, and an expert in Callahan Techniques® Thought Field Therapy. I am comfortable and effective in helping with individual, couples, family, and group psychotherapy. Since taking my first crisis intervention hotline call over 35 years ago, I have spent time with thousands of people. I have helped individuals survive and recover from child abuse in all forms. I have dealt with the death of a child, the unexpected death of a parent, automobile crashes, industrial accidents, criminal sexual assault, murder attempts, murder of a child or other loved one, school shootings, natural disasters of all types, terrorist attacks, military combat, the experience of war, political torture, and many other forms of traumatic stress. The knowledge shared here represents the result of those years of professional work and the experiences I gained in how people effectively heal and create change in their lives.

The wonder of my work lies in the fact that every interaction has given to me far more than I have offered in time and effort. Each time I connect with a person, I learn something about myself, how to help, and the amazing range of feeling and sensations available in life. And each relationship with a client feeds me hope and love. This book passes that hope and love to you.

Since I specialize in traumatic stress recovery, in this book I tell you many stories about how people live beyond terrible events in their lives as well as what happens when people become trapped by these traumatic events. Stories are printed in italics and are ended with this symbol ⌒⌒⌒⌒. My personal calling lies in helping people break free of these trapped states. I am *not* trying to focus on terrifying first-person accounts of horrific events resulting in death, destruction, torture, or unending pain. If you picked up this book, more than likely you have experienced enough scary stuff in your life already. For this reason, the stories I tell only include descriptions complete enough to help you identify with the people in them and find some hope in their successes. That said, you must judge what you can handle. Regardless of my intent, if the stories feel too overwhelming for you, skip them and start "tapping," or using Thought Field Therapy, to take care of yourself. I've included simple instructions for the process at the beginning of the book for just this purpose.

Using this Book

I've organized this book so you can use it in a variety of ways. Those of you who enjoy reading a book from start to finish before beginning to use the tools within it, can do so. However, those of you who have a "let's get to it mentality" or are hurting greatly and want to focus on a specific problem and get relief immediately can go to the table of contents or index and find tools to help you.

The book is divided into five parts. Each part by itself provides you with ways to think about and use Thought Field Therapy. Regardless of the where you are in the NOW recovery process, tapping offers a tool that allows you to examine your history and current situation in a calm and relaxed manner as you decide upon and take your next action step.

Part One includes this introduction and three chapters. It provides you with an overview of the approach taught in the book, gets you started using Thought Field Therapy, and helps you get comfortable with doing the work.

Part Two contains all you need to know about traumatic stress — its definitions, causes, effects, normal responses, and ways to determine how big a problem you have. These two chapters are full of examples and ideas about focusing on the important issues surrounding traumatic stress and using Thought Field Therapy to help you heal your traumatic stress experiences and your responses to those experiences.

Part Three offers a full explanation of the NOW model for recovery from traumatic stress. It details the process itself, what to expect, how it varies for different people with different histories, and how to know when you have fully recovered. The first chapter in this part gets you through disturbing symptoms, allowing you to move on to the next chapter, where you review and gain understanding of your past trauma. The last chapter helps you use that knowledge, understanding, and experience to get on with your changed life.

Part Four has three chapters on the issues that most often need to be addressed as part of the complete recovery process. You may have none of these issues or you may be affected by all of them: 1) traumatic grief and loss; 2) out of control behaviors, addictions, or bad habits used to cope with traumatic stress; and 3) ongoing effects of childhood violence in adult recovery.

Part Five focuses totally on Thought Field Therapy — the concepts, the tools, the procedures, and the ways to get the most out of the approach.

Whichever way you choose to read this book, you'll find you can quickly and easily begin using the approaches and tools offered. The reason for this is simple: Thought Field Therapy only requires that you follow the procedures. To benefit from it, you don't need to understand how it works or believe in its power. And you don't need to worry about doing the process correctly. Since Thought Field Therapy will not cause harm to you even if you do it incorrectly; either it works or it does nothing. Follow the steps offered and you'll either find your conditions improved or not. More than likely, however, you'll feel better.

Additionally, when you are in a state of overwhelming emotional upset, it becomes difficult to read or to learn. So, if you feel too upset to understand what you are reading, skip ahead, learn how to do Thought Field Therapy, and try doing the process on yourself. Afterwards, you'll find it easier to read the rest of the book. You will discover you are comprehending and understanding the material presented, because you will be calmer and your mind will be clearer. Plus, by beginning to practice using Thought Field Therapy, you will have undertaken the first part of the complete recovery process presented.

For some of you, this book will be the only one you ever read or need to read to live your life fully now. For some, this book will provide the missing information and skills that allow you to implement approaches offered in other books you've read. Once you learn the safe and easy way to overcome your past pains and future fears that is offered by Thought Field Therapy and the NOW process, you may find yourself reading many more books on your journey of self-development and self-help. Thought Field Therapy complements any other human potential methodology or tools you come across in books, workshops, or seminars.

Know, however, that the material presented here just scratches the surface of the body of knowledge and skills that can help you. If you do not get better from what you learn in this book, do not give up. Seeing no improvement or continuing to struggle with the effects of past trauma only means you need more or different help. Please, realize that you can be helped. If you need or want more resources, you can find suggestions for professional help, further reading, and research references at the end of this book.

You come to this place and time with a set of experiences that are yours and yours alone. Whatever else you learn from this book, I hope you learn to be kind and patient with yourself and to keep moving forward on your life's journey to more health, love, and joy. I hope you will find a way to heal the open wounds that keep you feeling the pain of the past so you can truly live in this present moment.

CHAPTER ONE

The Missing Ingredients Necessary for Healing Traumatic Stress

Staying on Task with Thought Field Therapy

The day began well. While the trolley to work had been more crowded than usual, I relaxed on the ride and read my book. Although work had been extremely busy for a long time, when I arrived in my office and sat down at my desk, focusing on the task in front of me generated a sense of confidence and pleasure within me and set a mood I liked.

Just as I had settled in and begun concentrating, I heard a very loud bang. I pushed my chair back from the desk and desperately scanned the room for a safe place to hide. Without any thought, I lifted myself out of my seat and pulled myself down under the desk. I crouched there, trembling and bracing for might follow..

After an uneventful moment or two, I peeked out from my hiding place and realized for the first time since I'd heard the loud noise that I was in my office. For the last few minutes, I had thought I was somewhere else. Looking around, I could see that nobody else had looked for cover. As I thought about what I had heard, I realized that the crashing sound most likely had come from the office next door. While it had been extremely loud, it simply indicated the continuing remodel that had started a few days ago, nothing else unusual or, more importantly, dangerous.

Despite this knowledge, my heart continued to pound a million beats per minute. I was perspiring profusely, and I remained trained on every sound, movement, and vibration in my office. As I climbed back into my chair, I could not begin to remember what I had been working on or how to get back on task. "Oh God, I hate feeling like this," I thought.

Then, I remembered that I could help myself, change how I was feeling, and get back to work and to "normal" by using a process I had learned, called Thought Field Therapy. Tapping with my fingertips a few times on the side of my hand, under my nose, at the beginning of my eyebrow, under my eye, under my arm, under one of my collarbones, on the tip of my index finger, on the tip of my little finger, and under my collarbone again, I felt myself calm down a bit. Knowing that I could make myself feel better always reassured me. I knew I was better, because I rated my level of upset and on a 1-10 rating scale it dropped from a 9 to about a 5. I wanted to get to level 1.

So, I went on continuously tapping the back of my hand about one half an inch towards my wrist from a point between my ring finger and my little finger. As I did so, I closed my eyes for a moment, opened my eyes, looked down to the left and to the right, then, while continuing to tap, hummed a couple of bars of a favorite song, counted to five, and hummed again. I tapped the same points I had started with again, beginning with the side of my hand. When I finished, miraculously I was back to my normal self. My heart had stopped pounding, I was no longer sweating, I was able to focus, and my sense of being present in that moment in my office had returned. My upset was gone. I no longer felt the need to stay aware of every detail of every sound, movement, and vibration.

As I reoriented to my work, I stopped for a moment to think about what had just happened. In the past, I had experienced a time when loud banging sounds did mean danger and there was nothing I or anyone else could do to stop the destruction and pain that would follow. After living though it, I had reacted many times to loud sounds instinctively. But it had been quite awhile since I had been triggered like today. I used to get set off in a similar manner by lots of things that happened around me or by people's actions. After I learned to use the tapping technique of Thought Field Therapy to eliminate the upset from my past trauma, I possessed a way to calm myself down and to relax when sound, sights, people's actions, or even seemingly nothing at all reminded me of past traumatic events and set me off. And this had allowed me to get back to work and to family and friend in an important and meaningful way. Over time, the tapping had decreased the occurrences of upset and their intensity when incidents like this one today occurred.

As I went back to work I decided I would give what happened today some more thought and talk it over with someone later. Taking action and not just waiting to get better has served me well since learning the NOW recovery model. Maybe I could figure out what triggered the upset this time. Maybe it was the stress of the last few days, a recent interaction with someone, or something else that had made me open to that sudden over reaction that I had not experienced for such a long time. One thing was clear to me: While tapping had helped heal the open wounds I had from my past traumatic events, I was still in the process of healing. I also felt certain tapping and the NOW processes would help me heal those wounds completely over time.

❧

Have you had a traumatic experience that left you feeling wounded? Do you feel as if that wound remains open, sore, and vulnerable? Do certain people, actions, noises, smells, subjects, make the wound more painful, thus sending you running in another direction, reacting in ways that seem irrational, or behaving in an unusual manner? Do you find yourself obsessed with the past or with the future? Do you have difficulty eating, sleeping, having loving relationships, working, concentrating, losing or gaining weight, quitting drinking or smoking or doing drugs? Is it difficult for you to live in this present moment fully and happily?

Your quest to live in a more fulfilling and joyful manner and to heal your wounds has led you to this book. No doubt, the experiences that fill or have filled your life contain pain and fear. One event or series of events in the course of your life may represent the source of the pain, symptoms, and fear that have stopped you from living fully. On some level or in some way, you have experienced what are called *traumatic stressors.* Maybe you were the victim of childhood physical or sexual abuse. Or maybe you found yourself in the middle of a school shooting or a terrorist attack. Possibly you are haunted by what happened to you while you were serving in the military. Maybe someone you loved died suddenly or violently, you were the victim of a car crash, or you accidentally killed someone.

It matters little what kind of traumatic event you experienced. All traumatic stressor events can leave open wounds that need to be healed. And open wounds affect how you live.

In this book you'll find what you are looking for: a fast, effective way to heal your open wounds, thus ending the pain and resolving other symptoms and fears. You also will find a way of making sense of your experience and life, which will let you find and make choices that allow you to live more fully, more connected to love, and with more purpose in the current moment—the *now.* As you continue the journey of your life, your past traumatic experiences need not cause you overwhelming upset or disruption any longer.

NOW and Thought Field Therapy

If you have been on the path of traumatic stress recovery or self improvement in any way, shape, or form, you know that many books and processes claim to offer the answer to your problems. You may be wondering how this book and the help offered within its pages differs or why it might prove more effective. While other books help you manage the pain and fear that limit your life, reading this book will put an *end* to that pain and fear. Additionally, it will teach you to use your experiences from the past to make choices uniquely fitted to your values and beliefs. Thought Field Therapy and the NOW traumatic stress recovery model, the two approaches and their specific tools presented in this book, embody the missing ingredients necessary for full traumatic stress recovery as well as for most self improvement methods to work completely. You can use them in conjunction with any other methods you have learned and liked, and you will find those methods becoming more effective and your success rate when using them increasing dramatically. Your desires to change your life are fulfilled more completely and quickly by including Thought Field Therapy and the NOW recovery process in your bag of self improvement tools.

Many self-help authors and teachers recommend *being in the now.* As such, *now* has become somewhat of a self-help buzzword today. When it comes to traumatic stress recovery, however, being in the now serves as an important aspect of creating change. So, it is important to know the meaning of this phrase and of the word itself. The word *now* as used in the self-help and self-improvement realm means staying *in the current moment.* In other words, *being in the now* refers to experiencing life without distortions created by your past and without negative anticipation of the future. However, getting into present-moment awareness can prove difficult, if not impossible, if you are caught up in pain from past events and anxiety about future actions. To *be in the now,* you must let go of the overwhelming feelings that hold you in the past and keep you from moving into your desired future. And, you must stop worrying about the future and imagining what it might be like based on your past, because those thoughts and visions stop you from enjoying your current moment.

In this book, the word *now* is used not only to indicate present-moment awareness but also serves as an acronym for two critical concepts that will help you achieve all the wonderful results promised in the self-help and self-development books available today. Let's take a look at those acronyms so you understand their use and their importance in the recovery and change process and in your ability to live your life fully.

First, to create change and to live fully in the present moment you must *not* be held in the past by the unhealed aspects of what has happen to you previously. You must heal the open wounds created by your past traumatic experiences. Thus, NOW stands for the primary objective of this book:

No
Open
Wounds

In conjunction with this concept, this book will teach you how to move forward safely in your life despite your past traumas and to heal your open wounds that were created by past traumatic events. So, when you see the word NOW, remind yourself to tend to any type of un-healed wounds left by past traumatic experiences or any wounds that leave you open to further hurt and damage.

Second, in this book the word NOW also stands for the action pro-cesses of traumatic stress recovery that give you the ability to change your life. NOW represents the three categories of action necessary for full recovery from past traumatic stress events:

Navigate the common symptoms of traumatic stress that stop you.

Observe and understand what has happened to you.

Work your life choices with integrity.

By taking these action steps, you stop reacting to symptoms created by your traumatic experiences and, instead, begin making conscious choices and taking positive steps forward. Moving through these cat-egories helps you close open wounds, understand what has happened to you in the past, make sense out of your life, and create the change you desire.

Navigating through the symptoms associated with open wounds represents a necessary first step to recovery, since the overwhelming bodily sensations and emotions related to what has happened to you in the past can impair your day-to-day living. This impairment can interfere with your ability to perceive, think, or behave in accordance with your nature. Instead of behaving in ways you know are correct or in ways you know you should, you react to overwhelming feelings in what appears to be an irrational manner. You also can suddenly shut down completely in mind or body. Or you can become impaired by your efforts to avoid reminders of the source of your wounds. The story that begins this chapter provides a wonderful example of some-one reacting to past trauma in some of these ways.

Using the NOW process, you first learn to use Thought Field Therapy to end the overwhelming distress that keeps you stuck. In fact,

Thought Field Therapy serves as the most important ingredient in your mix of traumatic recovery plans, programs, approaches, strategies, and action steps. This quick, self-applied, noninvasive, non-drug, safe technique, which was described as "tapping" in the story that opens this chapter, allows your wounds to heal and gives you a tool to use whenever old, reactive, and emotional patterns arise. Open wounds leave you vulnerable and with ongoing pain that impairs how you function. Open wounds also draw you back to the past, because their pain serves as a reminder of your past traumatic experiences. Thought Field Therapy closes those wounds and stops the pain associated with past traumas, thus allowing you to function effectively, to simplify your life, and to move forward rather than remaining stuck in the past.

Thought Field Therapy involves tapping in a specific sequence with your fingertips on meridian points on the body. Drawing on Chinese medicine's more than 6,000 years of theory and practice, Thought Field Therapy uses the same meridian treatment points as used in acupuncture. More than half the world's population uses acupuncture as the primary health care method, but Thought Field Therapy does not use needles, nor is it acupuncture either in theory or in practice. However, by stimulating these meridian points with five or six taps at each location in a specific sequence as you focus on your upset, change happens and healing occurs. As you saw in the example, the process includes a few other steps, but Thought Field Therapy can be completed in minutes and has lasting results.

Once you have "tapped" and the overwhelming upset is gone, you can move forward to the next steps of complete recovery — the NOW process. Thought Field Therapy helps stop the symptoms caused by traumatic experiences from controlling you and your life. This allows you to begin reviewing what happened to you. With a calm mind and relaxed body, you can observe the past in a useful way and come to some understanding of the events and their meaning in your life. Then, you can begin to actively engage in making choices about what you will do next. To move away from reacting to out of control symptoms and towards consciously making choices in you life requires tapping and asking yourself questions that only you can answer. Your efforts to find the answers that fit your history and identity serve as your active involvement in the process, and this allows you to make the best choices regarding the health, love, and joy you want in your life. Regardless of the source of your pain, you can become better, navigate through symptoms, observe and understand what has happened to you, and live your life with integrity. Integrity means living in an unimpaired condition or in a state of being complete.

Using Thought Field Therapy in Traumatic Stress Recovery

This book presents many ways to use and understand Thought Field Therapy, as well as many real-life examples and stories of how this process has helped people make progress in their lives. You can "tap" any time your negative feelings and sensations interfere with your thoughts, actions, or positive experience in the moment. You do not have to spend time preparing for or recovering from Thought Field Therapy. The tapping pattern provided at the beginning of this book constitutes the same pattern described in the opening story. "Just do it," as the Nike advertisement says, and you can get back to the important stuff—living your life in the now. Once you remove the pain from the past, you can begin making sense of your current life, create a future without unreasonable fears about moving towards it, and live now.

Starting this moment, whenever you begin to react negatively to your memories, current perceptions, or worries about the future, use Thought Field Therapy to reduce or eliminate bodily discomfort, mental confusion, or distortions. As mentioned previously, Thought Field Therapy is done by tapping with your fingertips on specific points on the body to activate your own healing systems. It takes only a minute or two to get results. You do not have to understand the theories behind it. You do not have to possess any previous knowledge or experience with tapping or even believe that it will work. Like taking penicillin, flipping on a light switch, or just breathing, you only have to perform the action for the positive results to occur. So, if you are aware of any upset at the mention of the past events, try tapping as instructed at the beginning of the book.

Stressors, Stress Responses, and Other Sources of Overwhelming Emotions

Your reactions to past events you have experienced — events that hurt, damaged, or destroyed parts of you or threatened to destroy your very existence — represent the primary source of the pain and fear that currently stops you from living fully. These events may have traumatized only your physical body, but for many people they often damaged the emotional, mental, and spiritual components of their being as well.

The events that threaten our existence are called *traumatic stressor events,* and we often experience *traumatic stress responses* to those events. Very often after traumatic experiences even small reminders of them will set off overwhelming physical and emotional reactions within you. These reminders are called *triggers,* and they come in many forms. Triggers may be memories, similar situations, smells, images, sounds, or anything that takes you into the past and causes negative sensations and emotions to arise. For example, in the illustration at the beginning of this chapter, the loud noise served as a trigger for the man in the story. (As you saw in that same story, Thought Field Therapy eliminated the triggered traumatic stress responses.)

More than likely, you already have a good idea of the past events — the traumatic stressors — driving your traumatic stress responses. But some people are unaware of experiences from the more distant past that may lie at the heart of their struggle. Stay open to the idea that the event you have identified as the cause of your problem may not be the only event you need to address in your healing process.

The kind of reactions that hold you captive and keep you from moving forward toward the life you choose come in many forms. You may have strong sensations, feelings, or reactions from the lingering results of traumatic stress events you clearly remember. Or the feelings that stop you from living your life in the moment may not appear to be huge, striking, or obvious reactions to anything in particular. They might arise as subtle and almost imperceptible conditions that persistently hold you back or that come up in troublesome ways. You easily recognize the pains and fears that jump out at you insistently, but it becomes more difficult to see those that live with you quietly and inconspicuously.

If you feel less clear about the source of your pain and fear, or if you feel afraid or in pain but can't put your finger on the source, the object of your fear, or the place where you hurt, you may have found some way to cope with your traumatic stressor events. Often with time and more general life experiences these feelings and sensation become less noticeable even though they may remain powerful influences in your life. However, coping with these subtle and persistent conditions by finding a way to put distance between yourself and the traumatic stress responses of your past can make it more difficult to overcome them.

The feelings and sensations that arise from past traumatic events always have a familiar quality, and you will recognize them even in subtle forms. To discover more about these feelings and where they come from, ask yourself over and over again, "Who are they?" Think about them as if they are pursuers, like the men following the main characters in the American classic Western movie *Butch Cassidy and the Sundance Kid*. In this film, two young outlaws ride, run, and climb at full speed in an attempt to escape the law. In scene after scene, we see the relentless pursuers riding just as hard after them. Each time the two outlaws try a trick to shake them loose, they look back in amazement wondering who could be that powerful and tenacious to just keep driving them further from a place of safety. Each time they see their pursuers close behind them again, Butch and the Kid ask, "Who are those guys?"

All of us have had a sense of the posse hot on our trail. For some of us, this feels like being forced in a direction not of our own choosing. For some of us, we live with a sense of persistent nagging. For others, we experience an urgent physical feeling in our gut that we may be called upon at any moment to defend our lives. Worse yet, we may feel the dread that we will suffer the torment of another event beyond our control. And, some of us may have deep emotional bonds holding us in place even though we want to move forward. You do not have to be held hostage or pursued by these feelings any more. You can use Thought Field Therapy and the NOW recovery processes to release their grip on your being and on your life.

In addition to traumatic stressor events, sometimes phobias serve as the source of the pain and fear in our lives. Phobias are irrational fears. If you have no reason to feel afraid—you just do—you have a phobia. Most people who have a fear of snakes have never actually had an interaction with a snake; this represents an irrational fear, or a phobia. If your fear of snakes developed after being bitten, the reaction to the presence of a snake would constitute a traumatic stress trigger, not a phobia. The same can be said of the fear of public speaking. If you have a strong reaction to speaking to a group and have been harmed by doing so in the past, the reaction characterizes a trigger, not a phobia. If, on the other hand, you have never spoken before an audience but you feel terribly afraid of getting up and speaking before one, your reaction denotes a phobia. The irrational fear of public speaking is the most common phobia. Thought Field Therapy easily ends this and other phobias, but the tapping pattern used differs from that used for traumatic stress.

Another less common source of impairment in people's lives comes from sensitivity to something in the physical environment or to the foods they eat. These sensitivities, called *Individual Energy Sensitivities* in Thought Field Therapy, are unique to the individual and overwhelm their capacity to function in some way. Often in chronic conditions, the source of the sensitivity interferes with the healing process and will have to be addressed. In more complex and rare cases, advanced Thought Field Therapy techniques will work to end the cycles of reoccurring illnesses. For the vast majority of people working on traumatic stress conditions, however, such advance treatment techniques are unnecessary. (For more information about what you can do in such situations and when to seek professional help, see Part Five.)

Stop Defining Your Life
by Traumatic Stress Responses

What you learn in this book will provide you with more than enough tools to rid yourself of pain from the past and fear of the future. The Thought Field Therapy approach always starts with the simplest solution and moves to the more complex ones, if needed. The NOW process helps you to heal and move forward in ways that make sense for your recovery. If you require more assistance than you find in this book, however, by all means reach out for professional help.

The traumatic events you experienced in your life that destroyed, threatened, or changed your physical, emotional, and spiritual existence also may have altered your understanding and way of being in the world completely. When this happens, you may stop living your life fully. You may hold yourself back or find that negative emotions make it difficult for you to feel fully alive. Thought Field Therapy can help you develop a new understanding that will allow you to live in the world along with your experience of traumatic events and thus begin living fully once again.

Maybe the traumatic event or events you experienced represent just a short detour on your life's journey, or maybe the force of these events has set the direction and quality of that journey. You may only see the negative outcomes of those events right now, but as you continue on your path and heal the open wounds left by your traumatic experiences you may find a positive side to their influence upon you. Once you can calm your mind and relax your body, you can make sense of your past and present life and act with purpose, both of which represent fundamental human needs. When you can meet these needs, you will find yourself living now. And all of this can be achieved by using Thought Field Therapy, as well as the NOW recovery process, as part of your traumatic stress recovery process.

Many factors influence the traumatic stress recovery process and impact the way we experience, endure, and heal from these powerful negative experiences in our lives. Understanding the recovery process gives you a way to map what has happened to you and the meaning you make of your life from the point of trauma forward. Most importantly, understanding how you arrived where you are today and what you value in life now will allow you to make better choices about what you do from now on. You can live better in this moment and in the future as you use Thought Field Therapy to cope with your negative feelings and sensations and as you apply the NOW traumatic stress recovery process to your life. Regardless of the source of your pains and fears, these two necessary ingredients for traumatic stress recovery can help you find more health, peace, love, and joy. They will also help you redefine your life. You don't want to live out the remainder of your days seeing yourself and your life as simply a product of the traumatic stressor events you have experienced.

While this book is focused on traumatic stress recovery, you don't need a formal diagnosis or even an understanding of the labels of Post Traumatic Stress Disorder (PTSD), Acute Stress Disorder (ASD), or Dis-Order of Extreme Stress Not Otherwise Specified (DESNOS) in order to benefit from the knowledge and skills you will learn from reading this book. In other words, you don't need to see a mental health specialist and be diagnosed with one of these conditions to use Thought Field Therapy. However, these labels and their uses, both positive and negative, are explained in the following chapters, and you might be able to discern if one of them applies to your own condition. Whether or not you ever have a psychiatric diagnosis to label your suffering or symptoms, the essential facts and information provided here will give you what you need to make more sense of your life's journey and to keep you moving forward.

That said, this book does not provide a complete course in the study of the traumatic stress field or in the study of Thought Field Therapy. You can learn much, much more about both of these areas than what has been included in these pages. However, this book will teach you the basic Thought Field Therapy concepts and skills so you can help yourself immediately.

Using the Stories of Others for Healing

As you read you will find lots of stories about people just like you who have overcome their past pains and future fears. Many of these stories are about my clients, who have shared their adventures with me. Some of these stories are about my life. Unlike the reference to fictitious characters, like Butch Cassidy and the Sundance Kid, mentioned above, the men and women and children you will learn from in these pages actually exist.

These stories describe experiences and have beginnings, middles, and ends. In most cases, the beginning represents a situation or condition in which the people find themselves; the middle shows you the action they take; and the end equals the changed state for these people, their eventual situation and condition. Sometimes these stories are told exactly as they happened, and sometimes they are changed to protect the identity of the subjects. Sometimes they have been altered a bit to illustrate the point being made. Listening to other people's stories and seeing the differences and the similarities between their experiences and your own will help you get clear about what you need to do to heal your open wounds and change your life for the better.

At times, the stories told in this book will seem like just a small piece of a bigger life or an event you only can appreciated fully with lots of background, but most of the time you'll find them so familiar you'll totally *get it*. You'll understand, because they serve as universal experiences. In other words, almost everyone has *been there* at some time in their life. Or, if you have not been there, you have seen someone you love in that place or in a similar place.

After each story, take a moment to enjoy what has happened and how the person has changed. While the tapping patterns used or the precise description of all the steps taken are not included in each case, you can assume that the self-help patterns provided in this book will work for the conditions being addressed in the stories. In Thought Field Therapy, we always start with the simplest procedures and work towards more complex treatments only as they are needed. As a professional helper, I try to make sure that all the people with whom I work learn Thought Field Therapy as a self-help technique. That means they learn the tapping methodology and can use it themselves without my assistance.

A reminder: While you are reading a story, or anything else in this book, you may find yourself triggered, which means that memories of your past or thoughts of the future upset you. If this happens go immediately to the extended traumatic stress treatment protocol at the beginning of the book, and take care of the upset by using Thought Field Therapy (tapping) before going on. Thought Field Therapy has nothing to do with unnecessary suffering. Do not stay in a state of being overwhelmed by negative emotions. You will get more out of your reading if you are not overcome or upset but instead feel calm and relaxed. I will be reminding you to tap many times throughout the book. Sometime these reminders may appear to you as unnecessary interruptions, but if you have been triggered by the stories or discussions you have read, these reminders — and your subsequent tapping — will get you back on track.

Overcoming Hopelessness, Isolation, and Addictions

Sometimes we experience such terrible things that we can't be expected to recover quickly or easily. So, be gentle with yourself if you have struggled for what seems like forever to get over your past traumatic experiences. When what has happened to you feels so scary that you cannot look at it long enough to understand what happened or to make sense out of the aftereffects of that traumatic event, you may wind up not only struggling with your situation and your desire not to face it but also feeling hopeless and isolated. Be aware that these conditions put you at risk for addictions and suicidal behavior.

Let's look at addictions first. To end the discomfort of an incomplete recovery process and to manage the overwhelming feelings that come with being unable to understand your current condition or what has happened to you in the past, often people turn to alcohol or other drugs to medicate the pain or to function throughout the day. Other

21

high-risk behaviors such as fighting, speeding in cars, or having unsafe sex accomplish the same goal as alcohol and drug abuse. They distract you from the sensations and thoughts that overwhelm you and make you uncomfortable.

Oftentimes using Thought Field Therapy to eliminate the upset feelings eliminates the need for self-medicating, and the dangerous behavior stops. Sometimes, if a habit has formed and is strongly entrenched, to heal completely you will have to directly treat the urge to use drugs or behaviors. Chapter 10 gives you information about how to relieve the underlying anxiety that drives these behaviors and to get back to a safer lifestyle. If using what you learn in this book does not eliminate your addiction problems and you are still feeling and acting desperate, seek the help of a person who understands addictions so you can make sure you remain safe. Addictions always win against reason alone. Tap, and get connected to others you can trust to help and support you in being safe and addiction free.

As for suicidal behavior and thoughts, this often accompanies feelings of hopelessness and isolation that follow traumatic stress experiences. The unstoppable and overwhelming sensations, thoughts, and emotions that make you believe you cannot manage living at a worthwhile level after a trauma can drive you to thinking you will be better off dead than continuing on in your current state. This condition is worsened by a sense that no one understands or even accepts you. Feeling hopeless that your overwhelming symptoms can ever improve is bad enough by itself, but when you add to this a sense that no hope exists that anyone can help, understand, or even care about your condition, you find yourself at high risk for self-destruction.

While open wounds left by traumatic stress experiences make us feel alone, Thought Field Therapy helps heal those wounds, thus curing us of the feeling of isolation as well. By removing our desperate feelings, tapping helps us become more connected to other people and less inclined to hurt ourselves or commit suicide. The reason for this is simple: hopelessness and isolation together form a deadly combination. In most people's lives, the capacity to endure horrible conditions and terrible pain is greatly enhanced by a connection to loved ones, family, and community. We can stand so much more pain and upset when we are connected to others, and hope always lives through that connection. Hope and love keep us alive.

If you are thinking or acting in self-destructive ways, keep reaching out to other people, and begin using Thought Field Therapy immediately. Seek out peer and, more importantly, professional help. Somewhere, someone will understand and accept you as you are. Hope exists for ending your unlivable conditions and for connecting to other people. Once you have recovered, you can become a beacon of hope for others. Once you have healed, you can reach out to those who are alone and hopeless by sharing with them your knowledge of traumatic stress recovery and Thought Field Therapy.

Some Really Great Things About Thought Field Therapy are:

- You do not have to know exactly what is wrong to make things better.

- You do not have to understand how it works to receive the benefits.

- You cannot hurt yourself by using it; the process either makes things better or does not work.

- Your beliefs and values will not change by tapping .

- Thought Field Therapy is *not* language or culturally specific;

- It works for all human beings regardless of gender, culture, language , faith, or belief.

This book's goals include helping you clearly see all the choices before you and assisting you in making the best choices for yourself. How you read and use this book constitutes your first choice. You can go to the end of the next chapter and experience Thought Field Therapy by doing some tapping without reading any further. (Or you may have already chosen to try tapping by using the information provided at the beginning of the book.) If you feel a great deal of emotional pain at this moment, I recommended you try tapping. Or, you can read on and learn more in the next chapter about the origins and concepts that underlie Thought Field Therapy before trying tapping. This is recommended if you have a calm mind, a relaxed body, and you like to understand a process before you experience it. You can then proceed through the book chapter by chapter, or you can skip to any chapter at any time — even right now — to focus upon your most pressing concerns about traumatic stress or upon specific problems, such as grief or addictions. Going to the table of contents or to the index also will lead you to the appropriate section if you are searching for an immediate deeper understanding or the resolution of a specific problem. In any case, the choice remains yours.

Each person heals in his/her own way. Use this book to heal in a way that feels most comfortable to you.

All you need to know to get started using Thought Field Therapy lies in the next chapter. So, why wait? Get started right now, this moment. Heal your past and change your future.

CHAPTER TWO

Closing Open Wounds
Using Thought Field Therapy

Sleeping at Night: Ending the Fear of the Past Repeating

Grace, a woman in her mid 40s came into my office seeking help with some difficult problems. She told me she'd struggled for as long as she could remember with the issues of dread and overreacting that interfered with developing relationships. Before we could even begin looking at these problems, however, we had to look at a more immediate concern affecting all aspects of her life. She had never slept well and reported that, at most, she could get three or four hours of sleep per night; thus, she existed in a perpetual state of exhaustion. Her sleep deprivation stemmed from an uncontrollable hypervigilance, which resulted in an inability to achieve a rested state. This problem had held her hostage for over 30 years.

Between the ages of four to nine, Grace and her sister were regularly raped by their father. Night after night, once everyone had gone to bed, he would come into the room the two girls shared. Grace learned quickly how to recognize his shadow on the hallway wall and waited every night for him to appear. As he would start moving towards their room, her consciousness would leave her physical body and hide in the curtains hanging in her room. In other words, she would have an out-of-body experience. Lost in another conscious place, if he chose her that night, she would not feel the physical and emotional pain of his assault on her little body. Disassociated from what was happening in the room, if her father chose her sister on that particular night instead, Grace would not hear the sounds of her sister's attempts to endure the pain of her rape.

25

Grace reported that falling asleep before her father came into the room meant that she would be roused as he pulled down the blanket and pulled up her nightgown and be caught in the horror of the event. Her shock at suddenly being awakened out of a sound sleep felt much worse than seeing him coming and disassociating. So, she developed a pattern of lying awake waiting for the safety of the first light of dawn. When she saw the shadow on the hallway wall, her conscious mind would leave her body and go to a place without feeling or sensation.

This sexual violence stopped at age nine, but the physical and emotional abuse continued until she left home at 17. For over 30 years, she had been held hostage by her body's defense mechanism, the memories of those painful rapes, and her fear that if she was not vigilant through the night she would suffer the shock of being ripped from her sleep by powers that would overwhelm and torture her. Right up to this first session with me, almost every night as she lay down in her bed her protective habits would rev up her mind and body. This caused her to think about the details from the day. She would relive the past day's events, mulling over all the possible meanings of the communications she'd had, both good and bad, and this would successfully keep her awake most of the night.

As soon we began working together, we used Thought Field Therapy to remove the shame and embarrassment Grace felt when she started talking about her childhood. Once she was more comfortable and could respond to my questions about what in her life needed to change, lack of sleep became the primary focus. After many years of work, both by herself and with the help of other professionals, Grace had arrived at a place where she could recount many of her childhood events. This made it possible for us to focus on what happened each night as she lay down in bed.

As she described her nightly pattern, we used tapping to eliminate her overwhelming fear and to find the knowledge that she was now a strong adult woman safe in her own home. As we did so, her mind and body calmed down and relaxed. She became able think about sleeping with ease. After that session, she started sleeping in a more normal pattern.

Grace is no fool, she knows that most rapes happen in a woman's own home. Now as an adult she is no longer overwhelmed by her past pains or her fears about the future. She can assess her risk of being raped again in a very different way and now can sleep peacefully each night. In fact, within one week she was sleeping six to seven hours per night and reported feeling much better.

Grace now taps a lot — at work, at home, out with friends, or whenever she needs to do so. Having learned most of the tapping patterns given in this book, she can always make things emotionally better for herself. Grace had been taken hostage by her internalized responses to childhood experiences. However, the hostage taker — open wounds from past traumas — was disarmed by Thought Field Therapy and could no longer control her.

<hr />

Shrinking the Shooter:
Putting the Memory into Perspective

In April 2001, an 18-year-old former high school student came onto campus and opened fire with a shotgun. He stood in a grassy area between two classroom buildings where he clearly could be seen by staff, teachers, and students. When he fired several shots into the administration building, a local police officer on campus immediately returned fire. The shooter retreated behind the building and, in a matter of moments, was wounded and apprehended by the police officer and a deputy sheriff.

When school resumed three days later, I was in one of the classrooms working with the staff and students providing critical incident stress management. After working with the students in a group format, I worked one-on-one with Dan, an adult staff member. As he talked about his experience, it became clear to me that he was having trouble dealing with his emotions. He described his worst memory as seeing the shooter firing his shotgun. Dan had been in the shooter's clear line of sight as he moved students out a back door and into another classroom. He was visibly upset by his memories, so I instructed him to begin tapping with his fingertips on treatment points on his body.

After the first round of tapping, he was calmer and reported that the picture in his mind was changing. When we started, Dan said the shooter appeared in his mind to be taller than the buildings, but as we tapped the shooter started to shrink. By the time we completed the third round of tapping, he reported that he no longer felt upset and the picture of the shooter in his mind had returned to a normal size. We both then returned to our duties with the students. At the end of day, Dan's memory of the shooting included a normal-sized assailant, and he was able to talk about the events with practically no effort or upset.

◆━━━━◆

What and Where is a Thought Field?

As you can see from the preceding stories, Thought Field Therapy works with a wide range of traumatic stress-related problems. Grace's story provides an example of a person using Thought Field Therapy to recover from a life-long struggle based on a series of traumatic events. In contrast, Dan's story provides an example of someone who used Thought Field Therapy to manage symptoms of a one-time traumatic event. The story at the beginning of chapter one illustrated how someone used Thought Field Therapy when experiencing a traumatic stress trigger.

These stories clearly show that Thought Field Therapy works. It may not be as obvious, however, what the therapy actually works upon. In fact, by now you may be wondering, "What exactly is a *thought field?*"

A home or office building exists in reality only after a designer has created a vision of that space and an architect has provided a blueprint that makes it possible to assemble the materials and construct the structure. The lines, calculations, and numbers representing the design all must be correct to end up with a sound building when completed. If, for example, the numbers representing the width of the building at each floor level differ, problems will develop in the construction of the structure. To solve the problem, a change must be made in the information on the blueprint.

Using this analogy, Thought Field Therapy works at the blueprint level by controlling what information exists on your blueprint; that information affects how you experience reality. A thought field is the place where the information defining your being and experience is kept. It is much like the paper on which the lines and numbers of the blueprint for a structure are recorded, but a thought field differs from a blueprint in that it is not found in a specific location in your physical being. You can't find it in a particular set of cells in your body or within a cognitive structure in your mind. But we can know it by how it functions within us and within our consciousness.

Human consciousness, which might be defined as the way we know we exist and hold an identity, is real to all of us. We are aware of consciousness and understand its affects on us even though nobody has every held one in his or her hand. Consciousness constitutes an emergent property of our whole being. That is to say, it cannot be known by any single piece or subset of the whole. Nobody knows exactly where it is or how it works, but it does. Your ability to know your experiences as different from other people's experiences—and the importance of this awareness every time you select a favorite drink or preferred color—serves as proof of its existence. Consciousness exists just as a thought field exists.

A *field* is defined as a connecting force across a medium or matrix that impacts energy and/or matter. Fields of all types have been studied since electromagnetic properties were discovered hundreds of years ago. A *thought* is a piece of subjectively known information that exists within us as an internal experience of the reality in which we exist. Thus, a *thought field* constitutes a force that holds and uses the fundamental information determining our being. Just as a blueprint provides a place for the critical information for creating a building to reside, a thought field provides the place for the critical information for creating our experience to reside. To correct a problem on a blueprint, bad information is erased and good information is added with a pencil or with a machine or computer that supplies a new design. To correct

29

a problem on a thought field, bad information is erased and good information is supplied by using the tapping methodology supplied by Thought Field Therapy.

If you feel you still don't understand the concept of a thought field, don't worry. Simply take from the short section above whatever makes sense. This chapter and the next will explain more fully the facts and theories about Thought Field Therapy. Regardless of your level of understanding of why or how Thought Field Therapy works, it will work for you when you use its tapping protocols. So, don't stop here, because you feel you don't *get it*. You don't need to get it to have Thought Field Therapy help you heal your open wounds and create positive change in your life.

The Development of Thought Field Therapy

Over the last 30 years, Dr. Roger Callahan has been the driving force in the discovery, development, and refinement of this revolutionary practice known by many as "tapping." In this book, Thought Field Therapy refers to Callahan Techniques® Thought Field Therapy. All articles and studies cited in these pages relate to Callahan Techniques® Thought Field Therapy (CTTFT), and all training discussed relate to it and are approved by the Association for Thought Field Therapy (ATFT). Each time Thought Field Therapy is mentioned within these pages, therefore, you can assume that it refers to Callahan Techniques® Thought Field Therapy.

Since making his first foundational discoveries, many of Dr. Callahan's trainees and other people using his methods have taken parts of his diagnostic and treatment protocols and made changes or renamed the processes. These derivations of Dr. Callahan's work have maintained, modified, and added a variety of elements. They are related to Dr. Callahan's work and recognizable in that they use tapping or other means of meridian treatment point stimulation in a sequence, have a nine-gamut series (described below), often employ kinesiology muscle testing, and/or refer to Dr. Callahan's discoveries. To the extent that these other approaches use elements of Thought Field Therapy techniques appropriately, they are effective in some situations. They may not be effective in others. For this reason, this book focuses upon Callahan Techniques® Thought Field Therapy alone.

Dr. Callahan and his associates used rigorous research and experimental methods to develop Thought Field Therapy. Understanding how this fast and effective approach was developed offers you a frame of reference that makes it hard to dismiss it as just some hokey, self-help craze or passing fad. Thought Field Therapy is not magic, nor was it revealed in a moment of cosmic attunement. It represents the result of Dr. Callahan's many years of methodical efforts and studies.

A radio operator and aerial gunner on a B-24 bomber in WWII before obtaining his Ph.D. in clinical psychology from Syracuse University in 1955, Dr. Callahan worked for years as a therapist, educator, and researcher before his first experiences with what led eventually to Thought Field Therapy. From the beginning of his career, his inquisitive mind and his commitment to finding ways to help individuals with anxiety and other debilitating disorders motivated him to explore helping approaches outside the mainstream. Prior to developing Thought Field Therapy, he accrued an impressive list of accomplishments and affiliations. These included becoming a fellow in clinical hypnosis in the early 1950s; serving as a trainer for Albert Ellis, the originator of cognitive therapy approaches; establishing the first Rational Emotive Behavior Therapy Center outside of New York; and, co-authoring the first double-blind study of psychiatric medications for children.

About 30 years ago, while in private practice treating anxiety disorders and continuing to explore what helps those who suffer from these issues, Dr. Callahan was introduced to muscle testing. Muscle testing, part of the practice of Applied Kinesiology, is used by chiropractors to discern the location of disturbances in the muscular-skeletal systems. Intrigued, he became formally trained in Applied Kinesiology and began to experiment with applications of this chiropractic approach for healing in the psychological realm. Dr. Callahan became the first person to use muscle testing as a reliable and valid way to diagnose the fundamental cause of psychological problems.

Once he had diagnosed the cause, he then used the same muscle testing methodology to find the correction for these fundamental impairing problems. Methodically, he discovered ways to identify and correct for psychological reversal, perturbation, neurological disorganization, and other causes of overwhelming emotional upset. (These conditions are explained in Part Five.) This revolutionary method of identifying the cause and the corrections for emotional problems using kinesiology, meridian energy flows, and other methods of healing served as the basis of what he came to call *Causal Diagnosis*.

Causal Diagnosis makes Thought Field Therapy different from other psychological approaches, because this technique effectively removes all the guesswork about a client's diagnosis and treatment. In all other psychological approaches, the therapist gathers a person's history as well as current signs and symptoms to place that person's condition in a category of disorder. Then, based on the therapist's best assessment, the therapist pursues the treatment generally used for that category. With Thought Field Therapy Causal Diagnosis, however, rather than placing a person in a general category and pursuing a general course of treatment, a person's specific needs and problems are addressed with appropriate required treatment. The relationship between a person's emotional states and meridian treatment points is unambiguous and precise. For this reason, Dr. Callahan was able to develop distinct treatment protocols for a large number of psychological problems, including depression, phobias, anxiety, panic, guilt, and trauma. He has taken this even further by putting it to use effectively in many areas of human performance and physical and mental health.

After thousands of applications of Thought Field Therapy Causal Diagnosis, Dr. Callahan identified recurring tapping patterns that provided the basis for the standard patterns of Thought Field Therapy treatments. This makes it possible for anyone to learn and use these tapping patterns without needing the knowledge and skills of Causal Diagnosis. While the general tapping patterns used are not as exact as Causal Diagnosis, many trained interventionists of all professional types generally find them about 90 percent effective in eliminating all traumatic stress symptoms. These tapping patterns, called *Thought Field Therapy algorithms*, are extremely effective in resolving both general and specific overwhelming emotional states. The word *algorithm* was borrowed from mathematics and refers to *a standard solution to a problem*. In this book, the tapping protocols and *Basic Steps* represent forms of algorithms.

Because algorithms are not as precise as Causal Diagnosis, this book instructs you to start with the most common tapping patterns for your problem and then to use other tapping patterns or treatments, which are also provided, in their most common order of use. The tapping pattern described at the beginning of the book represents the most common one used for traumatic stress. If this pattern does not work for you, then you will want to try another pattern or other steps as instructed in Part Five. When one algorithm listed in Part Five does not eliminate the distress, other algorithms (Basic Steps) or one of the *Next Steps* that follow them offered in that same chapter may make it work.

After you have gone through all the self-help suggestions and tools offered in this book, if you are not getting the results you desire or are still feeling upset about past traumatic events, you may need more advanced Causal Diagnosis. A practitioner trained in Causal Diagnosis can discern the exact tapping sequence necessary to help you. In addition to offering different algorithms, Causal Diagnosis practitioners have found that three to five percent of the general population will need to make additional changes in some aspects of their food choices or other lifestyle elements to achieve long-term cures. The impact of such changes is explained in later discussions of Individual Energy Toxins. However, Thought Field Therapy employs no general prohibitions regarding foods or lifestyle; these tend to be particular to each individual.

Once your primary traumatic stress symptoms are eliminated, you may be able to take on and begin healing other issues in your life. It may be necessary for you to address issues related to bereavement, family of origin, previous traumas, dysfunctional coping patterns, substance abuse, self-esteem, problem solving, decision making, and/or relationships.

On-going Development of Thought Field Therapy

Over 10,000 people have completed Callahan Techniques® Thought Field Therapy training workshops, and thousands more have used it. Within the psychological and counseling professions, Thought Field Therapy has been used effectively to treat a broad range of conditions. For example, one study by Caroline Sakai and others involved 714 patients from a behavioral and health services who were treated with Thought Field Therapy for 31 categories of problems or symptoms. All 1,594 applications showed statistical evidence for significant in-session reductions in self-reported distress. Conditions treated included trichotillomania (pulling hair), nicotine and alcohol cravings, Obsessive-Compulsive Disorder, depression, chronic pain, and variety of stress-related conditions. Thought Field Therapy will often provide relief when traditional psychological approaches have failed. Additionally, in his book, *The Pretzel Man*, James Schaefer describes his personal struggles with Obsessive-Compulsive Disorder and anxiety and how these problems were corrected with Thought Field Therapy after more than 20 years of unsuccessfully trying to do so with other forms of treatment.

Beyond psychological services, Thought Field Therapy now is used in many other professional settings, such as in physical medicine to improve a number of conditions. Most notably, Thought Field Therapy will improve heart rate variability (HRV). Established by basic research to be a stable and placebo-free measure, heart rate variability is considered the best predictor of mortality after a heart attack and measure of overall health. Nursing, psychiatry, chiropractic medicine, education, religion, sports psychology, acupuncture, physical therapy, and many other healing arts now use Thought Field Therapy as well.

Thought Field Therapy provides one of the most effective means of controlling symptoms of traumatic stress, and it does so in a matter of moments, and, in most cases, for a particular stimulus on a permanent basis. In fact, Thought Field Therapy has been proven so effective that it was adopted on a national level by the Surgeon General of Kosovo for treatment of traumatic stress disorders.

While in some cases, all the symptoms related to a critical incident may be resolved in one treatment sequence, sometimes each aspect of a memory or other related triggers that provoke negative responses may need to be addressed one at a time as they arise. If that happens, Thought Field Therapy can be repeated for each new trigger. In either situation, Thought Field Therapy provides for quick and complete symptom elimination rather than "management." This allows the therapy to focus on other aspects of traumatic stress recovery, such as reworking the trauma or integrating the trauma, as it is needed.

Resources for more empirical and theoretical Thought Field Therapy studies are offered at the end of the book. However, the best evidence of the value of Thought Field Therapy comes from your personal use of tapping. The proof of the pudding is in the tasting. The best test of Thought Field Therapy is in the tapping, so try it.

What Thought Field Therapy Does and Does Not Do

While Thought Field Therapy does, indeed, eliminate emotional upset and help heal the open wounds created by traumatic experiences, as well as the symptoms of many other conditions, there are many things Thought Field Therapy — luckily — does not do. Thought Field Therapy does not change your values, beliefs, knowledge, or aesthetics. Nor will it change personality disorders or eliminate normal human processes like grief.

Thought Field Therapy cannot change a person's belief or value structure. Values and beliefs are fundamentally cognitive or mental functions stemming from complex processes in the mind and consciousness. Your extensive value and belief systems is formed over many years as you develop. Reducing overwhelming upset allows a person the improved ability to draw on the strength of values and beliefs that already exist in that person.

Thought Field Therapy does not make you smarter. Individuals do not have access to factual information after tapping that were not already held prior to tapping. However, when Thought Field Therapy is used to reduce stress and anxiety, it has been shown to improve performance on intellectual tasks, such as reading or learning. Increased stress impedes cognitive functioning in a variety of ways. By reducing these stress responses and eliminating other mental and emotional disturbances with tapping, your functioning improves, thereby accounting for noticeably enhanced performance on familiar tasks. The same, perhaps, is true for memory. By removing barriers to memory, such as fear or anxiety, it becomes possible to improve your focus, which, in turn, improves your capacity to provide more-detailed reports. You master your memory more quickly, and your access to memories is increased when your fear and pain are reduced or eliminated.

Thought Field Therapy does not change reality, nor does it divorce you from fundamental human processes. You experience loss and integrate it into your being as befits your nature no matter what you do. You will grieve and experience bereavement even when you have eliminated the overwhelming emotions or recurrent intrusive images that accompany that loss.

Thought Field Therapy does not eliminate personality disorders. Personality disorders are descriptions of sets of individual traits developed over years that result in dysfunctional coping and relationship patterns. They do not represent the result of one event, tendency, or characteristic. Values, beliefs, knowledge, and aesthetics related to yourself impact the development and maintenance of your personality. In the same ways that Thought Field Therapy may improve your cognitive functions, Thought Field Therapy can ease and speed personality change. Thought Field Therapy makes considering or changing personality patterns much less stressful. However, it is not possible for you to "tap in a personality trait." This kind of change requires an active commitment on your part to developing and practicing the desired changes.

Changing life-long patterns requires conscious repeated efforts in new thinking and behavior. If these new thoughts and behaviors trigger overwhelming upset, you will not likely practice and incorporate these new thoughts and behaviors into your life. Thought Field Therapy can help your process of change by removing the overwhelming upset, thus allowing you to change. For example, stating a positive self-affirmation can provide the first step to changing negative self-talk. If your prior conditioning or past traumatic history causes you to become overwhelmed while making such a statement, the change you desire will not occur. By eliminating the upset, Thought Field Therapy makes it possible to change self-talk quickly. Thus, Thought Field Therapy allows you to accelerate the work of making cognitive and behavioral changes.

Starting Healing from the Place You Are Now

Now that you have a basic understanding of Thought Field Therapy, it's time to get started. The best place to begin making positive change is the place you find yourself right now. The following questions will help you identify if you have open wounds from past traumas that need to be healed.

- **Do you have pictures in your head of a terrible thing that happened to you in the past and you cannot stop them from entering your mind or eliminate them when they do?**

- **Do you have fears that stop you from going where you want to go, doing what you want to do, or closing your eyes to sleep?**

- **In the aftermath of a loss or trauma, do you have only one way cope and do you feel that the one way is no longer enough to help you get on with your life?**

- **Do you find yourself constantly dwelling either in the past or in the future? Do you have trouble living in the moment?**

If you answered "yes" to any of these questions, you may be experiencing a traumatic stress response. Following the simple steps of Thought Field Therapy will rid you of your overwhelming negative feelings and allow you to live in the present moment of your life. The now of your life differs from the memories and flashbacks of the events that happen in the past and haunt you still. It also differs from your imagination of the isolated and hopeless situations that keep you fearful and worried about what may happen tomorrow. Why? Because the now of your life represents what is happening at this moment.

Experiencing this present moment, right here and right now, frees you to make choices about your next moment. What do you choose to do? How do you choose to respond? Who do you choose to be with? Where do you choose to go next? Even if the worst thing in the world has happened to you in the past, you can recover, stay in the now, and make sense out of your life. However, you can't do that by living in the past or in the future. You can only do that in the now.

Give Thought Field Therapy a Try

You can start with a small issue or problem. Just pull up a piece of a memory or a small traumatic event from the past and start. If you need help finding a memory or issue, try one of these suggestions:

- **Recall the pictures of the terrible thing that happened to you the past that you often cannot stop from entering your mind or rid yourself of when they enter your mind.**

- **Remember the fears that stop you from going where you want to go, doing what you want to do, or closing your eyes to sleep.**

- **When you find yourself dwelling either in the past or in the future, what do you think about? What do you worry about?**

Once you have a picture or memory in mind, notice what you experience in your body. How does your body feel? Is it in pain? Do you feel specific emotions? Become aware of any discomfort or upset you feel at any given moment as you consciously recall these memories and pictures, because you will be asked to rate the level of your upset or pain during the Thought Field Therapy process. Continue to follow the instructions that follow. As you do so, pay attention to your feelings and bodily sensations. Notice if they are changing.

Basic Steps for Traumatic Stress

Step One.   As you focus on the problem, determine your Subjective Units of Distress (SUD) by rating the upset on a 1 to 10 Scale (1= no upset, 10=worst).

Step Two.   Using your fingertips tap about ten times each:

> Side of Hand,
> Under Nose,
> Beginning of Eyebrow,
> Under Eye,
> Under Arm,
> Under Collarbone,
> Little Finger,
> Under Collarbone,
> Index Finger,
> Under Collarbone.

Step Three.   Do the *9 Gamut Series*. While continuously tapping the gamut spot:

1. Close eyes
2. Open eyes
3. With your eyes look down and left
4. With your eyes look down and right
5. Whirl your eyes in a complete circle in one direction
6. Whirl your eyes in a complete circle in the other direction
7. Hum a couple bars of any tune
8. Count to five
9. Hum again.

Step Four.   Using your fingertips tap about 10 times each:

> Side of Hand,
> Under Nose,
> Beginning of Eyebrow,
> Under Eye,

> Under Arm,
> Under Collarbone,
> Little Finger,
> Under Collarbone,
> Index Finger,
> Under Collarbone.

Step Five.   Think about the problem in the same way again, rate your upset 1-10 as in step one.

Repeat steps Two through Five until:
Your SUD rating is a 1or 2, then go to Step Six.

Or your SUD rating stops changing then go to NEXT STEPS on page 247.

Step Six: The floor to ceiling eye roll.

While continuously tapping the gamut spot and holding your head level, roll your eyes on a vertical line from the floor to the ceiling over 6–7 seconds.

THE CALLAHAN TECHNIQUES®

Treatment Points
© 1994 by Roger T. Callahan

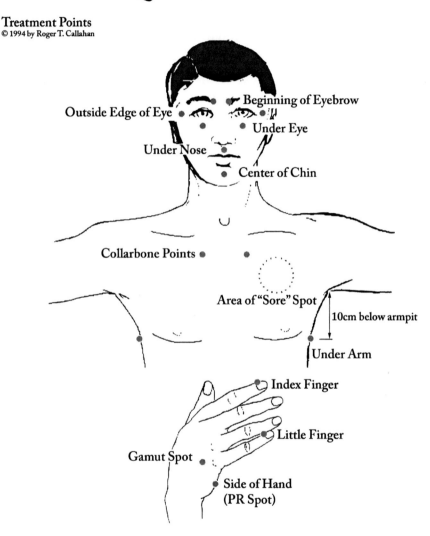

41

Thought Field Therapy makes much more sense once you have actually tried it and felt the changes described earlier in stories I've told. Knowing, in your own body and mind, the improvement that comes as your own upset diminishes serves as a more powerful lesson than hearing about the experiences of others. And now, as you can breathe and concentrate more fully, you'll find yourself able to comprehend the next chapter's discussion of the theory and practice of Thought Field Therapy more easily and completely.

CHAPTER THREE

New Thinking and Actions
Using Thought Field Therapy in Healing

Open Wounds Make it Impossible to Judge if You Are Safe

Open wounds make it impossible to know that you are safe. Joe, a 50-year old firefighter, was still having some problems even after completing a 12-week cognitive therapy outpatient treatment program for dealing with depression, changing his job location, and making the decision to stop trying to advance in his career. He had done all he could to reduce the stress in his life. Yet he still only felt safe to answer his door at home with his pistol in hand. He could not go out with his children and wife to public places, because he feared for their safety. And, worst of all, he constantly felt afraid that sharing his feelings just make him more vulnerable even though he had learned in his group therapy sessions the power of letting others help.

While his treatment had successfully reduced his risk of suicide, he was still miserable. He realized during treatment for depression that he suffered from Post Traumatic Stress disorder. He seemed unable to sort out when he was safe and when he was at risk for violence. Looking at his past and putting some important pieces together, he now understood the impact of over 25 years in the fire service in high risk settings.

The problem, as he understood it, started when he worked for 15 years in a low-income neighborhood. His duties included daily medical runs for domestic violence, gang-related shootings, criminal victimization, and responding to calls related to all the other suffering that comes from extreme poverty. As a young firefighter, he welcomed the opportunity to make a difference in people's lives and rose quickly to leadership roles. However, in these roles the constant threat of violence to himself and to his fellow firefighters under his command became the stressor that eventually pushed him over the line. After his fire truck responded to the shooting death of a police officer, the risk he and the crew faced hit him on a deep emotional level. After a few more similar events, he lost any sense of security. No longer did he feel as if the people he served welcomed his presence. More and more he felt that everyone in the area he served represented a threat to his well being.

Joe became more and more unhappy and afraid. His sense that danger was always there overtook his reason, leaving him fearful despite the fact that all indicators pointed to the fact that he was safe — safe at home, safe with his family, safe in his church and his community. He started carrying a gun everywhere and worried constantly about the safety of his wife and son. He stopped going out in public with his family, because he was afraid of what he would have to do to protect them. In fact, when a crowd appeared to focus on him, his fear overtook him, and he had to get out of that particular environment or somehow take control of the situation.

Once Joe learned and used Thought Field Therapy to resolve the overwhelming feeling that came with the memories of real dangers in the past, he was able to feel and act safe in the present. He quickly returned to using his reason to judge the safety for himself and his family in public settings. He was impressed that he could lay to rest the haunting incidents that occurred 20 years earlier in minutes. He could put the gun away and share his feelings without falling into the horrible sensations from past.

Living in the now requires that you not allow reminders of the past to upset you or, if those memories cause you upset, that you not get stuck in your emotions. Living in the present moment also requires not getting caught in fears that the past will repeat itself, thus causing you even more damage and hurt. If you find that you do, indeed, get stuck in upsets based upon reminders of the past or because of your fears about the future, you are living in the past and in the future rather than in the now. And this indicates that, like Joe in the example above, you are suffering from open wounds caused by past traumas.

Just as with other types of physical wounds, we tend to place much of our focus upon open wounds from a past traumatic event or events. If you've suffered an open wound of any sort, you know you feel every action taken in the wound itself. Every plan you make to take action includes thoughts of protecting the wound, and that will limit your life's journey until the wound begins to heal.

Physical wounds heal with time, stitches, bandages, air, and antibiotic ointment, but Thought Field Therapy provides a way to close wounds left open from traumatic events. As a physical wound heals and a scab forms, often you can return to almost normal activity. As an emotional wound heals, the pain and upset from a traumatic event subsides, and this allows you to turn your attention to healing—and to living—fully.

A Way to Think about Thought Field Therapy and How it Works

Now that you've heard about the Thought Field Therapy process and, hopefully tried tapping on yourself, and you've read the claims about how Thought Field Therapy works and some real-life success stories, you might be wondering, "How does Thought Field Therapy really work?" If you've tried it on yourself successfully, you might also be asking, "What happened to my feelings of upset?" or "Will the upset feelings return?" Understanding how Thought Field Therapy accomplishes such seemingly-miraculous results requires looking at human biology, physiology, anatomy, neurology, and medicine from the most scientifically-advanced perspective available.

Older methods for understanding the psychology and physical world just do not provide explanations for many recent advances in medical diagnosis and treatments. Current cognitive, behavioral, and neurological approaches cannot account for the healing that occurs with Thought Field Therapy either. A meaningful explanation of Thought

Field Therapy and other informational and energetic approaches can be found, however, in the new fields of science and medicine that incorporates human biophysiology using quantum physics instead of Newtonian physics. When we comprehend that electromagnetic diagnostic equipment, like magnetic resonances imaging (MRI), works because at a fundamental level we are energy, we also can understand how subtle energy can be used for more than just diagnosis. In fact, it provides an essential component in healing.

Drawing on quantum physics and information about the subtle energy of the body, the theory and the mechanism of action that makes Thought Field Therapy work is informed by investigations into what guides the formation, structure, and functioning of living cells and organisms. But most of us will never want or need to understand the hard science of tapping. Just remember that in any energetic system, the human body included, a control mechanism exists in which information is processed, stored, and communicated. Thought Field Therapy accesses this information through the body's energy meridian system. In Chinese medicine the meridians are the primary channels through which energy flows in the body. This flow provides a means of communications across all the systems of the body. Thus, tapping on meridian points provides a way to influence energy flow at the fundamental level of control.

When you focus on your upset, you are connecting to whatever memories you may have of past traumas and the accompanying negative feelings. Then when you tap on the meridian treatment points in the specific order described in the traumatic stress protocol, it sends a message to the control mechanism in your body—your energetic system—that something is not working and needs to be fixed. Since human beings are self-healing mechanisms and these fixes are built into their systems, you need only activate the system to *run* the *fix program*, or make a change. You can equate this to when a function on your computer freezes up. The tapping process equates to holding down Control-Alt-Delete together two times on your computer keyboard. When you do this, a coded message is sent to the central processing unit of the computer to restart the machine. When it restarts, it resets itself to full functionality, and you can continue working with your computer. In much the same way, when you tap in a specific pattern on your body's meridian points, the program controlling your responses and reactions resets itself and you are able to function fully again.

Using this computer analogy may seem a bit simplistic, but human nature asks us to make sense out of our experiences, and this provides a way to begin doing so. Remember, you don't need to understanding the mechanism of action or the underlying processes that make tapping work to get the results you want with Thought Field Therapy. You also can equate this to a computer: When my computer mouse freezes and the keyboard stops working, I don't really care why. I just know that if I do the simple things I have been taught to do in such a situation, the computer will respond and fix itself. Even though I do not fully understand what happens in the central processing unit of the computer, or in this case the thought field, I do know that sending the right code by hitting the right keys in the right sequence, i.e., tapping, solves the problem.

Saying that I do not understand fully how a central processing unit works represents a total understatement; I do not have a clue as to how electrons move around to make graphics appear on my computer monitor or to make a printer print. I have no idea how the messages are sent from the keyboard to the monitor or printer and how the data is stored on the hard drive and then later retrieved. Lots of people do know the specifics of these things, but you and I do not have to be one of these experts to take advantage of computer technology. Similarly, we don't have to understand how Thought Field Therapy works. We simply need to know that it does and how to use it. There are geeks in all fields. You don't have to be a computer geek to make computers work, and you don't have to be a psychologist, medical practitioner, social worker, or spiritual healer to make your healing systems work.

Facts and Theories Related to Thought Field Therapy

Dr. Callahan stresses in his teaching that becoming confused about the difference between fact and theory leads to misunderstandings and wasted time. So, what's the difference between the two? A fact

47

is something that exists in reality. A theory serves as an explanation of how or why something works. For instance, spending time considering the theory underlying heat, fuel, and oxygen coming together to make fire serves no purpose. We may never truly know how these elements interact to create fire, or, for that matter, if our theory is correct. On the other hand, regardless of any theory, we do know that smothering a fire with a lid or putting water on it puts out the flame. That's a fact. Why doing this works to put out the fire represents theory. You might say it works because a fire needs oxygen to burn, but this could still be deemed theory. And when you need to put out a fire, does it matter why putting water on it works?

We have some models to explain how Thought Field Therapy functions, but they represent theory. These theories, or explanations, are useful only to those who want to find better, faster, and simpler ways to activate healing. When working on yourself or with others suffering from traumatic stress responses, wasted time means prolonged suffering. And nothing good comes from such pain. Therefore, sorting out the *why* of a helpful process is not as important as how to use it to actually help.

Why overwhelming upset comes about or *why* it is eliminated takes us in to discussions of theory. *How* to use Thought Field Therapy for healing takes us into a discussion of fact. Yet, the human mind wants to understand everything. So, you might still ask, "Why does Thought Field Therapy work?" "Why is it possible to eliminate overwhelming emotional upset by tapping on certain points on the body?" These *why* questions lead you into the world of theories and abstract models of reality and away from reality and fact itself. The cause of the overwhelming upset you feel or the way it came about represents theory. You, I, or your therapist can speculate about how you came to feel the way you do and why you react in the manner you do, but it won't help the Thought Field Therapy process work. It will just take time away from using tapping to heal your open wounds and bring you into the present moment as you work through the complete NOW recovery process.

Instead of worrying about *why*, trust the facts, and add your own experience to the body of evidence that supports using Thought

Field Therapy in reality. The efficacy of Thought Field Therapy has been verified thousands of times. Available evidence in many forms confirms that Thought Field Therapy works. You can confirm this fact in moments with your own experiments with tapping. The results are predictable, repeatable, and verifiable by anyone who follows the simple procedures offered in this book. It is a fact that Thought Field Therapy works.

If you enjoy delving into theories, by all means explore the theories behind Thought Field Therapy. Since the human abstract-oriented mind likes to make reality comprehensible, you might even want to construct a few theoretical models of your own. Please remember, though, that these models just serve as a way of talking about concepts and considering them. On the other hand, Thought Field Therapy techniques give us a way to identify, assess, and address real feelings and behaviors. As such, they represent facts. And, while you are at it, challenge the models presented here and elsewhere that discuss why Thought Field Therapy works. Remember, human beings are meaning-making creatures that need to make sense of their experiences. Models and theories help us do that. Maybe you are the one who will expand our understanding and move us toward new applications. But be sure to tap away any overwhelming negative feeling you have before you engage your mind in the building of conceptual models. Everything makes more sense when you don't feel pain or fear.

Communicating Your Reality Clearly

Another reason exists for possessing a good understanding of the difference between facts and theories. A key element in the Callahan Techniques® Thought Field Therapy revolves around the concept of dealing with facts and communicating shared reality clearly. And your reality matters the most. Thought Field Therapy uses a 1–10 rating scale throughout the tapping process to help you clearly see changes in your reality. If you recall, you are asked to rate on a 1–10 scale how much distress you are experiencing as you begin the Thought Field Therapy process. Then, as you complete the tapping process, you report changes again on a 1–10 rating scale. The number 1 represents no distress as you focus on the issue being addressed; the number 10 represents the worst possible distress you can experience.

In Thought Field Therapy, this scale rates the Subjective Units of Distress (SUD). The advantage of the Subjective Units of Distress rating is found in its ability to precisely communicate your reality. "Feeling a little better" does not mean the same thing to everyone. These words can be subjectively translated. However, moving from a Subjective Units of Distress rating of 8 to 4 indicates a clear, objective change that will direct the next step in the Thought Field Therapy process. Again, "Feeling really bad" means different things to different people; it's a subjective statement. Moving up the scale from a 4 to a 9 serves as an objective rating that tells you what step to take next and offers a distinct picture of what is going on in your process. Additionally, the Subjective Units of Distress rating indicates how you are changing in reality regardless of the theory you use to explain why your feelings and sensations are changing. You can find a more complete explanation of how to use the Subjective Units of Distress to stay clear about your reality as you help yourself or others in Part Five.

A Relaxed Body and Calm Mind
Begins the Recovery Process

Traumatic stressor events can have a long-term impact on your overall understanding of the world. They change our lives beyond what happens in the moment of the actual trauma. The wounds inflicted on us when we experience trauma shape how we view, understand, operate in, and experience our world from that point forward. For this reason, beyond eliminating the emotional upset that remains after a traumatic stressor event, often trauma survivors need to take time to heal the their damaged manner of looking at the world as well.

However, what has happened to you will never change. You cannot undo time nor experience. Human beings with physical bodies remain subject to the laws of the universe, and, as such, Thought Field Therapy cannot and does not change the objective reality of your world. Yet, if you use Thought Field Therapy you will find your ability to clearly perceive the world and to think and to act deliberately enhanced by the fact that you no longer suffer from overwhelming feelings and sensations related to your past experiences. Indeed, you take the first step in the traumatic recovery process when you achieve a relaxed body and a calm mind.

For you to use the tapping process effectively, it is critical for you to understand the concept of *what* actually does change during Thought Field Therapy. Do not expect a change in the level of sensations and emotions in your body to change your external reality. Do expect that as the feelings and sensations in you body lessen you will be able to perceive and process information about the world around you in a different manner. As a human being, you can only make the choices available to you at any given moment. The options you see for yourself are based upon your understanding of your experiences and your environment at that time. After tapping, you are less emotional, which means your body relaxes and your mind becomes calmer. This, in turn, allows you to achieve a new clarity. Your view of your situation and your options simply become clearer and your ability to make choices based on your true preferences is enhanced. In addition, your perception and understanding of your current situation and choices tends to be expanded; so, you see the different options and can choose to make objective external changes for yourself that you might not have made previously.

The NOW model of recovery asks you to take actions like tapping first to change your internal responses and that achieves that relaxed body and calm mind state. You follow this with the actions of reviewing and understanding what happened, because you then can do this more effectively. Tapping brings you to a place where you can understand and see all the options before you and act in an unimpaired, complete, sound, and honest way.

If the traumatic stressor events that are at the bottom of your struggles come from deep in your past, you may have to use Thought Field Therapy and apply the NOW recovery model to those remote events in your life as well as to your current issues or, more specifically, to solve your current problems. In other words, those events in your distant past may actually represent additional open wounds that need to be healed before you can experience full recovery from your current issues. Often our current symptoms are impacted by more than one traumatic event, and we have to look beyond what seems obvious to find complete healing. (If you think this applies to you, you may find it helpful to read Chapter 11, which deals with understanding the connection of current responses to childhood events.) Whether a one-time event or a life time of events have wounded you, healing comes as naturally to human beings as breathing. We need only find a way to allow it.

Tapping Allows To Get to the Heart of the Matter: How Would I Live With Killing?

I had just finished a presentation of Thought Field Therapy applications at a naval hospital and had asked for a volunteer on whom I planned to demonstrate tapping. The participants, chaplains, doctors, nurses, case managers, and other professionals in the mental/physical health services, were military and civilian service providers caring for injured service members. The man who came forward, a recently-commission chaplain, had been an enlisted marine prior to this.

When I asked with what issue he wanted help, his response was clear: An earlier presenter's discussion about the impact of killing innocent people in the current war had left him stuck with a picture in his mind that troubled him. American soldiers and marines are trained in techniques of reflective firing while in boot camp. This means that when certain targets are recognized, or specific identifiable indicators are visible, soldiers fire immediately and automatically. While this has been a big part of making the U.S. Army and the Marine Corps the most effective combat force in history and has saved many soldiers and marines in the field, it unfortunately results in the killing of innocent women, children, and civilians at higher rates than in the past. The chaplain said he had experienced this while deployed in Iraq, and the presentation had not only brought back these memories clearly but the emotional upset that accompanied the actual experience of being in Iraq and killing innocent people as well. As he talked briefly about the *presentation he had just heard and his current upset, I could see the change in his eyes and throughout his whole body. He was not in this his body, the room, or the country. He appeared to be right back in the place and the source of his memories.*

We started Thought Field Therapy immediately to relieve the traumatic stress response the chaplain was feeling as he remembered being in combat in Iraq and killing innocent people. After two treat-ment sequences, he returned to the present time. The change in his eyes and body was apparent to everyone in the room. He now was able to remember the event in Iraq without the upset.

As the chaplain sat down, most of us in the room had one question on our minds: "If this had happened to me, *how would I live with the knowledge of that event?*" In other words, "How would it impact me and the way I look at and respond to myself and the world?"

This was neither the chaplain's therapy session nor what I thought of as a safe place to start the next stage in the process, which would have involved exploring this man's values and beliefs as im-pacted by the reality of his traumatic experience. Before leaving, I made sure that another officer would check in on this good man harmed in the line of duty. I knew he would need to do more work around this traumatic event. He would need to explore such ques-tions as: "Was it a legal killing per the rules of engagement," "Was what I did moral," "How can I give my experience meaning in my life?" and maybe "Can I forgive myself and/or others involved?" Thought Field Therapy does not have answers to these questions. This man would have to sit with someone who could help him sort through these issues, someone who understood and offered support and not judgment. Using the NOW traumatic stress recovery process also would afford him a way to process some of these questions and the impact his experiences had on his life.

You also will need to look at the reality of your past traumas and your current life. Using Thought Field Therapy will allow you to face what has occurred and what is now, but what you do with this information—how you deal with it and move forward with your life—represents a personal choice. Using the NOW model of traumatic stress recovery provides a framework for understanding what has happened to you and what it means to you. For those of you struggling with difficult questions related to past traumas, the NOW process, which is explained in Part Three of this book, will help you answer them, offer you support, and help you discern how to move forward with your life in a meaningful manner.

Challenge Yourself to Make Important Changes

Despite all that you've been told so far, you may be wondering how Thought Field Therapy compares to other modes of traumatic stress recovery. You may actually have tried some of these other methods with some success (or no success). Although if any of them had totally healed your open wounds you wouldn't be reading this book.

Currently, the mental health and behavioral health fields tend to use only evidence-based approaches to traumatic stress recovery. Most academic and research groups, as well as most professional-membership organizations, consider studies that show a *statistically significant improvement* with control group comparisons as acceptable evidence that a recovery process works. This means the study shows that a particular approach helps more people than another approach or than doing nothing at all. Random chance does not serve as enough proof that one mode of recovery works better than another; actual experiments on controlled groups of people must be applied. However, achieving statistically significant improvement does not require a very big difference between control groups, and many individuals actually may not be helped at all even in these studies.

If you like, you can look up some of the more traditional forms of evidence supporting Thought Field Therapy and related techniques. There are over 50 references to studies, articles, and books found in the traumatic stress data base funded by the U.S. Department of Veteran's Affairs. The PILOTS Data base and other sources are listed in the resources section of this book.

But you do not need to rely on mathematical models or studies to see the power of Thought Field Therapy. As Dr. Callahan has pointed out, when you use Thought Field Therapy you will experience a *clinically significant improvement* without having to look for the small changes found using statistical tests in traditional research approaches. Clinical improvements constitute the results you experience in the change in the level of distress you rated in the tapping protocol. Clinical improvements represent the changes in your own ability to function in ways that you determine important to you. The big changes in your own behavior, which can be detected without having to compare little details statistically, provide strong evidence for Thought Field Therapy's efficacy.

Evaluate Thought Field Therapy and the NOW traumatic stress recovery approach for yourself. You can do your own research and collect your own body of evidence by tapping and doing your own recovery work. Make a list of what you would like to change in your life right now. Don't work too hard at this; just ask yourself, "What do I want to change?" Remember why you picked up this book. Ask yourself, "Why did I feel it would be helpful for me? What problem did I hope it would solve in my life?" What changes will make your life better? As you read this book you will become a witness to many change experiences in the stories shared, but the best evidence about the efficacy of tapping will be what you learn and change about yourself by using the Thought Field Therapy techniques and applying the NOW model.

If you are among the small group of people who for some reason find yourself dissatisfied with the approach presented here or the results you achieve with Thought Field Therapy, do not give up. The techniques presented here are self-help and, as such, are limited and not comprehensive or complete. If you are not getting the results you want, it does not mean you are in a hopeless situation. Reach out to others who have experienced what you have experienced. Find a professional with the knowledge and skills you do not have. If you already knew everything you would not be reading this book. Sometimes finding someone with more training and experience with Thought Field Therapy represents all it takes to create change and to get you moving in recovery.

Do What You Must, But Tap First

When people seek professional help for their problems, most often they already know what decision or action will improve their situation. At least they know the initial steps to take. They don't always take those steps, however, because they are stopped in their tracks by their overwhelming emotion. The pain of a loss, the horror of the reality they have to face, the acceptance of limits, or the demands of the environment in which they find themselves constitute the source of overwhelming negative emotions and sensations that freeze their thinking and immobilize them.

You, too, know what actions are right, healthy, and would bring joy to your life right now. You know what actions will move you further on your life's journey. As you learn about traumatic stress recovery using Thought Field Therapy and the NOW traumatic stress recovery process, you will be able to take those actions you know inherently will help you heal and take you where you want to go. Why? Because your steps no longer will be blocked by fears and emotions that impair your ability to think, decide, and act. You will understand how to be where you are in time and place comfortably. You will be more aware of the current moment and able to envision and to create a future that matches your essential self, the part of yourself you will have come to know through the experience and expression of health, love and joy.

Trust what you know about yourself, your values, your beliefs, and your desires to lead you on. The shortest distance between two points is a straight line. So , the point where you found yourself as you started this book and the point where you want to end up may be closer together than you ever imaged prior learning Thought Field Therapy. Before you can begin to move towards that desired point, however, you have to rid yourself of the blocks to action. Using tapping when you are in pain and fear will end the overwhelming feelings that stop you from thinking as well as from acting. As you become aware of the open wounds from the past that cause you pain or fear in the present, tap.

Tapping in Public

Do not wait to be alone. Do not wait to be with someone supportive. Do not wait to avoid the strange looks from people around you who are ignorant of the importance of caring for yourself. Do not wait to for the pain and fear to subside on their own.

Find a way to do what helps you while you are in the midst of your upset. Find a bathroom or some other place to be alone, if that is what you need to feel safe enough to tap. Give the people you are with any excuse you can come up with in that moment to get to a space where you can tap. Or, don't offer any excuse at all, and get to a place you feel safe so you can tap. Or just start tapping. If you need to say something to explain what you are doing, here is a list of things you can say:

"I know this looks weird. I'll explain what I'm doing in a minute."

"Give me a second to calm down a bit. This helps me."

"If you are as upset as I am, try this with me."

"I saw this on TV, and it helps."

"My therapist suggests I do this when I get upset. I want to take her advice."

"I want to show you something and see what you think of it. Try this."

Once you tap and calm down you can share as much or as little as you want about what is going on with you. Sharing your story is very personal, and, as you will see in later chapters, often difficult to do. Sharing your knowledge of Thought Field Therapy, however, always is fun if you remember that how those with whom you share this process respond to the information you give them represents their choice and not your responsibility. Accept that until they experience tapping for themselves they will not fully comprehend the process.

To begin moving along that shortest line to covering the distance from open wounds to complete healing and recovery, become a shameless tapper. You can even tap away your shame and embarrassment about tapping so you can tap shamelessly. (If you feel the need to do so, see the basic steps in the Part Five for the appropriate tapping patterns.)

Stealth Tapping

When you cannot find or get to a safe place to tap, you can care for yourself by performing the technique with pressures instead of tapping. After you become familiar with the protocols and using Thought Field Therapy, this allows you to do it quietly with anyone present.

If you are with people with whom you do not feel it is safe or appropriate to reveal your condition or your need to take action to help yourself, you can still do Thought Field Therapy effectively using the extended trauma protocol with pressure instead of tapping. Here's how you do it: Press firmly on the side of your hand. Press with your finger on the place under the nose. In a way that makes it appear you are giving the topic at hand some thought, hold you head with your fingers at your brow and then under your eye. Fold your arms so that you can touch and press the place under you arm. Lean on your collar bone or appear to be scratching or rubbing the collarbone point. Press on the fingers under the table if you are at a meal or a meeting. When you do the nine Gamut series just press the point on the back of your hand and just imagine you are doing the eye movement and do the hum-count-hum to yourself silently. It is all right to slow it all down or speed it all up to have your movements take on a more natural rhythm. With a little practice you can get good at taking care of yourself this way.

So far, you have learned that you do not have to suffer overwhelming negative emotions, you have the tools to heal your open wounds, stop your pain from the past and your fears of the future. Now, it is time to start looking more closely at the events that caused you to need a book like this. Part two, deals with coming to an understanding of the nature of traumatic stress responses — causes, normal and abnormal reactions and responses — and what you need to know to make sense of your experiences.

PART TWO

What You Need to Know
About Traumatic Stress

CHAPTER FOUR

Traumatic Stressor Events
and Traumatic Stress Responses

Telling the Story Leads to Taking Back Control: Working Through the Layers

Jean was referred to me by the local prosecutor's office. She needed help preparing for a preliminary hearing concerning the man who had assaulted her. As the session began, Jean started to respond to my simple question, "What happened?" but soon found herself unable to do anything besides cry. At my direction, she began tapping to help her reduce her upset and to help her relate her story. In a minute, she was able to begin telling me what had happened.

As she described the events she had experienced, she again became so upset that she had to stop talking. This time she was able to report that as she remembered what had happened to her she now was filled with feelings of anger and rage. These emotions, however, constituted a different focus than the one she had mentioned when she started the session, the first layer revolved around the difficulty she had talking about the traumatic event without overwhelming emotion. During the first tapping sequence, she was thinking about how much pain she had felt when she was assaulted; we tapped to relieve that pain. We performed a second tapping sequence for the second layer of anger and rage she was feeling at this point in the session. She then finished telling the story of the assault.

As Jean talked about the upcoming hearing, the next layer of overwhelming feelings arose. At the thought of being in the same room as the perpetrator she felt her heart pounding and breathing stopping. She then tapped for the anxiety associated with that upcoming event.

This made it possible for her to visualize herself being in the room with her assailant and actually testifying. Then Jean imagined her husband and parents in the courtroom watching the proceedings, and her upset returned. She acknowledged that her current feeling, which she identified as guilt for putting her loved ones through the hearing, was unreasonable and that she had done nothing wrong. Yet, Jean could not tolerate the feeling that she was hurting people she loved. Since her family culture made it unacceptable to ask them to not attend court to support her, we tapped to rid her of this layer of irrational guilt.

At that point, Jean reported she felt complete with our session and knew what she had to do to finish her preparation for the next day. She would go home and tell her husband and her parents what had happened to her, because she wanted them to hear the facts from her in a safe place before they heard them in open court. The fact that she felt both willing and able to take this action indicated that Jean had moved from a place of feeling like a victim to feeling like a woman who had regained her power and ability to do what she felt was important to her. She would be able to prepare her family and take care of them just as she always had in the past.

Jean did not request further assistance. She felt ready to be a credible witness and to do what needed to be done. Once she had managed her overwhelming feelings, using her natural support systems Jean made sense out of what happened to her and what it meant in her life. Before she left my office, she was given written tapping patterns to use if her feelings became overpowering again.

⟐

As you saw, after each tapping sequence, it became possible for Jean to think about what had happened to her and what would happen in a new way. As she cleared each emotional upset, she gained clarity and began thinking about additional related issues. These new thoughts brought up additional layers of powerful emotions that needed to be addressed. In this example, Thought Field Therapy eliminated each layer as it occurred. In a very short time, she was able to return to her normal level of functioning.

The tapping patterns given to Jean were the same patterns provided in this book. So, rest assured, they will work as well for you on a variety of issues as they did for her. For many of you, tapping one time will clear several layers at once.

It is normal to become dysfunctional after your life is threatened. Healing is normal also. The choices you have to make about what is best for you, as well as for those you love, will become clearer as you know more about the normal human healing and coping process and how it relates to traumatic stress and stressor events.

What are Traumatic Stressor Events?

Equipped with the basic knowledge of how to use Thought Field Therapy, you can safely delve deeper into the concepts associated with traumatic stress and recovery in order to help speed your healing. Coming to a clear understanding of the terms and concepts used when discussing what has happened to you and how you responded to these past events provides a framework and a guide for sorting out your experiences. But thinking about these concepts may bring forward memories of what happen to you and set off overwhelming feelings and sensations. If this happens, tap to take care of yourself. By the end of this chapter, you will have gained a new way of looking at your past experiences, your responses to them, and the actions that led you to this place and time.

Current research offers no agreement about how many people have been exposed to traumatic stressor events. We can, however, assume that by their mid 20s, at least 60 percent of all college students have undergone a traumatic stressor event. Assuming that most college students come from a higher socio-economic background and grew up in fairly safe environments, this represents an astounding number. If we include other populations, such as those who live in less protected environments or who have high-risk jobs, that percentage rises considerably. For example, a soldier or marine going on a deployment that includes combat operations most likely will experience a traumatic stressor event as will someone growing up in a low-income, urban area where guns, violence, drugs, and gangs exist as a part of daily life.

Keep in mind that the event you call *traumatic* may not be called traumatic by another person. Despite your differing experiences of the same event, you both are correct in your assessment. A person may react to an event with traumatic stress responses, while another might not. Both people remain normal.

So, how do you know if you or someone else has experienced a traumatic stressor event? How do you know what constitutes a traumatic event? You might possess a mental picture of what a traumatic stressor event looks like, especially if you or someone you know has experienced one, but health care professionals actually have defined this term. This formal definition, which makes it easy for them to decide if someone has experienced a traumatic stressor event, is found in the American Psychiatric Association's *Diagnostic and Statistical Manual of Mental Disorders* (DSM4-TR). This offers a set of definitions and diagnostic criteria referenced by all the mental health care systems in the United States, including insurance companies, the Veteran's department, and the legal system. As a layperson, looking at this definition may help you begin to understand the term *traumatic stressor event* and to recognize if what you experienced fits into this category.

According to this manual, a person has been exposed to a traumatic stressor event *if both of the following were present at the time*:

1) The person experienced, witnessed, or was confronted with an event or events that involved actual or threatened death or serious injury or a threat to the physical integrity of self or others.

2) The person's response involved intense fear, helplessness, or horror. *Note:* in children, this may be expressed instead by disorganized or agitated behavior.

To meet the American Psychiatric Association's criteria for having been exposed to a traumatic stressor event you also have to be aware of the actual event while it is occurring and of the fact that the event has or can cause great harm to you. Additionally, your response to the event must involve strong feelings. This last stipulation explains why a traumatic stressor event experienced by one person may not be experienced as such by another person present at the same event, nor may it be deemed as such if that second person were to be examined by a health care professional. Each person experiences and responds to a situation in his or her own way. Because the criteria for determining if what a person experiences is a traumatic stressor involves both the actual external event (a tangible threat) and an accompanying internal response (awareness of horror), the definition a traumatic stressor event will vary from one person to another.

Many known and unknown factors determine how each of us perceives and experiences a situation. Certainly, individual histories, expectations, and resources at the time of an event play a part in our awareness of the danger and the feelings we experience. If you experienced the event yourself, you can easily judge by the criteria offered whether or not the event in your past falls into the category of a traumatic stressor. You know the details of the event and how you responded to it. However, be careful about rushing to judge whether or not another person's experiences meet your personal — or the professional — standard for being a traumatic stressor event. Without knowing the person's history and situation well, you cannot know if that individual perceived it as a life-threatening experience accompanied by feelings of horror or helplessness. You also have no way of measuring the other person's awareness or feelings at the time of the event.

For example, imagine you are part of the inpatient staff at a psychiatric facility, but have had no training as a psychiatric specialist. Your experience of a patient with delusions and hallucinations attacking another patient likely would differ greatly from that of someone trained to work in that setting and experienced in such situations. You might feel very helpless and hopeless without any knowledge and skills to intervene. However, with training and practice, as well as with the help of a good team, such an event might actually leave you feeling pumped up by your ability to help.

How we respond to events in our lives has nothing to do with moral courage or any other single factor either. Even the most courageous people find themselves affected by traumatic stressor events. The truth of this statement can be seen when looking at those who suffer from Post Traumatic Stress Disorder (PTSD), an anxiety disorder that can develop after exposure to a traumatic stress event. The percentage of living recipients of America's highest recognition for bravery, the Medal of Honor, suffer from PTSD at an almost equal percentage to living combat veterans without such medals acknowledging their courage. Even the most courageous and best of us are susceptible to overwhelm.

Also, a one-time, life-threatening event may not become a traumatic stressor event, but when that same event is repeated it may, indeed, become one. The fact that something didn't bother you the first time you experienced it offers no certainty that that same event will never become a traumatic stressor. All stress is cumulative, and high-intensity events create stress that can change the way we perceive and experience these events over time. The resources you have available to respond to an event at any given time can make the difference between that event being a normal stressor or a traumatic stressor. For example, swimming across a lazy river to tow a child on a float back to the beach might stress you a bit. Now, imagine that same swim after a twenty mile hike, a four hour climb down a rock face, and no sleep for 24 hours in an unsupported rescue. That effort might exhaust and overwhelm even the strongest emergency responder.

Your previous experiences usually become resources; you learn from them, and become better able to cope with the same or similar circumstances in the future. However, too many similar traumatic experiences, or too many too close together, can mean your experiences add to your stress. Coping with the death of a child always is difficult but dealing with the death of eight children in less than a month feels close to impossible for most of us. The more stress you experience, the less available resources you have for dealing with life events. The less available resources you have at a particular time, the more likely you will experience a life-threatening event during that period as a traumatic stressor event.

Traumatic Stress Responses vs. Coping Mechanisms

When really terrible things happen to us, we have many ways to respond that help us survive the event and then live through its aftermath. In general, we call these *coping mechanisms* and, in most cases, they constitute normal responses to traumatic events. The spectrum of normal responses can range from our minds or bodies shutting down to them becoming hyperactive. We may respond totally differently at the moment of the event than we do a short time after the event ends. Changes in our response can happen again after a day or a week as well, and our response can be different months later. We may be upset initially, then much better for a while, and then we might find ourselves stuck in certain negative emotions or behaviors just when we think we should have forgotten the event and moved on with our lives.

Luckily, human beings are extremely resilient and often bounce back to health after a traumatic stressor event. When life pulls at us and stretches us, we stay connected to the love, joy, and health of our essential being, and we snap back into shape. Just like a rubber band doing its job to hold something together, we get stretched but continue to hold things together time after time as we expand and contract to meet the demands placed upon us. This expanding and contracting can be likened to our coping mechanisms.

However, sometimes a rubber band gets stretched too many times, and it loses its ability to snap back into its normal form. Sometimes the task it is asked to perform simply is too big, and the rubber band breaks completely. When this happens to us, instead of simply finding ways to cope with traumatic events, we develop *traumatic stress responses*. In such cases, traumatic stressors stretch us past our limits and cause us to break emotionally, mentally, or physically. Sometimes we may not break, but we are unable or less able to function as we did before the traumatic stressor events. When a rubber band gets stretched too far for too long, it loses its elasticity. In much the same manner, extreme stressors can impair our functioning and be destructive to our nature.

The first step to healing any of these responses involves navigating through the obstacles to becoming functional. For this reason, looking at the symptoms that make up your traumatic stress responses provides a good place to start understanding any impairment with which you might be struggling. This is especially true since many traumatic stress responses are generally accepted as indicators of psychological disorders, and traumatic stress responses can, indeed, lead to psychological disorders.

Common Traumatic Stress Responses

The DSM4 contains 17 symptoms representing dysfunctions in three separate categories. Each of these categories reflects another dysfunction that often occurs after a traumatic stress event, and, as such, they reflect the ways in which traumatic stress responses are manifested. The first category discusses ways someone might re-experience the event. Having or sharing memories with another person when you choose to remember the event constitutes a positive response or behavior. On the other hand, experiencing images, memories, dreams, or sensations that pop up in an out of control manner represents a negative condition. The second category deals with ways in which people avoid or come into contact with the bad feelings and thoughts associated with a traumatic event. Behaviors that allow you to avoid anything that sets off a sense of re-experiencing the event, such as not feeling your bodily sensations, not remembering, or not engaging with other people or activities, would fall into the unhealthy stress responses covered in this section. On the other hand, those behaviors that allow you to do the opposite would constitute healthy stress responses. The last category details what happens in the body to keep you from calming down and relaxing when you are safe again after a traumatic stressor event. Sleep problems of all kinds, not being able to think in a clear and focused way, and overreacting to others, situations, or noises are a few traumatic stress responses that fall into this category of responses.

After experiencing traumatic events, additional problems can indicate serious impairments in your life. As mentioned, specific psychiatric diagnoses may even apply to your situation and symptoms. For now, though, just use the categories listed above as a way to consider the nature of your own traumatic stress responses. Or, to determine if you are suffering from any of the more common and serious traumatic stress responses, ask yourself if you have any of the symptoms on the following list:

1) Recurrent and intrusive distressing recollections of the event, including images, thoughts, or perceptions. In young children, repetitive play may occur in which themes or aspects of the trauma are expressed.

2) Recurrent distressing dreams of the event. In children, there may be frightening dreams without recognizable content.

3) Actions that indicate that, or feelings as if, the traumatic event is recurring now (including a sense of reliving the experience, illusions, hallucinations, and disassociative flashback episodes that include those that occur on awakening when intoxicated). In young children, trauma-specific reenactment may occur.

4) Intense psychological distress at exposure to internal or external cues that symbolize or resemble an aspect of the traumatic event.

5) Physiological reactivity on exposure to internal or external cues that symbolize or resemble an aspect of the traumatic event.

6) A need to make an effort to avoid thoughts, feelings, or conversations associated with the trauma.

7) A need to make an effort to avoid activities, places, or people that arouse recollections of the trauma.

8) An inability to recall an important aspect of the trauma.

9) Markedly-diminished interest in participating in significant activities.

10) Feelings of detachment or estrangement from others.

11) Restricted range of affect (e.g., unable to have loving feelings).

12) A sense of a foreshortened future (e.g., does not expect to have a career, marriage, children, or a normal life span).

13) Difficulty falling or staying asleep.

14) Irritability or outbursts of anger.

15) Difficulty concentrating.

16) Hyper vigilance or overactive and oversensitive senses.

17) Exaggerated startle response, the body is over reactive and unable to calm down

As you take note of which of the above items are part of your experience, ask yourself the following additional questions:

- **How frequently does that condition occur?**
- **Which, if any of symptoms, are a constant in your life?**
- **Which symptoms come and go in your life?**
- **Under what conditions do symptoms occur—when, where, and with whom?**

The above list, which actually consists of a variety of traumatic stress responses, offers you one way of thinking about what happens to normal people as they attempt to come back to their everyday way of being after a traumatic event. Each of these responses reflects the body's and the mind's way of protecting you from harm at the time of a traumatic event and a way to be ready to react if the event continues or reoccurs. They serve as coping mechanisms. Once the event has ended, the body and mind do not need to continue coping in this way. Continuing to respond as if the event is still happening creates conditions that impair your function and recovery, and that's when your coping mechanisms become traumatic stress responses or psychological disorders.

The more rarely you experience these symptoms and the more specifically you can identify the conditions that set off these reactions, the better. After traumatic experiences, often even small reminders of these events will set off overwhelming physical and emotional reactions within you. These reminders, or conditions that cause us upset, are called *triggers*, and they come in many forms. Triggers may be memories, similar situations, smells, images, sounds, or anything that takes you into the past and causes negative sensations and emotions to arise. However, Thought Field Therapy eliminates these trigger responses. The fewer the triggers, the better. If you can identify what triggers you and when, however, you can easily begin tapping for these triggers, resolve your upset, and set your healing process in motion.

Everyday Stressors and Stress Responses vs. Traumatic Stressors and Traumatic Stress

The distinction between everyday stressors and traumatic stressors is just as important as the distinction between everyday stress and traumatic stress. Stress occurs in all human systems as we respond to environmental factors or changes in our activities. For example, walking up a flight of stairs, which represents a physical stressor, causes your body's heart rate to change. In addition, the stressor of stair climbing causes changes in breathing, temperature, release and absorption of sugars and other nutrients, and concentration of energy and strength. These changes constitute your stress responses to the stressor and should be seen as positive changes.

The human system has built-in safety checks to balance its whole system. These tell you when you need to stop or to change what you are doing, thus keeping you from harming yourself. If you listen to them, they actually help you become stronger and increase your endurance. Traumatic stressor events, on the other hand, represent those life-threatening events that cause changes that overwhelm your body's normal checks and balances; they push you to unsafe levels of exertion or exhaustion.

Not all stress responses are bad; when a stress response turns into traumatic stress, it becomes a problem. Paying attention to changes occurring within you (stress) as events or forces impact you (stressors) increases your awareness of the present moment. Most of times the stressors around you provide opportunities to engage, grow, or strengthen yourself in the moment even as you undergo stress responses.

In the brain, human beings respond to stressors by focusing or activating different nerve pathways for perception, decision making, and commanding the body's actions. These pathways differ in response to traumatic stressors. The physiology of the brain and the whole body are changed immediately as the fight-or-flight survival mechanisms kick in during traumatic stressor events. Sense of time, distance, and even space can become distorted during a stressor event. At such times, our perceptions can become focused on items we seldom notice, and we may act in response to these experiences in unpracticed and often untested ways. Sometimes when we react under traumatic stress, later we cannot place the events that happened to us and our responses to those events in a spatial/temporal map in our memories. Putting what happened into a place and time represents a normal cognitive process, yet when we respond to a traumatic event this response can become inhibited and impaired.

Emotionally, as we become aware of a life-threatening situation, we experience the traumatic stress as a whole person. Bodily sensation and internal feelings provide us with information and awareness of our emotions. As a situation changes, our emotions alert us to a need to resist or submit to the conditions around us. The type and intensity of our emotional responses are drawn from our intuition, experience, training, and past actions in response to similar situations. Sometimes our bodies even direct us to shut off our feeling when our emotions normally would run high. This can lead us to express our feelings in unusual ways within ourselves or externally with others.

For example, under traumatic stress, someone who never cries may bawl or someone who is always loud and expressive will become quiet. When traumatic stress occurs, you can become overwhelmed by your emotions and feelings. Or you can get so focused upon your emotions that you cannot think and, therefore, may act thoughtlessly. Sometimes you can become so focused upon your internal sensations that you become immobilized and cannot act at all. Sometimes you have to shut out your emotions and sensations completely just to survive.

All of these responses fall within the normal range of traumatic stressor responses. In most cases, how you respond to a stressor, however, is an automatic reaction, not a conscious one. In other words, in a traumatic situation or after one, you likely won't choose your traumatic stress response. You'll just react. Also, often after powerful traumatic stressor events we need some help getting back to our normal way of being. So, don't be surprised or upset if you find yourself unable to stop your traumatic stress responses on your own.

And therein lays the large difference between normal stress and traumatic stress. Day-to-day stressors create day-to-day stress in the body that we handle with some sleep, healthy food, and the opportunity to calm the mind and relax the body. With some support and good problem solving, we resolve our stress and continue on stronger than ever. Traumatic stressors, on the other hand, create traumatic stress responses that impair how we function in our lives. Our system's attempts to react to extreme conditions and forces can have extensive and long-lasting impact on our normal modes of being. In worst case scenarios, traumatic stressors can result in traumatic stress responses that not only change how we function in the world but also rips to shreds our expectations and beliefs about ourselves, others, the world, and even God. This changes not only how we behave but how we think about and respond to everything around us.

Sometimes after we experience traumatic stressor events the actual physiology of the whole body, including the brain, changes. Our ability to activate and regulate changes in heart rate, breathing, temperature, energy consumption, and strength may be thrown out of balance or lost completely.

You can think about what happens by thinking about your car's electrical system. It has a generator (or alternator) to make a spark to start the engine or charge the battery. It also includes a distribution system to that spark where it needs to go for the engine to work and a battery to provide a source of power to run the engine when the power demand exceeds the generator's capacity. The battery also provides the power for the engine's starter. Additionally, the electrical system contains a regulator that measures and controls the direction of the flow of electricity. Sometimes the electricity flows from the generator to the engine, and sometimes it flows from the generator to the battery. Or it could flow from the battery to the engine. When the regulator and the whole system work within its design limits, all is well and your car runs great.

What if something goes wrong? What if a part in the generator wears down and is unable to produce the optimum amount of power? What if you move to a very cold place and the battery does not work as well? If the demands of the system fall within the design limits, then the regulator will make the necessary adjustment and these new stressors will be met by an adequate stress response, and you will continue driving down the road. If the system undergoes a traumatic stressor event, like a crash that smashes the battery case or dislodges the regulator's normal adjustments, neither the regulator nor the battery will be able to perform their jobs. This creates traumatic stress in the system, and the car breaks down.

Unlike human beings, cars are not self-healing mechanisms and, as such, require external help to get back on the road. Human beings do have ways to heal and re-grow certain parts and make repairs to their systems. Like the example above, sometimes the events in our life are within our human design limits and a simple correction by the regulator component keeps us going as when the auto's electrical system has to send more electrical juice to one part of the system to adjust or compensate. However, sometimes the problem exceeds the adaptive limits of the regulatory component and some parts break or shut down completely requiring repairs. Sometimes human beings need a little help, too. The knowledge you are gaining and the use of Thought Field Therapy and the NOW recovery process are the help that will, in most cases, keep you on the road.

Time: A Factor in Determining the Severity of Your Problems

Most of the time, after a traumatic event we are able to recover normal functioning, return to appropriate responses, and resolve the upset on our own. Since such healing generally is expected to occur naturally, the psychiatric diagnosis used in the field of traumatic stress recovery include specific timelines to allow for normal processes to occur without having to label someone as having Post Traumatic Stress Disorder. For example, if you have just experienced a traumatic stressor event, you can expect the first few hours and days after the event to be hard, but you should also expect to start getting better during that time. The intrusive images that pop into your head should be less frequent and less intense after a day or two and even better after a week or two. This is normal. As long as you can sleep, eat, and continue to interact with the people in your life, it probably is safe to give your natural healing mechanisms a chance to work. To help yourself heal, keep talking to others about what is going on inside of yourself, and tap to relieve overwhelming emotions.

However, using the same example, if you continue suffering from any of the above symptoms thirty days after the event, and if those symptoms are severe in nature, a health care professional would more than likely attach that label Post Traumatic Stress Disorder (PTSD) to your condition. Acute Stress Disorder, another diagnostic label used by professionals evaluating people after traumatic stressor events, gives you at least three days to achieve normal responses before attaching this particular psychiatric label to your behavior. What does such a diagnosis actually mean to you? Simply, that traumatic stress responses are negatively affecting your life. In the terminology of this book, it means you have open wounds from the trauma you experienced, and you now need to heal them.

Extraordinary, repeated, or prolonged exposures to traumatic stressors can impair our day-to-day functioning. Sometimes even our entire way of understanding the world becomes impacted. If these events happen to children, the response they must make to survive can create distorted or unhealthy perceptions of the world around them and how to best live in that world. For adults, sometimes the events force a stress response that can completely shatter their perception of their environment and leave them unable to make sense of the world. Traumatic stress responses that go beyond human design capacity cause chronic mental and physical illnesses, dysfunctional patterns of social interactions, and other impairments to living life fully.

If you are not sleeping, your eating patterns are out of the norm, your alcohol or drug-use patterns are excessive, the pictures in your head or bad memories keep coming back and their intensity increases, you need to seek out help. Try taking healthy action. Try some Thought Field Therapy. Try talking with a friend. If you continue to get worse get some help from a professional health care worker who has training and experience in traumatic stress recovery. You do not have to wait any particular length of time before you start tapping, talking with others, or seeking help. Be aware of how you are responding to your environment and of what those around you are saying about your behaviors and responses. As you go on with your life after a traumatic stressor event, expect the symptoms to be less of a factor in your daily activities. If things are not getting better, get help from some one you trust.

Many factors will effect how much traumatic stress you experience from the events of your life and your response to that stress. These include: 1) types and lengths of exposures to traumatic stressor events, 2) your age and developmental level at the time of exposure, 3) the support systems available to you for recovery, and 4) the personal family and cultural norms you have experienced. These things also determine how quickly your open wounds will heal, if they will heal on their own, or if you will need help with the recovery process. Most of you will find the information and techniques presented in this book sufficient to activate and speed your healing, but do not wait to seek out professional help if you are unable to keep yourself safe and healthy at any time. Your safety and quality of life, as well as that of your loved ones, are your primary responsibility.

Phobia vs. Traumatic Stressor

When identifying traumatic stressors, be sure not to overlook the possibility of a *phobia*, rather than a traumatic stressor, as the source of your upset. Phobias are overwhelming physical responses to: specific environmental conditions (storms, heights, or water); animals (big dogs to the littlest bugs); bodily fluids and injections (including the mere sight of blood); or situations (public transportation, closed spaces, crowded rooms, or flying). This list is just a very small part of a very long array of phobias.

Phobias differ from traumatic stressor triggers in that most people cannot recall any history of traumatic events associated with the source of the upset. There is no apparent connection to the past that drives their pounding heart, changes in breathing, out of control responses, or loss of reason. These symptoms are set off by what others think of as nothing. In short, phobias appear as irrational fears, which constitute the very definition of a phobia. Sometimes what looks like a phobia might actually be a trigger from a traumatic stressor event. The ability to recognize the difference between phobias and triggers will assure that you are using the correct tapping pattern. Thought Field Therapy will eliminate these fears in minutes. For example, the following story illustrates how tapping helped someone with a bug phobia. As an expert in Thought Field Therapy and traumatic stress recovery, I have had the privilege of training many groups all over the county. It is always a joy for me to hear how well Thought Field Therapy works.

Bug Phobia: "I Can Kill 'em or Let 'em Live; It Just Doesn't Matter"

I was picked up at the airport and taken to the hotel for a training workshop by a woman who had taken a Thought Field Therapy workshop from me four years earlier. As soon as we were in the car, she reminded me of who she was and what she had worked on. I remembered her clearly as the woman who had wanted to go out to her hot tub to take a soak, but could not go by herself alone or even with her family. Her fear of cockroaches prevented her from this enjoyment. If she saw a cockroach, she would, as she said, "Just freak out and lose it for hours."

She had no memory of being attacked by a gang of wild cockroaches or of being tortured with cockroaches by a sibling as a child. She had never been diagnosed with a disease spread by these bugs.

Yet, when I met her she suffered from a specific phobia, an irrational fear that stopped her from enjoying her home and family. She had a bug phobia, or, to be more exact, a cockroach phobia.

As she drove me to the hotel, she told me, "I remember clearly that night four years ago when I went home and went out the patio where the hot tub is. As soon as I saw a cockroach, I stepped on it and heard it crunch. Since then, I can let them live or kill them, but I have no reaction to them." In fact, she related that she goes through her home with no fear of seeing one of these creatures. And now, thanks to Thought Field Therapy, when she gets home stressed out from the day, she can rest on her patio and in her hot tub with or without her family and without any concerns.

❧

Phobias come from human survival mechanisms gone awry. This explanation, more a theory than a fact, will fall into place for you as you learn more about Thought Field Therapy. Remember, you do not have to have a comprehensive theoretical understanding of Thought Field Therapy to help yourself or others right now.

A fear of cockroaches, for example, may constitute an irrational fear or, in another case, it may be the outcome of having a traumatic experience involving this bug. If you ask, "When did the anxiety start?" and the answer comes, "After waking up as a child in a room full of cockroaches," then you are dealing with a traumatic stress trigger and not a phobia. You need to tap for traumatic stress in this case rather than for a phobia. If you are uncertain if your upset is caused by a phobia or a traumatic stress response, tap first with a phobia pattern and then with a traumatic stress pattern and see which pattern of tapping works best. Notice in the basic steps section in Part Five that the patterns for traumatic stress and for phobias differ.

I once treated a high-ranking executive of a multi-billion dollar corporation for a fear of public speaking. This represents not only one of the most common phobias but also one that creates devastating limitations in people's lives. This mature accomplished man had one fear in life—speaking in front of an audience.

Public Speaking Fear: "So What Was the Problem?"

In his role, Mike was required to make a presentation at the annual stockholders meeting. He would start thinking about it months in advance and his anxiety would continue to mount as the date approached. With all his will, he was able to get through it but was completely physically and emotionally exhausted by the time it was over. This pattern had gone on for years. Mike had tried all the standard cognitive approaches and they had helped him get to his speech and through it a bit better. He had tried drugs to alleviate his stress, but the side effects for him were more than he could stand and they affected his performance. He even had tried to change the corporate charter so he would not have to present at the meeting, but this turned into a legal nightmare. When he heard one of my radio advertisements, he called in desperation.

After two Thought Field Therapy sessions, Mike was able to think about making his presentation with no anticipatory anxiety and able to talk about past events with no discomfort. He had two sessions only at his insistence. He was done after the first session, but he could not believe getting over his phobia could be so easy.

Mike called after that dreaded presentation to tell me it had gone well. He said that while speaking and afterwards, he could hardly remember what the problem had been and had trouble believing that the silly tapping exercise had done anything other than distract him.

⌘

This is an excellent example of what in Thought Field Therapy we call the *Apex Problem*. Often once the phobia has been eliminated, it is as if the phobia never existed. Something about not having the feelings or sensations of upset in the body that accompanied the phobic response makes it hard for the person to remember they ever had fears of such a silly thing. You will see the Apex Problem arise in those you help as they struggle to make sense out of a successful Thought Field Therapy application. They will be unable to wrap their minds around the fact that the dramatic improvement they felt was caused by the tapping. This understanding of the Apex Problem is helpful in explaining the change you feel when using the traumatic stress tapping.

Additionally, someone who does not have an understanding of healing that includes approaches outside of traditional medicine may not be able to recognizing the power of tapping in their own healing process. Yet, as mentioned, an understanding of Thought Field Therapy or a belief in it is not necessary for it to work—or necessary once it has worked. No need exists to convince someone that tapping has caused their healing, even if it has. It only matters that they are free of their upset and their traumatic stress responses.

This little detour we have taken in talking about phobias is important in your understanding the differences between conditions that may feel very much alike and knowing what to do to help yourself. Phobias do not have the same origin and so need a different tapping pattern than do traumatic stress responses. The outcome of tapping for phobias and traumatic stress is very much the same. The upset is eliminated quickly and you may feel as if the phobia or trigger was never really a problem as a way to explain the change. And finally consider your phobic response as a traumatic stressor event. Every time you were forced to endure exposure to the phobic object or condition you may have experienced traumatic stress. For example, if someone phobic of water is thrown into a pool, that person finds it life-threatening and feels horror. Tap for these traumatic memories as they arise.

Traumatic Stressor Events: A Pragmatic Definition

If you look carefully at your life, you'll find you can make a long list of events in which you were threatened with death or serious injury. What happened to you may no longer threaten your life, but you will never be the same after having gone through what you experienced. The same is true of people who have been tortured, have witnessed terrorist attacks, or have seem family or community devastation of some sort, since such events change a person's sense of self forever. However, if you examine your list for events when you had emotional responses involving intense fear, helplessness, or horror, the number of events that could be called traumatic stressors becomes somewhat limited. Individually-inflicted human violence, community-wide disasters caused by humans, acts of nature, or acts of God, these all represent sources of traumatic events. For anyone, the list of events could be endless, but again each person responds differently to each event; only you know what traumatic stressor events you have experienced and what felt stressful but did or didn't leave you with open wounds to heal.

When you started reading this book, you may not have known the term *traumatic stressor event*, but you probably already knew the events that served as the sources of your problems. Trust what you know. Even if you are not fully aware of all of that happened to cause your current condition, you can still heal and feel better. You do not need someone to tell you if you have suffered a traumatic stressor event or to give you a list of specific things from your life that qualify. You don't even need the American Psychiatric Association's criteria to help you decide if you have, indeed, suffered a traumatic stressor event.

If you have had or are having a traumatic stress response to an event, that event was a traumatic stressor event. The next chapter gives you more ways to assess if you are experiencing traumatic stress responses.

Take a moment now to stop reading and check in on how you are feeling as you think about the events in your life that might qualify as traumatic stressors. If you become uncomfortable, or if you notice changes in your bodily sensations, emotions, or ability to think clearly, you may need to do some tapping before you go on to the next chapter.

CHAPTER FIVE

Assessing Your Traumatic Stress Responses

Healing Yourself to Heal Others:
Overwhelmed by Other People's Events

During a Thought Field Therapy session, Alice, a client of mine was sharing an experience that happened to her at about age eight. She was now in her 40s, but as an eight-year-old child she had suffered a horrible level of violence and pain. She had been sexually, physically, and emotional brutalized by a violent group of adult male pedophiles while being forced to watch and participate in their similar assaults on other children.

At some point as she told me her story, I began to cry. This does not constitute unusual behavior for me; I will laugh with a client, and I will cry with them. In this situation, however, my own upset continued to increase as the details of her horrific suffering became too much for me, and I found I could no longer listen. For this reason, I stopped her recounting of the events and treated myself with Thought Field Therapy using the basic traumatic stress tapping pattern.

Once I had reduced my own upset from this vicarious traumatization, she continued to tell the rest of the details of the event. We then used Thought Field Therapy to help her with her overwhelming feelings. Additionally, I was able to help her by being a witness to her story of the violence she experienced and, after the telling, to guide her in making sense of these events and of her life post trauma.

Before I learned Thought Field Therapy, I would have stopped Alice from telling me her story. Even as skilled and committed as I then was to helping others, I would have found a reason to avoid the powerful feelings that arose and to protect myself when she recounted her traumatic stressor event. I might have used the excuse that it was too painful for her to continue. Or, I might have suggested she needed to process these events piece by piece, and we should stop and process one or two parts before going on. Had I done so, through my re-sponses — emotional or otherwise — Alice might have gotten the message that she was not permitted to hurt me with this story. Thanks to Thought Field Therapy, we were able to continue and to find some healing for her in the process.

I didn't realize until the next week that my being overwhelmed had actually provided Alice with a big pay off. When I asked her a question I often use to start sessions, "What stuck with you from the previous session?" Alice replied, "That in all my life, it was the first time anyone had ever cried about what happened to me as a child."

This meant a great deal to her and to me. Our professional re-lationship has continued to grow, and she now feels safe sharing her experiences, a first for her in several ways. Prior to this, she had never felt safe enough in a relationship with another person, in particular with a man or an authority figure, to reveal her story. Additionally, she now knows she does not have to take care of her therapist and that her therapist will be there to help her. And she knows that tapping works.

Are You Having Traumatic Stress Responses?

In the last chapter we mentioned some typical traumatic stress re-sponses, but let's take a look at the wider range of responses that might occur when you experience a traumatic stressor event. This will help you determine if or which ones you might be having in response to the traumatic stressor event or events you have experienced. Remember you do not have to completely fulfill the formal criteria for Post Trau-matic Stress Disorder to suffer from events that have happened in your life. Other ways exist to determine if you are suffering from traumatic stress responses.

Your traumatic stress responses may be conscious. You may be aware of your feelings, your thinking, and how you are behaving at the time when they affect your life. Or you may only be aware of these responses as you review your interactions with other people or your behavior or thoughts after the fact. You also may only be aware of these responses when you look at what you are not doing or who you are avoiding. Besides noticing your patterns of avoidance and engagement around issues you find difficult, pay attention to the sensations in your body as you think or talk about other people's traumatic events.

Human Connections Can Lead to Traumatic Stressors

While listening to people recount their experience cannot be compared to witnessing an event directly, for many people doing so feels the same as being there. As in the story that begins this chapter, I witnessed a traumatic stressor event through some one else's account of it, and doing so evoked traumatic stress responses within me. Such accounts may consist of people's stories, pictures, videos, or recording of events. Feeling sympathy or empathy with strangers may connect you to their traumatic experiences. Family history may connect you to the traumatic events of war, genocide, or culture-wide disasters. The love you have for your child or significant other may connect you to the traumatic events they experienced. For instance, the lovers and families of all the marines and soldiers who serve during times of war often have traumatic stress responses. Knowing the violence or threat of violence your loved ones undergo and the very real sense of horror and helplessness you feel in response to their situation can become a traumatic stressor event for you. More precisely, such an experience is called *vicarious traumatization* or secondary trauma. You won't find these terms in the DSM4, although they should be included in the manual. Basically, it means that when something terrible happens to someone with whom you feel connected by love, their experience often constitutes a traumatic stressor event for you.

Take a moment and let yourself think about the following questions, and, as you do, notice what happens in your mind and body.

- Are you afraid to hear about other people's life and death events, because the injustice of their experiences overwhelms you?

- Are you afraid to hear about other people's painful losses, because it reminds you of your own losses and creates unbearable pain within you?

- Are you afraid to hear of other people's struggles to find their way back to joy, love, and health, because it only intensifies your own sense of hopelessness?

If you are overwhelmed by other people's stories, it may be that your resources are so depleted by your own experiences that any pain or suffering may be too much to manage. It may be that their story is too similar to your own, and it triggers your own responses. It may be that even when you are feeling strong you are so connect by love to that person and their story you become overcome with emotion. In any case, tap to remove the overwhelming sensations and feelings and get into the present to heal yourself and your loved ones. Generally, the more your life history is filled with traumatic stressor events, the greater your susceptibility traumatic stress responses.

A Childhood of Violence, Pain, and Hurt: Extreme Traumatic Stress Responses

What happens when terrible things occur to children? What if these terrible things happen over and over throughout their development? If one event can change how an adult perceives the world or the way an adult relates to himself, others, and God, what do such events do to the untested beliefs of a child? In fact, just as one event can completely shatter the beliefs an adult has about the world, being raised in an environment of continuous traumatic events practically ensures failure, loneliness, and destruction for a child. Indeed, when bad things happen to a child directly or to those around the child, the child typically forms the belief that "only bad things happen" and that becomes his or her way of understanding the world.

When children are exposed to a one time event but have good support systems, they likely will have a quick and complete recovery. Often just a little Thought Field Therapy to relieve any overwhelming fears will allow the love of a caregiver to do the rest of the healing. However, when the "bad things" continue in children's lives, then these traumatic events and the traumatic stress responses that go with them become the foundation on which the children build their relationship to themselves, others, and God. The result of many years of overwhelming physical, emotional, or sexual abuse, as well as exposure to violence, both threatened and actual, over extended periods can cause destruction of core functions and or development of extreme coping mechanisms. This level of exposure leads to a condition called Disorder of Extreme Stress Not Otherwise Specified (DESNOS) by the mental health practitioners. Disorder of Extreme Stress Not Otherwise Specified constitutes another one of those definitions not currently in the DSM–IV that should be there.

Typically, Disorder of Extreme Stress Not Otherwise Specified causes people to become unable to establish the boundaries that keep relationships physically and emotionally safe. Extreme coping mechanisms make them unable to make and trust decisions about their actions and choices. Their thinking about everything and everybody becomes black and white. They no longer have regard for the value of themselves or others. They learn that to stay safe they must always be perfect and get it right. Or they learn to stay safe by always being ready to change to meet the immediate expectations of the environment and people around them. This leads to beliefs, values, and personality traits that affect the way they see the world, people, and relationships, and how they react to the world.

Since Thought Field Therapy does not directly change values or beliefs, it is impossible to tap away personality disorders. Personality disorders are descriptions of sets of individual traits developed over years that result in dysfunctional coping and relationship patterns. These fundamental characteristics are not the result of one event, tendency, or response.

Values, beliefs, knowledge, and aesthetics concerning oneself impact the development and maintenance of personality. In the same ways that Thought Field Therapy may improve cognitive functions, it can ease and speed personality change. Tapping makes reconsidering or changing personality patterns much less stressful. However, as mentioned, it is not possible to *tap in a trait* or to *tap out a belief*. For some individuals with histories involving a lifetime of traumatic stress, complete recovery from traumatic stress responses may involve more than just ending the intrusive images or understanding what happened to you. It may also involve changing the world view that underlies personality. Notice that in the sentence above the emphasis is on the words *for some individuals*. Do the work of recovery, and you will be pleased at how fast your life can change for the better.

A Sense of Safety in an Unsafe World

A feeling of being safe shields and protects us from constantly reacting to fear and allows better access to our coping resources. As you consider your traumatic stress responses, work from a place of safety or the most safety you can create. In the service of creating a safe place in my office for those seeking help, among other things I would tell my clients that while they were in my office nothing bad will happen to them—they were safe. September 11th changed that for me. Parents were calling me and asking for help with their children who had seen the events on TV. What do you say to a child who asks, "Is a plane going to fly into our house?" Saying, "That can't happen to our house," will only get the "Yes, it can; I saw it on TV" argument. Children, like most people, cannot be talked out of their feelings or what they know to be true. When the child feels fear, I suggest two things: tap for the fear and reassure the child that whatever happens he or she will not be alone. "Daddy and Mommy will always be here, and whatever happens, we will get through it together," are the words that most often bring the needed comfort and sense of safety.

Today in my office I offer no guarantee of safety. However, I do guarantee to those who come to me for help that in my office whatever happens to them happens to me, too, and they will not be alone. This brings a sense of safety even without the guarantee of safety. Now, I encourage parents to talk honestly with their children about what scares them, use tapping to get rid of their children's upsets, and to reassure them that Mommy and Daddy will also be there to get through it together. Remember to make the connections with others who you trust to be with no matter what happens and work from a sense of safety.

Being Here and Now

For most of you reading this book, the discussion about vicarious traumatization or childhood abuse may be informative but not critical to understanding your problems or recovery. But one feature of traumatic stress response remains common to almost all those who suffer from it and it has to do with one's sense of time and place.

The essence of Post Traumatic Stress problems lay in a mental and physical inability to distinguish the difference between the *there and then* (when the event happened and you were unsafe) and the *here and now* (where you currently exist safe and sound). If your body and mind cannot tell the difference between the *there and then* and the *here and now*, it will react as though the event is happening again. When that happens, all the neurochemical flooding that comes with traumatic event responses will trigger physiological activity in the body and perpetuate the over-activation of your coping mechanisms. And you will feel as if you are reliving — or constantly living in — your traumatic stressor event.

Research indicates that these hormonal releases and the subsequent chemical interactions that occur in such circumstances actually can cause damage to the brain and other organs. Thus, having a person who has been formally diagnosed with Post Traumatic Stress Syndrome relive a traumatic event in their mind, in written word, by audio or visual stimulation, or in any other form causes them physical damage, because their body cannot tell the difference between what really is happening and what is not. At best, approaches that ask people with this condition to trigger their symptoms through any type of process may teach them something about functioning in this triggered condition, but they will not eliminate the under lying condition itself. Using these exposure techniques may help survivors of traumatic stressor events become better able to function at an extremely high level of stimulation or to function in a state of complete disassociation, but this ability will not bring joy or love into their lives. Rather, finding a way to integrate their memories into their lives and take action to make their lives better by getting them to the *here and now*, such as with Thought Field Therapy, will allow them to accomplish this.

The NOW Test of Traumatic Stress Recovery

Let's return to the rubber band analogy we used in an earlier example. How do you know if a rubber band still retains the ability to snap back or has been stretched beyond the point of no return? And how do you know if you, like the rubber band, can return to normal functioning or have incurred permanent damage from the traumatic events experienced? The importance of knowing this cannot be understated. If you can know your triggers and heal your traumatic stress responses to them, you can protect yourself from further harm and dysfunction in your life. By doing so, you ease the tension on the rubber band, allowing it to do its job without worry about it snapping or becoming stretched beyond repair. In other words, you allow yourself to face daily life without the fear of triggers causing you upset, pushing you into past pain, future fears, or constant traumatic stress responses.

You could ask a health care provider to make this evaluation for you by performing a formal assessment and diagnosis. However, the formal assessment and diagnostic process requires that you find someone with training, experience, and time to complete it for you. Also, the results of those tests are only as good as the person giving the test and the information you provide. How much you trust the tester and thus are open in your responses factors into the results as well. In fact, when finished, the analysis might be incomplete and likely will be subjective.

An easier way exists to analyze your condition. You can do a quick read on your level of impairment simply by telling the story of your traumatic experience from beginning to end. I call this the *NOW Test* for evaluating you state of traumatic stress recovery. If you can tell the whole story with *appropriate affect* then, in all likelihood, you have recovered from the event or are well on the road to recovery. To discern the level of impairment of someone you love or know, ask them to retell the story of their traumatic experience and notice if they do so with appropriate affect.

Appropriate affect means expressing sadness when telling a sad part of the story. You might even cry if the story is really sad, but melting down into a puddle of tears and being unable to continue constitutes *inappropriate affect*. If you find yourself unable to continue with the retelling because you have become filled with anger or rage, that also constitutes inappropriate affect. Appropriate affect means laughing when something is funny, although you might need to allow some flexibility in evaluating what is funny. Laughing when the story is not funny even to those with seasoned sick senses of humor constitutes a bad sign, as does being emotionally shutdown while telling the story. The telling of the story from the head only — without any connection to feelings, emotions, or body expressions — suggest incomplete recovery as well.

Notice if you tell the story as if the events are, indeed, a memory of something that happened in another time and place with all thoughts and feeling available as recollections. At the same time, while you are telling the story, you should have all your current thoughts and feelings about what happened accessible. After you complete the story, you also should be able to allow the listener to respond and not feel the need to run away. Leaving immediately or needing to hide in drugs or alcohol use or other dangerous behaviors to avoid people and their responses to your story after recounting the traumatic event does not indicate that you are healed or healing. Instead, it indicates someone with open wounds who is in need of healing.

The NOW Test

If you would like to take the NOW Test by telling your story and judging your degree of appropriate or inappropriate affect, or to use it with someone you know, follow the steps below. In case you have some difficulty telling your story or feel uncomfortable doing so, I've provided some guidelines and questions the person listening can ask. The questions provide some structure to create a story with a beginning, middle, and end and will encourage you along. The questions also lead you through various aspects of the internal and external components of the story. These are just suggested questions; you can, of course, simply allow your story to unfold as it will.

When you are ready to begin telling your story, read and heed these precautions first:

- **DO NOT DO THIS TEST ALONE! Telling your story to others provides immediate feedback on how you appear to someone else as you recount the traumatic stressor event you experienced.**

- **Know the Thought Field Therapy traumatic stress protocol and be able to use it.**

- **Do not allow the telling of your story to become harmful to you or to your listener in anyway. Be sure to stop and tap at any point if you feel the need.**

- **Stay aware of your responses, and if any part of you says stop, then stop and take care of yourself.**

- **Do this with someone you trust to take care of you and themselves as you tell the story.**

This is your story, so you tell it your way. The following is an outline just to get you started.

1. Pick *one* event, and start from the beginning (just before the event began) of the story.

a. How did you come to be in that place?

b. Who was with you?

c. What were you expecting?

2. Go through the event as it occurred in time.

a. What was the first thing you noticed that was different from what you expected?

b. Once it started, how long did it last?

c. Go step-by-step through each thing that you or others there did and the physical and emotional reactions you and those around you had as it happened.

d. In each part of the story, share what you sensed in your body, the thoughts in your mind, and the emotions you felt.

3. Find the ending of the story.

a. When did you know the event had ended? What was the last action or response?

b. What title do you give this story?

c. How do you make sense of out of your responses? Can you see a reason for your actions?

d. What is unfinished in this story? What feelings remain to be expressed? What injustice remains to be addressed? What gratitude is yet to be shown? What honors still need to be recognized?

4. Find the meaning the story gave your life.

a. What memories from this event and the aftermath do you value and want to carry forward?

b. What life lesson do you take from this event for yourself, for you loved ones, for those who will experience this type of event? What do you want others who may face a similar event to know?

c. Who do you want to share this part of yourself with?

d. How do you want to change the world you live in and will pass on to the next generation?

Considering Your Test Results

By definition, traumatic stressor events cause damage to those who experience them. Most of the time human healing mechanisms protect and repair this damage, closing the open wounds, allowing each person to heal and to return to his or her previous level of functioning. **As you told your story, did you notice any open wounds?** These become apparent in the places where you, or another story-teller (if someone else was telling their story to you), slip out of the *here and now* and into *there and then*. You can also find them in any parts you left out of the story, because it was "just too hard to say or hear" or any segments you told without a sense of connection to the emotion. Did any of the memories or thoughts about the place, time, and other people in the story trigger inappropriate or dysfunctional responses as you told the story? These indicate open wounds as well.

Thought Field Therapy can help you eliminate triggers and remove traumatic stress responses. This leaves you able to tell your story with appropriate affect, because you will have healed your open wounds.

When you can tell your story with appropriate affect, you are well on your way to navigating through the common blocks to complete recovery. You are ready to begin the NOW process of traumatic stress recovery. The first part of the NOW recovery process involves finding a way to keep the emotional and behavioral traumatic stress responses from overwhelming your life. This NOW test will help you see how far you have come in the healing process naturally and how much healing you still need to do.

The second part of the NOW recovery process entails making sense out of the events you experienced and the responses you have to those events. The more complete your understanding of the event and reactions the better. Thus, the more reasonable and rational your story is, the better. As you tell your story, the person listening will be able tell you if it was possible to follow the order of events, make sense out of your reactions to the events, comprehend how you made decisions, and relate to how you managed your emotions. Also, you should be able to observe your own story from a safe place even as you are telling it; this means you can remain removed from the story itself.

The frame of reference you use to understand what happened to you in the past is based upon your whole life experience and world view, not just one event. The criteria or rules you use to deem something reasonable and rational was built over time, and the previous traumatic events you have gone through form part of the foundation of your understanding of how you and others react in life and death situations. What makes sense to the person who has lived a life with many traumatic stressor events may not make sense to someone experiencing a life and death situation for the first time. Your life does not consist of one story or one event. So, you may have to look at many stories, or events in your life together to get the understanding you need to help you heal one or more traumatic stressor events.

If you can **Navigate** through your story without being overwhelmed, then you have come a long way in your recovery and healing. (If you can't, simply go back and tap for the issues that still cause you overwhelming upset.) If you can **Observe** by telling your story from the *here and now* and even understand to some extent what happened to you, then you have come even further in your recovery process. Having engaged in these two active processes, you are ready for final part of the **NOW** recovery process — taking as much control of your life as you can. This represents the **Work** of using what you have learned about yourself: Making choices based upon *who* you are not *what* you have gone through . . . and living those decisions.

The suggested structure for telling your story includes giving meaning to what has happened in your life. Once you have found the lessons in your experiences, then you can apply them to your relationships, your work, and to your life's goals and visions. In this stage of the healing process, we talk about living with integrity. Integrity is defined as a state of wholeness that guides your choices and actions. When you do not feel overwhelmed by your traumatic stressor responses and can, through your observations of what happened to you in the past, understand the events and your responses, then you have access to many more choices in this moment. You have choices that will let you focus your awareness, behave in a way befitting your values, and experience the health, love, and joy available to you.

Telling your story, beginning to end, provides one way of beginning the assessment of your traumatic stress responses and focusing your recovery process. The goal is to live in the now, which happens when you have No Open Wounds. You achieve this goal when you have completed your healing and the NOW process. How do you know when you've arrived at complete healing? When you can answer, "Yes," to each of these questions:

- **Can you navigate your symptoms?**
- **Can you observe and understand your experience?**
- **Can you work the choices available to you with all the knowledge and the wisdom available to you?**

While Helping Others, Don't Forget to Help Yourself

As a professional, my area of expertise lies in Traumatic Stress Response and Recovery so I have listened to thousands of stories. From the first crisis call I took as a volunteer in college over 35 years ago until today, helping individuals overwhelmed by life's events has been my calling. Thought Field Therapy has given me a way to stay in this business of helping. When I learned Thought Field Therapy, I had been doing this work for over twenty years, and I was getting pretty burned out and fatigued. I had held many a hand and been witness to lots of violent stories. As my clients shared their stories, I would do what I had learned as a professional and knew as a compassionate man to be helpful. Yet, we all have limits to our capacity to endure traumatic stress, and I was close to my limit and near a time when I could no longer expose myself to vicarious traumatic stressors safely. At that time, a colleague introduced me to Thought Field Therapy. The tapping process gave me a way to bring an end to my clients' suffering and to my own sense of being overwhelmed by their experiences. By using Thought Field Therapy, I could be successful with my clients and no longer be at risk for compassion fatigue, a form of vicarious traumatic stress response common to professional helpers.

The next story provides an example of how stress, in particular from repetitive stressors, accumulates over time. And, as stress adds up, we respond by becoming more and more stressed until that stress actually becomes overwhelming traumatic stress. It may not begin as traumatic stress, but it becomes traumatic stress over time. This story also shows you how even the most knowledgeable and skilled person can be overcome by exposure to traumatic events even when they think they are prepared to face horrible life events. Last, it illustrates the importance of continuing to search for the help that allows you to return to normal living after traumatic stress responses impair your ability to live fully.

Stuck with the Symbol and Being Triggered Everyday

At a conference workshop on self-care, I asked for a volunteer to demonstrate Thought Field Therapy. A woman who had already shared some of her history came forward. She was a well-trained healthcare professional with extensive experience in traumatic stress recovery work. Two years earlier, she had coordinated an extensive organizational response to a bus accident in which many passengers and staff at her facility had died or were seriously injured. She clearly had done a very good job in providing for the survivors, families, employees, responders, and her own staff. She had even sought out a therapist to help her work through her own responses to this once-in-a-lifetime set of circumstances.

Now, years after the event, her problem revolved around the fact that she still encountered triggers, including her company's logo, in her daily life that stimulated overwhelming emotional responses.

This affected her sleep, her response to requests for certain kinds of help from others at work, and her willingness to accept advancement and promotions. Her traumatic stress responses were wearing on her, but she had stopped seeing her therapist after a year when she had seen little improvement in managing her triggers. While she managed to function day–to–day, she acknowledged she was at high risk for both burnout and compassion fatigue in her job.

When I suggested we try some tapping to relieve the over-whelming feelings associated with her triggers, she said she was fa-miliar with tapping since her therapist had used it with her. However, she reported that it had not worked on this issue. It turned out that she was not doing Thought Field Therapy. Her description of the tapping patterns and procedures used made it clear her therapist had not used current Callahan Techniques® Thought Field Therapy.

Using the Thought Field Therapy trauma protocol, she was able to end her emotional upset in a matter of moments. Several other pro-fessionals in the workshop verified an observable change in her physi-cal appearance, as well as in her subsequent discussions of the event and response to seeing the company logo. The next day, she reported that her fiancé said that for the first time he could see a positive physi-cal change in her when as she discussed these issues. It was the first time he had seen her talk about the incident without all the color drain-ing out of face. He was impressed by her experience with Thought Field Therapy and the fact that when he showed her the logo of the company for which she worked, she didn't react at all; previously she had become very agitated.

The story above describes how to use tapping to treat vicarious traumatic stress for a professional who was not part of the incident but who was connected emotionally in many ways. But vicarious traumatization works the same way for someone who has simply listened to a friend tell the story of a traumatic event in their own life. Tap when you are overwhelmed by emotions. Whatever level of knowledge and skill you have, you can work with yourself. You also can work with those you love and care about by using Thought Field Therapy. If, however, while you are trying to help others—just by listening to them or by helping in a crisis intervention center or during a disaster—you begin to feel overwhelming emotions yourself, you need to take care of yourself as well.

I tell you this story to encourage you to, please, always take care of yourself as you help others. Once you learn how to use tapping on yourself, you will find you will be inclined to help others. Or, you may have picked up this book with the express desire to help someone you know who has experienced a traumatic stressor event and is suffering the aftereffects of that experience. In either case, with Thought Field Therapy, no reason exists to wound yourself in the process of helping others.

Your Traumatic Stress Responses are All That Matter

The important traumatic stress responses are the ones that are yours. They are all that matter when it comes to assessing and healing your ills. The ways your mind and body reacted at the time of the traumatic event and afterwards serve as part of a natural human system. These systems protect and restore you to your highest level of functioning. Each person generates a combination of responses that work the best for him/her in that moment.

Has the rubber band has lost it snap? Is your body, mind or spirit unable to tell the difference between the *there and then* and the *here and now*? Is getting all the way through the telling of your story utterly impossible? Is it impossible to trust another human being because of what happen to you? Do not worry if you answered "Yes" to some of these questions. An affirmative answer only means that there is work to be done.

Armed with Thought Field Therapy, some more concrete information about your own traumatic stress responses, and an awareness of where you are in your healing process, you are ready to move on to the NOW traumatic stress recovery process. The next part of the book presents each of the action processes in the NOW recovery model in depth and offers more suggestions for recognizing where you are in your recovery process and additional tools for moving forward towards complete healing using Thought Field Therapy.

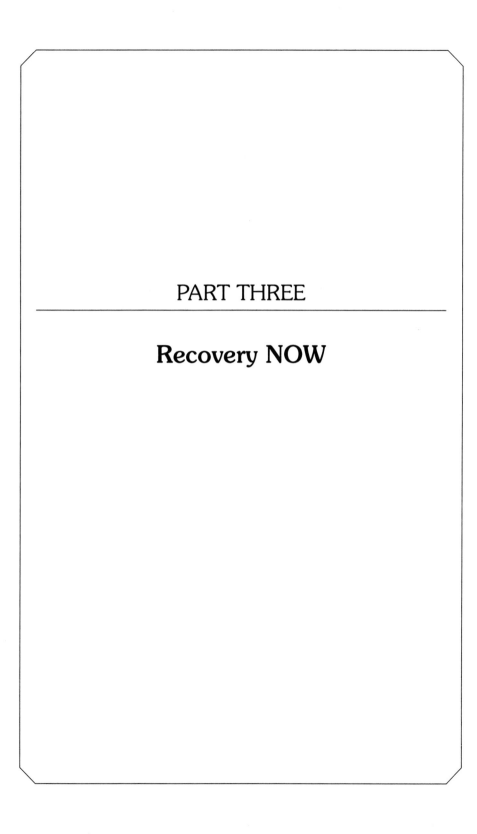

PART THREE

Recovery NOW

CHAPTER 6

NOW, Navigate to Health, Love and Joy

Equipped with the ability to tap your way out of overwhelming upset, you are ready to now work on more fully understanding your current condition and moving towards complete healing or traumatic stress recovery. Although Thought Field Therapy represents a huge step towards healing the open wounds you bear from past traumatic events, the actual healing process — and, therefore, the actual recovery process — starts with getting clear about where you are, where you want to go, and how you will get there.

The word *navigate* means to travel through, on, or over a distance. In terms of your recovery, it means that you have set a course towards health, safety, and being functional. To reach your destination, you must navigate the distance between where you currently stand, which may feel like a terribly unsafe, unhappy, or unhealthy spot, to a safe, healthy, loving, and joyous place that exists somewhere in the not-too-distant future.

The acronym NOW, which stands for Navigate, Observe and Work, serves as a description of naturally occurring processes that begin the moment you feel overwhelmed by the sense of horror and helplessness accompanying a traumatic event. Most of the time, we move through this series of actions spontaneously, returning to an even higher level of functioning in our lives afterwards. Even though traumatic stressor events impact many people every day, this natural process helps many of us to move on rather than remaining dysfunctional long enough to be labeled with Post Traumatic Stress Disorder. More often than not, we move from unconscious reactions that cause impairments in our functioning to conscious, purpose-driven decisions and actions without even having to becoming aware of how we make this transition. However, by increasing your awareness of your own natural NOW process, rather than allowing it to function unconsciously, you will increase your ability to speed up your own healing mechanisms. And often the increased awareness makes us all the more focused and able to deal with stress, make decisions, and move towards our goals beyond closing the open traumatic stress wounds.

You take the following actions naturally to heal from traumatic stress:

Navigate the obstacles of traumatic stress symptoms that stop you.

Observe and understand what has happened to you.

Work you life choices with integrity.

Recovery from traumatic stressor events is *not* a passive process. You cannot do nothing and expect to get better. Healing requires active engagement. That said, when your natural systems of healing are working, you may be unaware of what is happening, because your internal and external resources move you toward that healing quickly and easily. This may seem like being in the healing *zone* — it just happens without conscious effort on your part. You can liken this to when world-class athletes report that they suddenly find themselves 'in the zone' and make the perfect play or take the perfect shot. All of their natural ability, training, and hard work come together to make the activity feel effortless in that moment.

Effortless, however, does not equate to inactive or passive. Athletes condition their minds and bodies and practice constantly. Years of study, review, experimentation, change, and repetition create the zone. When we experience a traumatic event, though, most of us lack the internal and external resources to move into our healing zone. We haven't trained like athletes to heal from traumatic stressor events. So, even though our bodies have a natural tendency to heal, and they know what process to undertake to accomplish healing, we may not be able to get into the zone. Instead, we get stuck in traumatic stress responses. And when we get stuck, we continue to suffer impairments in day-to-day functioning rather than healing from the traumatic event.

Plus, if we remain stuck long enough, we also can develop bad habits while trying to become functional or to end the pain and frustration of our traumatic stress responses as well. These can include such things as self medicating, distracting yourself with high-risk behaviors, or avoiding all emotions. If you become stuck while at certain key developmental points in your life, you can develop unhappy, unhealthy, and lonely ways of seeing the world and being in the world as well. These bad habits or limited ways of understanding the world then become additional roadblocks that you must navigate around or through in your movement towards healing.

All of this happens unconsciously; most of the behaviors and habits enter into your life while you remain unaware and creep further and further in until they are well settled and difficult to extract. Becoming aware that something is wrong—that your behavior or thinking has changed—and taking action to correct the problem constitutes an essential active process in recovery.

In fact, awareness represents the first action step, and the most important step you must take, to engage in your healing. Awareness represents the starting point. Once you become aware that you are stuck, then you can use what you already know and what you are learning about recovery—such as reading this book—to keep moving. If the sensations of pain and fear that you experiencing remain your primary focus, then use Thought Field Therapy to calm your mind and relax your body. This will allow you to move away from pain and fear and toward awareness of what you know about your condition and the resources available to you

The resources that bring you to and keep you in the healing zone are: loving parents, supportive friends, caring lovers, a sound family, good health, good preparation prior to exposure to traumatic events, and opportunities to easily return to a safe place. Unlike athletes who have to practice their skill a lot before they can find themselves in the zone, your existing resources can help you get into the healing zone easily. Additionally, as you become aware of the recovery processes, this in and of itself activates more healing resources.

Each category of action in the NOW process contains a series of questions about yourself, what happened to you, or how your experiences have caused you to change. Your active involvement in the recovery process requires that you find answers to these questions. Doing so will increase your awareness about what happened to you and how it has affected you and your way of being in and seeing the world. Read the questions carefully and thoughtfully. Then look for responses that are equally as thoughtful and that fit with your beliefs about who you are now. Some questions will seem more important to you than others. You'll find some answers in the stories of what others have done and learned as well. Some answers will come easily and completely all at once while others will come slowly and will change over time, requiring a great deal of your energy to finally complete them. No matter how you complete the questions, arriving at the answers serves as *your active role* in the complete traumatic stress recovery process.

Starting from a Safe Place

To set a course of travel you must first know your starting location. Once you know where you are, you will be able to select the direction in which you need to move to get to your destination and that will tell you what hazards lie ahead. These can't be identified if you don't know your current location. To begin the NOW process and to start navigating towards your healing and recovery, you must now identify your current position. To do so, answer these questions:

- **Where are you? What is your physical location?**
- **Who is around you, and what is your relationship to these people?**
- **What is expected of you at this moment?**
- **What sensations are you feeling?**
- **What emotions are most prominent within you?**
- **What images or thoughts currently occupying your mind?**
- **Are you safe?**

The answers to these questions may seem easy and straightforward or difficult, complex, and vague. The ability — or inability — to focus on these questions often is determined by how safe you feel you are from continuing traumatic stressors.

Your answers will offer you an important detail: They will tell you if you feel safe right now. Any condition (person or situation) that represents danger to you represents the first hazard you must navigate through. As you start the recovery process, you have to find a way to end any ongoing traumatic stressor event(s), get out of whatever situation causes you continued traumatic stress, or, at the very least, place yourself in a safe place and time. You must create an environment that shelters you from physical and emotional harm. Until you can see, assess, and know that the danger no longer is present in this moment, you will have an *on-guard* mind/body set that perpetuates your traumatic stress responses. Of course, if dangers still exist in your life, then having an on-guard mind/body set serves you and should not and cannot be eliminated. However, for healing to occur, you must be safe enough to rest and to restore your mind, body, and soul. If you feel exhausted or depleted in any way, as you would if you were hungry or thirsty, your primary biological survival needs will take precedence over any attempts to relax the body or calm the mind and to get to a level of actual emotional healing.

If you actually are safe and are not experiencing any real traumatic stressor events at this time but you still think you are in an unsafe situation because you are reliving past traumatic stressor events, you likely are suffering from symptoms of Post Traumatic Stress Disorder. You still need to place yourself in a safe place, and you will need to do this by using Thought Field Therapy to reduce your upset and bring you back into the current moment so you realize that you are, indeed, safe.

Even when you find yourself in present-moment situations that continue to cause you stress, Thought Field Therapy will help you calm yourself. You can use it any place and any time, but no matter how calm you are at any given moment, certain actions, like driving drunk at high speeds on a motorcycle, remain unsafe. Remember, being safe does not always depend on other people; sometimes it depends on you. No substitute for common sense and good judgment exists. Feeling the connection to yourself and the people around you, being able to recognize real threats versus imagined dangers, knowing when you are being triggered to past events and experience, and remembering to tap when this happens, keeps you safe.

If you are having trouble recognizing the validity of your feelings about a situation or a relationship, you can use your awareness of others to help you make choices that move you in the direction of safety and healing. You can compare your experiences with those around you, thus doing a *reality check* to see if the *here and now* you are experiencing is the same as the *here and now* of others. For example, if you think you hear a fire alarm or smell smoke but know you sometimes hear or smell things that are not there, look around you to see what other people are doing. If everyone is heading towards an exit, then you probably should, too. If no one is moving or asking about the funny smell, then your *here and now* indicator is confused and you may need to tap and sort out what triggered you. If you are home alone with no one to use for comparison, using your dog's or cat's responses to the *here and now* may help you know when you have slipped into the *there and then*. If they are sleeping soundly, you can likely be assured that you are safe. Sometimes getting directions from a reliable source helps us navigate to safety.

So, ask yourself, "Am I as safe as I can be?" Be reasonable about what this means. In some places and times, danger is part of the location and the role you have chosen. Given the choice you made to be where you are, are you as safe as you can be? If you don't answer with a strong, clear, "Yes," start moving out of your current situation immediately or change what you can so you can get to a safe place right away. You may need to change your location. You may need to change the people with whom you are associating or the nature of your relationship with them in some way. You may need to rest and restore yourself to better respond to the situation in which you find yourself. Only from a safe place can you start to sort through what has happened to you and become aware of the reality of your current situation. Then you can begin making choices about your future.

Are Your Symptoms Allowing You to be *Here Now*?

Once you are feel safe and unthreatened by traumatic stressor events (real or perceived), the next step in the process involves dealing with Post Traumatic Stress Responses you might be experiencing. Part of knowing where you are involves knowing the factors and conditions that you are currently dealing with. Some of these may have been revealed in the answers to your questions as well. Those symptoms represent the obstacles you must navigate through as you move towards recovery. Those dysfunctional conditions make it difficult to clearly see where you are at this moment, where you want to go, and how you will get there.

If you aren't sure if the symptoms you experience can be classified as Post Traumatic Stress Syndrome or if your traumatic stressor responses represent problematic ones, try asking yourself the following questions.

- **Can you see in all directions around yourself?**
- **Can you hear subtle and beautiful sounds as well as loud and scary ones?**
- **Can you be patient and let things in the moment unfold as they will, or do you have to force some action?**
- **Are you engaged with the people around you or just keeping an eye on them?**
- **Are you involved in risky behaviors just to avoid feeling anything but the rush necessary to know you are alive?**
- **In this moment are you avoiding people, places, or things, because they set off negative sensations, feelings, memories, or thoughts?**

Asking and answering these questions will increase your awareness of whether you are choosing to live a life of health, joy, and love versus just reacting to triggers or protecting your open wounds. If you answered "Yes," to the first four questions and "No" to the last two questions, you likely are well on your way to healing from your traumatic stressor event(s). If you are not getting clear answers to these questions, you may be stuck in problematic traumatic stressor responses or even Post Traumatic Stress Disorder and not living your life fully. Tap for any specific triggers that may be setting you off.

Stop Running Away and Start Running Towards Recovery

A common traumatic stress response involves running away from whatever causes us discomfort. While avoidance often seems the best immediate solution to dealing with nasty stuff like the traumatic events you have experienced, and this serves as a perfectly good first response, it doesn't help you get clear about where you are, where you want to go, or how you will get there. And it certainly doesn't help you heal the open wounds left from your experience.

Sometimes we do have to hastily navigate around something unexpected in our path so we don't crash into it. However, once you've navigated around the thing that threatened to cause you pain (or did cause you pain), where do you turn next without getting totally off course? How do you get back on track?

Unfortunately, too many people don't realize they have swerved and gotten off course, and so they don't start navigating again to correct it and redirect themselves towards their desired destination. Instead, they look for new destinations that most often involve continued ways to avoid pain. Only now they are avoiding the pain from the past traumatic event, and this doesn't allow them to move forward toward and into a future where the wounds they have incurred are healed.

To avoid the pain, many people become numb. They simply choose not to feel the pain or, for that matter, any other sensation or emotion. Going numb serves the same purpose as running away, because it allows you to avoid—not feel—your emotions. When you are unaware of the sensations and feelings in your body, you have difficulty thinking, or reacting or knowing what you really desire. What happens to the quality of your life if you cannot feel? It becomes empty and dull and without preferences. It's no wonder then that over time coping by feeling numb or running away from feelings often leads to self-medicating with alcohol and other drugs, because these help you cope with the resulting lack of direction in your life. Sometimes risky or compulsive behaviors can keep you from the feelings you do not like by replacing them with the adrenaline rush of doing something dangerous or the repetitive motions of compulsion. All of these responses become just another way that you become more unsafe in the world. Being fully in the moment with all your senses active represents the safest condition.

If the description above sounds more like you in any way, you can skip ahead to Chapter 11, which talks about taking control of addictions and bad habits. You may find it useful, and it is okay to skip ahead and come back after you feel more in control of your emotions or responses to your traumatic stressor events.

Rather than spending your time and energy in avoiding what you experience, a better approach to dealing with the negative, fearful, or anxious feelings lies at your finger tips. Instead of running away from your pain and anxiety, actively engage in moving towards your desires. When you encounter triggers, use them as an opportunity to heal by remaining aware and using Thought Field Therapy and the NOW traumatic stress recovery process to navigate through these triggers.

As discussed earlier in the book, triggers come in many forms. They may consist of memories related to a past trauma or similar situations or they may consist of smells, images, or sounds related to the traumatic event you experienced. Triggers represent anything that takes you into the past and causes you to have negative sensations and emotions related to your traumatic stressor event. If you can tap your way through the trigger so the emotional upset dissipates or disappears, then you can look at the trigger more clearly and try to understand why it causes you to move from the current moment into the past. You can increase your awareness of why it serves as a trigger and take another step towards healing your open wound.

Each time you are triggered, you lose your grip on the difference between *there and then* and *here and now*. If you decide or take actions based on a sense that you are somewhere else at another time and in danger, you place yourself at a high risk of making decisions you will regret when you regain your awareness. You are most safe when you are in the *here and now*, and your best decisions will be made based upon an awareness of your current situation. Thought Field Therapy eliminates trigger responses and allows you to look forward. The Now process helps you to increase your awareness and understanding of your triggers so you can make more informed decisions based on the *here and now* as well as on the future you would like to create for yourself.

Choosing Your Destinations

The journey to full traumatic stress recovery leads to somewhere. The result of your work, change, and movement will take you to new place. Finding that place means more than just ending the overwhelming emotional and physical responses from past traumatic stressor events and their current triggers. The destination you choose may be the same as the one you had chosen before the traumatic events, or you may choose another one. In either case, you can arrive there with no open wounds and fully recovered. However, you must know where you are going. You must have a destination, a goal, a vision towards which you are moving.

In Chapter three, you were asked to create your own body of evidence for the effectiveness of Thought Field Therapy and the NOW model of recovery. Doing so involved making a list of the things you wanted to change, and then using tapping to help change them. This list provides a good starting place for looking at where you are, where you want to go, and how you plan to arrive at your destination. When you have a list of symptoms you want to rid yourself of or a clear sense of what is wrong or not working that you'd like to improve, you have found your current location in life. You also have located the direction in which you'd like to move and the motivation to get moving.

Even in the simplest forms of life, motion is either towards something or away from it. Single cell critters move towards those things that bring them what they need to flourish and move away from those things that are destructive to their essence. These simple creatures seem to possess a source of knowledge that effectively provides information about positive and negative forces. Scientists have a very incomplete understanding of how this occurs, but they have seen this phenomenon even at a cellular level.

Humans respond the same way. We receive information that tells us to move away from anything that causes pain, fear, or out of control behavior. And we move towards anything that gives us pleasure. However, human beings are not simple-cell creatures. We possess a much-more-complicated sense of direction and choice of movement that varies from moment-to-moment and circumstance-to-circumstance. Our reasoning ability causes us sometimes to realize that we are moving in the wrong direction, necessitating that we change not only our direction but sometimes even our destination.

Plotting a Safe Course

Now that you have a safe starting point and a sense of your destination, you can plot the course you need to take to get there. Like most people, you likely will find the journey from where you are to where you want to be cannot be taken by traveling a straight line. The stops and detours you take along the way may constitute pleasant side trips made simply for the fun of it. Or you may pause to meet obligations or commitments, or something unexpected might sidetrack you. Sometimes you make a turn off the main road to explore new terrain or something that looks interesting only to find you have taken a long detour that brings you back to the path you were on at the start. Or you may discover a road you prefer that leads to a totally new destination. As you begin thinking about your path, here are some questions to consider:

- **Are you alone, traveling with another, or in a group?**
- **How much baggage (connections to the past, tools, or gifts)**

are you carrying, and what will you want or need when you arrive?

- **What feels better to you: getting there quickly or slowly so you can see everything along the way?**

- **What resources are available to you? How is your health, and how strong and numerous are your support systems?**

Your answers to these questions represent but a few factors that come into play as you plot your next move on your trip. Give some thought also to the factors that influence how you plan your trip in general. For instance, look at the people in your life and at your relationships. You may want to move towards those individuals with whom you feel safe and away from those individuals with whom you feel unsafe. Your values and beliefs about right and wrong set limits related to what you will and will not do. The feelings and sensations in you body can direct you, working almost like a compass or a navigation system, and you can also trust your heart to give you good directions when you are not feeling overwhelmed.

As always, though, overwhelming upset make it difficult to assess the reality of a situation or condition in which you find yourself. Out of control emotions will make it difficult for you to take advantage of — or even see — your available resources.

Remember, you can also use those you trust to direct you to safety. If you are lost, acknowledge this fact, ask a trusted guide for directions or to help get you to your safe destination.

Pace Yourself When Using Exposure Therapies

As you deal with the symptoms that impair your normal functioning, be careful about how much you try to heal at any given time. With your destination known and your course plotted, the speed at which you proceed is critical to a safe journey. First, address those things that reduce the overwhelming feelings you have and help you feel and be more in control. However, do this one symptom at a time.

Go slowly. When you engage in any work dealing with traumatic stress, stay aware and proceed with caution. In the NOW recovery model you are asked to face your past and confront the anxieties that stop you. This represents a form of *exposure therapy*. Completely and quickly eliminating the overwhelming feelings and sensations that arise during exposure therapy, however, differentiates Thought Field Therapy from other exposure therapies.

Other books and approaches to healing teach you how to overcome your blocks to success or recovery by telling you to *re-experience* the events that trigger you and to manage your responses differently until you are no longer triggered by them. This sometimes is accomplished by thinking about the event differently, giving it a different meaning, by disassociating from the feelings as you go through them, or by learning you can survive the experience of being triggered. Some exposure therapies ask you to write and then read the story of the traumatic stressor events you have experienced while others ask you to imagine being in that situation again. Some such therapies even give you video or audio play back from actual similar events or computer stimulations to stimulate your response. Still others have you travel to the actual locations where your trauma occurred or to recreate the actual events.

These exposure approaches can help you come to a better understanding of the traumatic stressor events and your common responses to those stressors by having you re-experience the events from the *here and now*. However, if you experience the situations in a way that places you back in the *there and then*, such exposure puts you at risk for the same kinds of physiological and psychological damage that occurred *there and then* when the traumatic event actually occurred.

These exposure therapies are powerful regardless of the type of exposure used. However, as you tell your story of the traumatic stressor event during Thought Field Therapy, if you start to feel overwhelmed or uncomfortable you are told to stop telling the story and to tap to eliminate the overwhelming distress. Thought Field Therapy allows you to end the symptom, think with clarity, and to assign meaning to the events that fit your values and beliefs. This is very different than being told in exposure therapies to manage your reaction or symptoms in a different way such as; to get used to it, to think of it in a different way, or to change the meaning of the events. You are encouraged only to tell the story from the *here and now* and never to be in or remain in the *there and then.*

If you choose to participate in any other types of exposure therapies, be careful of how much you take on. Sensing the traumatic events as if you are *there and then* only makes things worse. If you cannot tolerate a brief thought of your traumatic stressor event or if even small triggers send you back into the *there and then,* you are not ready for further exposure.

Most professional therapists and researchers understand the power of these traumatic stressor events. In most cases, the exposure work is handled in a progressive process. In other words, you are asked to expose yourself a little bit at a time to the memories of your past trauma, taking on more and more as you learn to handle it. Often you are not allowed to do these kinds of exposure therapies until a professional monitoring your process is convinced you are staying in the *here and now* as you do other types of therapies.

If and when you consider using exposure therapies that do not include Thought Field Therapy, ask yourself if the professional helping you understands your limitations. Ask yourself, "How will I or my helper know when it is time to stop?" And ask yourself if you can keep yourself safe in the *here and now* while you go through the process. Keep evaluating if the exposure therapy you choose, and any approach you choose, is making you and your life better. People who are unable to successfully complete exposure therapies often think it is their fault, and that they are beyond help. Actually, not completing exposure therapy only means this was not the right approach for you at that time.

You are responsible for your recovery. You pick the approach, you choose the pace, and you set the limits.

Trust your own process!

Before going on to next chapter consider this story, which shows you how having a set of action steps for healing can sometimes get in the way of healing itself.

Sometimes when Thought Field Therapy clears problematic symptoms, the rest of the necessary healing process falls into place all on its own. As a specialist in traumatic stress recovery, I spend a lot of time with people who are stuck in their recovery process. They come to see me, because they want help getting unstuck so they can heal. I give them the added professional insights, techniques, and support they are seeking. Once in a while, though, I am pleasantly surprised by the wonder of the natural healing processes at their best. At those times, I just sit back and watch.

I Gave Him the Ring!

When someone puts a gun in your face, it's pretty common to only remember seeing the gun. A woman in her 30s came in to see me after being mugged. It had been over a month since a thug had found her alone on the street and grabbed her purse. As she had turned to see what was happening she saw the gun pointed at her.

The man had yelled "give me your ring." She had complied, and he had run off.

Afterwards, the woman filed a police report and went on with her evening. The only problem was that since that night, the image of the gun barrel directed at her kept popping into her head at all sorts of weird times.

As I showed her how to use Thought Field Therapy, she had no problem bringing up the picture in her head of the gun and rating the level of distress she was feeling. In minutes she had told me about the whole event, and we had tapped when ever her emotional level of upset increased. Each time we did the tapping sequence, her feelings diminished. She learned the protocol for tapping traumatic events, and we talked about when to use Thought Field Therapy on her own. With that, she gave me a check for my services and said, "Thanks."

I suggested, however, that maybe we were not done working together, because in my model of traumatic stress recovery she still had two action processes to complete. She needed to answer the questions "Am I safe now?" and "What's happened?" I explained the model to her.

She said, "Well, let's see . . . Am I safe now, and do I feel safe? Yes. What happened? He put a gun in my face and demanded my ring. I gave him my ring and then called the cops. That's petty clear to me, and I see no other way to have handled such a situation. So, what does this all mean? How have I changed? Not much! In my world, people get mugged pretty regularly. God allows a lot of things I would not, but God and I were managing to get along before my ring was stolen, and I don't see thing have change much since then. Thanks for the tapping. I'll call if the gun thing comes back."

Once the intrusive image was gone and she was no longer impaired, this woman had clear answers to my questions about what had happened to her and what it meant to her life. Her healing process simply moved from beginning to end easily and effortlessly with no prodding from me and no conscious attempt to do so on her part.

Sometimes even a great model is a waste of people's time. So, use what you find helpful on your road to complete recovery. Don't bother with the rest.

Now that you know your location in time and place and are safe in the *here and now*, you can turn your attention to where you have been. Looking back provides a wealth of knowledge that will help in your movement forward.

CHAPTER SEVEN

Observing and
Understanding What Happened

Once in the *here and now,* you posses the best chance of not becoming triggered and feeling overwhelmed emotionally, mentally, or physically. At this point, you can incorporate your past experience into your overall body of knowledge and wisdom. You can embrace it, learn from it, and use it to help you move forward safely, joyfully, and successfully. For this reason, the second set of NOW action recovery processes—Observing and understanding—involves making sense out of your past traumatic experience.

To begin, try to answer the following questions about the event that happened to you:

- **Was your reaction to the event within your control?**

- **Could you have done anything else given the resources available to you at the time?**

- **What do you want or hope to do differently if the same thing were to happen again?**

- **How were your perceptions, reaction, and decisions different than usual?**

If in your heart and mind you have complete and satisfactory answers to these questions, then you are well on your way through the Observing and Understanding part of the recovery process.

Human nature causes those of us who have experienced traumatic stressor events to carry difficult questions, such as those asked above, in our minds and hearts. Therefore, it serves us best to have a way to answer them when they come up. If you have experienced a

119

trauma, at some point in your life you will find yourself asking these same questions or very similar ones. For the purposes of the NOW recovery process, you will want to ask and answer as many questions as possible. This will help you observe and understand not only the traumatic stressor event itself but to become aware of your reactions and responses to it as well. So, also ask yourself the following questions, and answer them to the best of your ability:

- **Are you able to describe to your satisfaction what happened around you during the traumatic event you experienced?**
- **Can you recall your responses to the event in a step-by-step manner?**
- **Were these responses reactions or decisions?**
- **Can you see the difference between making choices and reacting in this situation?**
- **Are you able to understand your reasons for each action?**
- **Do you know what others say represents reasonable expected behavior in this situation?**

The answers to these questions sometimes seem like "no brainers." Of course, you would do some things differently given a second chance, and it may be clear in your mind why things happened the way they did. However, sometimes things just don't make sense. Things you did or those that others did, or why the events unfolded the way they did become nonsensical without more background information and knowledge of human and physical systems and processes. Therefore, do not worry too much right now if you have unanswered questions. By observing what happened and adding some missing pieces, you will come to a better understanding of the traumatic stressor event you experienced, your reactions to it, and the decisions you made about it. That's the purpose of this part of the NOW process. Your own self reflection, other's experiences, and general knowledge from related fields of study will help fill in the missing pieces. Reviewing the events makes the place and order of events clear as well, which helps you reduce any remaining risk of slipping back to the *there and then*.

Sense of Time and Space Keep You in the *Here and Now*

When taking the NOW test for recovery, you where told that being able to share your story with appropriate affect serves as a way of checking if you have gotten stuck in your recovery. Telling the story also requires that you place the events that happened into a time and place and make sense of your responses. When you do so, you help yourself put the whole experience into a time and space context, which helps you continue being *here and now* and not *there and then*. Stories have a beginning, middle, and an end. They take place somewhere.

Becoming clear about these facts gives your traumatic stressor event a timeline and a spatial context that allows you to separate from it. Separating from the event allows you to see it more clearly so you can understand it and your reactions and responses to it, and to remain aware of the fact that the event and you constitute two different things entirely. It also helps you keep the event in the *there and then* and yourself in the *here and now*.

The following story focuses on a woman moving through a traumatic event. She chose to use a professional helper—me, but professionals are not the only helpers available in your life. You can find the support you need to keep moving forward and to work through your triggers and your traumatic stressor responses with Thought Field Therapy. And you can use Thought Field Therapy by yourself or with the help of people in many different parts of your life.

Remember, telling your story out loud to anyone changes your understanding of it. Watching how others respond to your story gives you more information about how others understand what happened to you. Hearing other people's stories about what they did in similar situations enhances the validity of your judgments about your responses. Observing and understanding what happened to you in the past helps you stay safe in the present moment, because you now know more and have more options about how to respond if a similar traumatic event happens to you again.

Looking at the Pictures

Suzy, a woman in her late 20s, had completed three sessions with me a couple of months earlier when she called to make another appointment. She had come in about six months after the death of her fiancé. He had died in her arms as they waited for help after a car crash in a remote area. Suzy, her fiancé, his best friend, and his girlfriend had been spending a couple days in the country. That night they had been drinking, and, at some point, they decided to go to town for more alcohol. She and the friend's girlfriend stayed behind. The two women watched from the front porch of the house where they were staying as the lights of the car went off the road about a mile away and then ran to the scene.

Suzy's fiancé was conscious and able to talk but pinned in the crushed vehicle. His friend, who had been driving, was nonresponsive, and the women were unable to get under the vehicle to check on him. Suzy did what she could with her first- aid training while the other women ran back to the house to try to speed help on its way. My client was left to hold her fiancé as he slowly drifted away from her. For a few minutes, they talked of their love and future plans. He had no external injuries that she could see, but internally he we was crushed and bleeding. He was dead when the emergency responders arrived about half an hour later.

In our first sessions, Suzy and I had used Thought Field Therapy to address the intrusive images and memories that haunted her about the time alone with him as he died. These images were making it difficult for her to live her life. After learning tapping and working with me during a few sessions, she was able to care for her daughter once again and to go back to work, two things she had been unable to do after the accident and prior to using Though Field Therapy.

During this follow-up call, Suzy said she had decided it was time to know for sure what had happened that night. She said, "I'm ready to look at the pictures."

I knew what she meant; she wanted to come in to my office and be with me while she read the accident report and looked at the pictures within it for the first time.

Despite being told by emergency responders at the scene and later by the medical examiner that she had done all she could have done, Suzy was having trouble understanding why she did not get her fiancé out of the car or see the injuries that killed him. Her memories of certain aspects of the evening were very clear, but, as often happens when we are on overload in a crisis, for Suzy some facts about those hours were not known, recorded in memory, or accessible in present time.

In our session, Suzy and I looked at the new information from the files. As she worked through her memories of that night, she tapped several times when feelings would start to overwhelm her. By the end of the session, I had seen the light go on in her mind several times as she looked at pictures and read the report. With the additional facts, suddenly things about that night made sense to Suzy in a way they had not before. Her sense of loss was not eased much by knowing more about the details of her fiancé's death, but at least now she could understand both her actions and responses at the time and since then.

Unexpectedly, reading the report also provided her with information about the length of response time, which was shorter than she remembered. This eased some of her anger at the local sheriff's department. After the session, she reported that she could put to rest much of what had been on her mind about the incident for a long time.

<hr />

Suzy's Thought Field Therapy work and her efforts to observe and understand the traumatic stressor event she experienced provide a good example of the first two actions processes of recovery. First, this woman was able to eliminate many of the symptoms that were impairing her functioning and stopping her from being and feeling safe. Then she was able to review the events from that evening in a way that helped her make some sense of her own actions and of what had actually happened. By completing these two healing steps, she moved closer to finding some kind of meaning for these traumatic events in her life and to living her life with more integrity.

Reworking the Traumatic Event

"We are meaning-seeking creatures thrown into a meaningless world," said Victor Frankel, a survivor of the horrors of a Nazi extermination camp. Those who, like Frankel, survived Hitler's concentration camps suffered traumatic stressor events, to say the least, and the killing of six million Jews has to have seemed like a senseless act to them that could never be made or found meaningful in any way. Yet, to be functional as humans, we must create meaning or find it through our beliefs. The extent to which each of us has to have structure, order, or purpose for our actions varies greatly, but in all cases this drive for meaning requires that we use the best understanding of what has happened to us within the context of our world view. To do this, we must make sense of what has occurred. By confronting our past traumatic stressor event(s), we can accumulate the information necessary to satisfy our human need to make sense of our existence in a rational way.

The NOW process of observing and understanding the traumatic stressor event(s) you have experienced helps you put the pieces of what happened to you into a *temporal and spatial map*. Again, this assists you in understanding how and why you responded in the way you did and the impact the events and your reactions had on your life both then and now. A *temporal map* offers a timeline of events. A *spatial map* provides a sense of location and movement of events. You need these maps to handle all the information about your experiences, because that is how humans process information. When our minds are working well, specific parts of the brain assign a time stamp to an event, while another part assigns a location to that same event.

This description of how our minds assign times and places to events offers a simplified version of one element of a theory that explains why we encounter problems with memories and flashbacks related to traumatic stressor events. When we experience a traumatic event, the parts of the brain that assign time and location stamps are by-passed and information goes directly to brain centers that direct our responses. While we don't completely understand brain activities during and after traumatic stressor events, no doubt exists that the mind and body work differently under traumatic stress than under normal stress or other conditions. So, when you become triggered or are trying to pull up some information while experiencing traumatic stress, your sense of order and control disappear, become unbalanced, or change. With this sense of altered order and control, everything you feel, sense, and think feels unfamiliar and dysfunctional.

What happens to you when you experience a traumatic stressor event is bad enough by itself, but if you cannot make any sense of your experience and what you did or did not do, you may begin thinking that you are just plain crazy. In reality, little that exists can actually be called crazy. We call that which no one can make sense of crazy. People in this world think and behave in some pretty strange ways. What many would call "meaningless, irrational, stupid, silly, scary, or just pain nuts" to others simply constitutes a way to cope.

As you use Thought Field Therapy and the NOW traumatic stress recovery process, you will learn more about your own behavior and the nature of what makes us strong or weak, conscious or unaware, functional or dysfunctional, and connected or disconnected. This will help you make sense out of people's behavior — yours included. By collecting information about your own specific situation and conditions, adding knowledge about normal human processes, and using the concepts of the spatial/temporal map, you can find order, structure, or reasoning in almost any situation and behavior. And, in the process, you'll find that you are not thinking of yourself or others as crazy.

As you revisit your past traumatic event in your memory and re-examine it without becoming overwhelmed or upset, you can create the time line and lay out the location of the action. While you do so, however, remember to keep checking on your internal physical sensations and emotional feelings and to tap as you feel the need. The act of observing your traumatic event does not require that you suffer through it all over again; in fact, doing so just gets in the way of understanding the event.

Looking Back in Another Way

As you search for answers to the questions in this chapter, if you still find yourself struggling, confused and uncertain, even after tapping, look at it your traumatic stressor event as if someone else experienced it. This will help you avoid upset while observing this past experience. Then ask yourself the following questions:

- **How do you know the things you do about this event?**
- **Are you sure the events happened in that order or in that location?**
- **How is it possible that you performed that particular action in a specified time frame?**
- **Do you normally see things from that angle or focus or perceive things in that manner?**
- **Do you often track the movements of others in the way you did during this event?**

You might find it even more effective to share your recollections with someone else who experienced the same traumatic stressor event. To do so, they, of course, have to have a good handle on their own traumatic stress symptoms; they may need to work on them before joining you in this process. Often the other people's spatial/temporal map looks different from yours. Their focus during the events may also be different. By seeing the events from another angle, theirs, you gain a fuller picture of what happened.

No matter how you tackle it, the task during the Observing and Understanding phase of the NOW recovery process involves building an abstract, symbolic representation—a map of sorts—that helps you answer questions about what really happened during your traumatic experience. Doing so fills in the gaps in your memory, making it possible for you to have a complete picture of past events. Your clear awareness in the *here and now* as you look back at the *there and then* allows your memory to remain intact and embedded within a more complete and extensive informational context. The more expansive and complete your map, the more useful it becomes for gathering information.

However, the map does not represent reality but rather your reconstruction of reality. Also, your experience of the event will differ from the experience of the event related by someone who shared the event. That is because you are different people and come to both the event itself and the retrospective observation of it with different histories, capacities, and resources.

If you were alone when the traumatic stressor event happened, you may find it useful to find other information sources about what happened. Police or investigator reports, pictures, or news reports all can supply some helpful insights. Consulting with an expert in these types of events will help you put the pieces together as well. For example, if you were raped, you might want to seek out an expert in sexual assault investigation, recovery, or others who have been through the experience. Such experts can help answer the many questions that may arise as you review the events. These might include: Is this a normal reaction? Did I do the best thing? How did that come about? Why did a particular thing happen that way? Could I or someone else have done it differently or better? Was it my fault? Who bears responsibility for the occurrence of these events?

If you have a question about why or how something happened, someone has an answer. Telephone hotlines, crisis centers, rape recovery programs, and combat stress recovery services are examples of resources that can offer you the information you want or need. A large body of knowledge exists about normal responses to abnormal events, because so many people have already gone through the same healing processes you are going through. If you need or want to know something about the nature of a specific traumatic stressor event or response to it, ask someone who has had a similar experience. Sometimes doing so is as simple as making a call or attending a support group.

As you ask your questions, keep in mind that each person judges an acceptable set of answers by a different set of standards. Sometimes you may want to know every detail. Sometimes you will be satisfied with just broad strokes and little detail.

Plotting and Time-Stamping the Event

If, even after using Thought Field Therapy, you still suffer from some reoccurring intrusive memories or images related to your traumatic stressor event, you may need to add into your memory the information missing at the time you experienced the event. Remember, the mind skips over some data as it tries to focus on responses to the traumatic event. This leaves gaps in the information you have stored in your mind. You can input this information by plotting the events on your spatial and temporal map and adding a running time stamp to the replay in your head.

If you are visually oriented, imagine it this way: you see pictures in your mind as you think about the traumatic stressor event you experienced. You then simply add some data to the picture to clarify the *there and then* in comparison to the *here and now*. This exercise becomes fairly easy with a little practice.

Here's another way to think about it: on a video replay, you see numbers off to one corner that give you the exact year, month, day, hour, and minutes the event was recorded by the video camera. The next time you remember your traumatic stressor event or are caught in a flashback experiencing it as if it were happening again, add that set of numbers as you see it. Put the year, month, day, hour, and minute of the event into the picture. Also, add a world map in another corner that shows the location of the event. Make it an interactive map that you can click on to expand or compress to get a useful scale. Think of this like you were finding an address on the Internet; you can get a broad view to find the location in the city, and then narrow the view to get the specific site you want. Once you have added these features to your memory playbacks, it will become much easier for you to compare the time and place of the *there and then* and the *here and now*.

If you are not visual and see black when you close your eyes, then you have to imagine without the mental pictures. You may imagine the passing of time or the changing of location by imagining what you body feels as you move from location to location. You may have to track time by your heart beats or cycles of sleep just as time passes on the clock or calendar. Most people — about 80 percent — are primarily visual in their mental information processing ability. A high percentage of people tend to be kinesthetic, processing information through movement and the sensation of movement. Others are auditory, processing information through what they hear. No one uses only one sense, but most of us have a primary way of operating. However you prefer to process information, find your way to put a time and a place to your memory of the events of your past that help you clarify that they are occurring in a different time and place from where you exist now.

Going Beyond the Moment

As you try to really know and understand the traumatic stressor event again and you observe your memories or other informational sources, you may find symptoms arise again or new ones appear as you gain a new understanding of the powerful events you experienced. Or, from your new clarity you may see the same events from another perceptive, which can cause new upset. This quick change in mental, emotional, and even physical condition is not unusual, because Thought Field Therapy works so quickly that you may find yourself finishing with one picture in your head or an emotion you feel and moving on to the next without being aware of it. Tap for each of these upsetting sensations as they occur. Once these are removed with tapping, however, you will be able to think clearly again.

When you think about the event with new mental clarity and find yourself becoming aware of a change in your level of upset as you focus on the new picture, tap to help resolve the new upset. You will have to navigate your way clear of these new symptoms before returning to your attempts to observe and understand the past traumatic event. Don't be surprised if you find yourself using Thought Field Therapy again and again. Eventually, you will reach the point where you can understand what happened to you during that traumatic stressor event, how you responded, and how you feel about the event and yourself in this current moment. Once you get to this place, you can move on to working your life with integrity.

The following story illustrates one woman's efforts to observe and understand her traumatic stressor event and her responses.

Getting Your Feelings Out of the Way

Bea, a woman in her mid 30s, felt stuck in the past in many ways. Three years ago she had held her son in her arms as he died. An innocent victim of a drive-by shooting, the young man had made his way back into her living room before collapsing. Since that time, she replayed these moments over and over in her mind. She was overwhelmed every time something reminded her of her son. Most everything in her home and in her life served as a trigger for this traumatic event, and each time she became triggered she would find herself right there with him in her arms all over again, watching his face as he died.

When offered the opportunity to try something new, Bea said she was ready to try Thought Field Therapy. She said, "What do I have to lose? Just the mention of the bad memories puts me right back there."

After the first round of tapping, which reduced the level of upset she felt as she spoke about her son's death, Bea reported that the picture in head was changing. She was seeing not just her son's face but more of his body and her arms and legs as she held him. After tapping again, Bea's level of upset continued to improve and the picture in her head continued to change. She could now see the carpet on the floor and was aware of the light in the room. Tapping once more, she began describing her son and herself in the whole room.

That's when she abruptly stopped, and tears started to pour down her face. Bea related that now she could see her other son standing in the doorway to the room. He had witnessed the whole thing, and she now felt a flood of feelings for her living son, who also had been harmed by his brother's murder.

At this point in our session, clearly Bea's level of upset was at least as high as when she had started, but now she was feeling additional emotions to those she had when she started. Bea tapped for the feelings of guilt and sadness she had when she realized how the intrusive memories and overwhelming feeling had interfered with her caring for her living son. While she knew she had done the best she could, she felt horrible about how alone her son must have felt these last years. After a little more Thought Field Therapy, Bea was ready to go home and give some serious thought about how to help her living son and to discuss this with friends and family. Most importantly, she wanted to hear about her living son's experience of his brother's death, and she wanted to do so without getting triggered and caught up in her own needs.

The goal of the NOW recovery process revolves around making different choices about how you live your life. In the story above, Bea *Navigated* past the overwhelming vision of her son's face as he died in her arms. This allowed her to *Observe* what happened in a more complete way and to understand she was not the only one harmed by this event. The *Work* in her life was refocused as she chose to tend to her living son in a different way.

Sometimes the process of Observing and understanding requires much more time and energy than in the story above. For some of you, such clarity takes tapping for many injuries you suffered over a lifetime. For some of you such knowing and awareness comes only after examining the coping mechanisms and survival strategies you have developed throughout your life.

When the Planes Hit the Twin Towers — Understanding How the Pieces Fit Together

A therapist specializing in anger management referred Fred, a man in his late 20s, to me after it became clear that his presenting problems involved more than just jealousy issues. Fred was a good-looking man who currently made his living in the building trades but had also made money in the visual arts and as a musician. The problem that brought him to therapy revolved around the difficulty he and the woman with whom he was living were having. He said he was quick to become angry and upset about anything she might do that reminded him of her relationships with other men. His way of acting this out involved withdrawing and refusing to speak to her for days at a time or speaking to her only in a very angry and abusive tone. Because of his behavior, he was afraid he was about to destroy the relationship and lose her.

The first therapist learned Fred had been in New York City on 9-11 and had been fairly close when he witnessed the collapse of both the Twin Towers. This did not represent the first trauma he had suffered in his lifetime, however. His mother had been killed in an airplane crash when he was very young. His father's alcoholism caused further traumatic stress events. Fred had had extensive outpatient and inpatient treatment as a child and adolescent and he had been a substance abuser. The therapist felt concerned that many of Fred's problems were related to these traumatic stressor events.

In his first session with me, Fred revealed that 9-11 had been a life-altering experience for him. He said he stopped drinking shortly after the towers collapsed, because he realized that if he continued to drink he would drink himself to death. He said he had been an active alcoholic for most of his adult life and drank on a daily basis. Once he realized he was in a self-destructive spiral, he was able to stop drinking and invest himself in his relationship with a new girlfriend. However, he was constantly reminded of the Towers' absence, since they had been his reference point through most of his life in New York.

He and his girlfriend left New York and moved to San Diego eight months after he stopped drinking. Fred tried everything he could think of to stop his many post 9-11 traumatic stress-related symptoms, but he could not sleep, nor could he get the sights and sounds of that day out of his mind, or stop thinking about the people he knew who had been killed. Nothing helped. And in the few weeks he lived in San Diego, his symptoms seem to worsen.

We first worked on Fred's relationship issues. Using Thought Field Therapy helped Fred get the jealous anger and rage out of the way. When he had thoughts about his girlfriend being with other men, he then was able to connect his anger to the fact that his girl-friend had been raped two years before he met her. Often as they would begin being sexual, he would have thoughts about her rape and about what had been done to her. He would then get caught in a confusing whirlwind of thoughts, become unable to continue be-ing intimate, and would withdraw from her. Unable to talk with his girlfriend about the thoughts going through his head, the relationship was deteriorating rapidly.

With this information, we began to tap for his vicarious pain, anger, and rage about what had been done to his girlfriend. With re-duced upset, he began to develop a plan to start discussing these issues with her and to be more open with her about the problems that he was struggling with.

In this first session, we also did Thought Field Therapy for is-sues related to Fred's witnessing the fall of the Twin Towers. By the next session, which only occurred a month later, he reported that his re-lationship with his girlfriend was much better, and he had begun once again enjoying sexual relationships with her.

He was very aware, however, that he was currently struggling with what he wanted to do with his life and where he wanted to live. Even though he had been born on the West Coast, he had spent most of his life on the East Coast. He felt uncertain about what direction his life would take in San Diego with his girlfriend. This conversation led to a discussion of problems he was having with his family of origin and with establishing a relationships with his alcoholic father. During this session, he also revealed to me that his mother had been killed in a plane crash when he was eight years old, a fact I already knew, and that it had complicated his life terribly. Fred admitted that he had never re-ally dealt with these issues as a child and, subsequently, found himself going though a series of inpatient and outpatient treatment programs. He eventually ended up living in a residential adolescent treatment facility from the age of 16 to 18.

At this point in his recovery process, Fred was willing to use Thought Field Therapy to help treat some of the unresolved grief about his mothers' death. This made it possible for him to talk more fully about how not being able to discuss his feelings with family or anyone else had impacted him as a child.

It was also in this session that he began to talk about the difficulty he was experiencing with writing or doing his visual arts. He said that the last piece of art he had created revealed such ugliness that he couldn't deal with doing anymore of this kind of work. We did some tapping around the overwhelming fear he experienced dealing with that violence.

I saw him again a month later, and he had begun playing music again and was making headway on having more open and honest discussions with his partner about who he was and what he wanted in the world, as well as what she wanted. We spent a good deal of time again working on his desire to return to New York, where his girlfriend's family still lived and where he had an extended support network. Yet, he was still concerned about the discomfort he felt in New York post 9-11.

During this session, he also began to discuss an insight he had about one of the planes crashing into the Twin Towers. As he watched it hit the towers, he had wondered what it was like for those people on the plane to crash into the building and what it was like for his mother when the plane she was flying on had crashed. As he watched the events unfold before him, he had asked himself, "Did she know? Did she suffer, and what must it have been like for her?" Telling me about this evoked feelings in him that were tremendously overwhelming and upsetting. Again, we used Thought Field Therapy to help him deal with these excessively strong feelings, many of which appeared to be directly related to what he experienced as an eight year old trying to make sense out of his mother's death. At the end of the session, he was again encouraged to continue working with his music and to continue discussing with his girlfriend what their plans would be for the future.

I saw Fred once more, a month later, at which time he reported that he and his girlfriend were about to be married. She was pregnant, and they had decided to return to New York to be with her family and his friends. He was not apprehensive about returning and was actually quite excited about the possibility. We did more work to help him focus on his relationship with his father and to deal with feelings he had about the way he had been treated after his mother's death and the years he had spent in treatment. Once more, by having him focus on the upsetting memories and tapping, he was able quickly to access new information about the events and to think about them in a new way. As we ended the session, he assured both of us that he will continue to tap, use the coping skill he had learned earlier in life, and keep struggling to make more sense of his life.

⌘

This story illustrates how quickly a combination of problems can be dealt with using Thought Field Therapy. As each problem presented itself, it became necessary to resolve the overwhelming emotion related to it and then to follow the discussion to the next level of overwhelm that blocked Fred's ability to cope and to make sense out of his life.

You have completed the Observing and Understanding steps of the NOW recovery process when you decide you have enough information to make sense of your traumatic stressor event and your responses to it. When you begin to integrate the event, and your understanding of it, and your responses and reactions to it into your life, you are well on the road to recovery. Your wounds are healing nicely. The next chapter examines further how making choices as a person with no open wounds leads to a full recovery and a move towards health, love, and joy. This represents the work of living with integrity.

CHAPTER EIGHT

Working Life with Integrity

The final test of your recovery is measured by the degree to which you have stopped living your life by reacting to traumatic stress triggers and symptoms and begun consciously choosing your actions in a manner congruent with your values and beliefs.

As you live your life are you:

- **Choosing your job or career?**
- **Choosing the people with whom you live?**
- **Choosing the individuals you love?**
- **Choosing how you spend your precious time and energy?**
- **Choosing your words and actions in all aspects of your life to satisfy your values?**

The answers to these questions represent only a few of the choices you make as you live your life day-to-day and year-to-year. Full recovery from traumatic stressor events, however, includes going forward in life with *integrity*. Integrity means in a state of completeness with no impairments or dysfunctions. Integrity also means living in accordance with a standard of conduct congruent with your values. While you make choices all the time, the goal of recovery revolves around making choices about how you live that leads you to a life of health, love, and joy. And these choices must come with and out of integrity, which can only happen on a consistent basis when you are no longer driven by traumatic events you have experienced.

Think about the questions you answered a moment ago. Now, answer these two questions:

- **Are you making these choices in accordance with your values?**
- **Are you living and making choices from a place of integrity?**

Integrating the Changes

Can you currently say you suffer from no open wounds? This question does not infer that you have never suffered a traumatic stress "injury," nor does it mean that the wounds and the processes of healing from those injuries have not changed your life in some way. It simply means that the wounds have healed enough for you to move though and forward in life without noticing them any longer. Even if the wounds have healed, you may bear some scars from your past traumatic experiences. And sometime scars itch or hurt a little when the weather changes or you notice them when you look in the mirror, but if they have truly healed you likely almost have forgotten about them. Like someone who limps after a really severe leg injury, the way you walk in the world may permanently have changed even though your injury has completely healed and your physical therapy has ended. You may no longer notice the change in your gait as you move through your days.

When it comes to traumatic stressor events, having totally healed wounds means your overwhelming symptoms have stopped interfering with your day-to-day life, and you have navigated through the hazards of recovery well enough to review what happened during the traumatic stressor event and to make sense of it. Also at this point you can see some reason in the order of the past event, your reactions to that event, the reactions of other people who were with you during the traumatic stressor event, and your responses after the event ended. You should have gained some understanding about how your experience has changed you or how you see the world, and you now should be able to put that understanding to use in your life.

Your traumatic experience, the injuries it caused, and the healing process you had to undertake have made you stronger in some areas of your life and weaker in other areas. An athlete who injures a tendon or ligament in a leg and undergoes physical therapy to help heal it, often finds the leg that was hurt becomes the stronger leg. That said, the athlete might become prone to injuring that particular part of the body. In psychological terms, a child who suffered abuse may grow up to always react with extreme sensitivity to angry outbursts by others.

However, as the wounds heal, this person may also develop an excellent ability to read other's emotional states. So while such a person may not be easily suited in a career in law enforcement, they may be a wonderful educator or counselor.

One philosophy of life says, "That which does not kill you makes you stronger." Another philosophy says, "Only by experience will you learn the lessons of being fully human." No matter to which philosophy you subscribe, you can count on the fact that everything that happens to you changes you in some way. And when you change your values, priorities, and preferences often change, as do your choices.

When your wounds have healed, which means the overwhelming sensations that accompany past memories of traumatic stress have stopped and you can observe and understand what happened, then you can use that knowledge and make integrity-based choices. You will see different choices available to you in the *here and now*. Thus, full recovery from traumatic stress includes working with your current choices and not the choices you had before the traumatic events happened to you. It means making choices in the *here and now* and not in the *there and then*. It means bringing everything you've learned from your traumatic stressor event into the current moment and making decisions and choices based on your current beliefs, values, desires, goals, etc.

Before you were fully healed, you might have made choices based upon the *there and then*. For example, you might have decided not to do something, because you still harbored a fear that what happened before could happen again. Or maybe your emotional upset, which continued to be triggered by your day-to-day life, made it impossible for you to see clearly enough to make any sort of decisions. If you were in a terrible automobile accident, for instance, before you engaged in the recovery processes and learned to tap, you might have decided to give up activities like going to church, visiting friends, or attending family events if they required that you drive. After healing from the traumatic stress of the auto crash, however, you now find that you can choose among these activities with no concern about driving.

In the NOW test for recovery, you are asked to share how the traumatic stressor events in your past life and your reactions to them have informed your definition of what you deem important and valuable. You address these questions:

- **What memories from this event and its aftermath do you value and want to carry forward?**

- **What life lesson do you take from this event for yourself, for your loved ones, or for those who will experience this type of event?**

- **With whom do you want to share this part of yourself?**

- **How do you want to change the world in which you live and which you will pass on?**

Of course, these questions can take a lifetime to answer fully. At this time, you only have to find partial answers, but the answers must be complete enough to inform your decisions about your relationships and other behaviors. Finding fully satisfactory answers to these questions provides indications that you are fully recovered from the traumatic stress responses that interfered with your life. Take a moment to answer them now.

A Standard for Full Recovery

The following standard for complete recovery is based on a model of traumatic stress recovery offered by Mary Harvey in an article published in the *Journal of Traumatic Stress* in 1996. Written using the terms we have been using in this book, it leads you through a variety of recovery steps beginning with regaining control of memories and ending with the making of value-based choices. By reviewing the list you can check off how many of these items you have completed.

- **You are in control of your memories—you can recollect the experiences of your past and you choose when and what you recollect.**

- **Other reminders of past experiences, like images, sound,** smells, or situations, do not trigger responses that take you out of the *here and now.*

- You can have current thoughts, opinions, and emotions about what has happened to you and to others in the past with no confusion about where you are in time and place.

- You have stopped self-destructive coping behaviors used in the past.

- You have accepted yourself and possess genuine feelings of concern, care, and love for yourself.

- You have ways to connect with other people in a trusting and loving way.

- Your life now has purpose, meaning, and a sense of fulfillment.

- You are able to be honest with yourself and others.

- You are moving forward unimpaired emotionally, feeling complete as a person, and with a strong, clear sense of personal values.

Were you able to check off all items? If not, you may protest that this list constitutes an unrealistic standard. You might say, "Even before any traumatic events crashed into my life I could not meet this standard. So, why should I hold myself to such a standard now?" Fair enough.

So, go back to the beginning of the list and as you think about each item, ask yourself these two questions:

- Was this true for you before the traumatic event?

- Is it true for you now?

Hold open the possibility that you and your life may actually have improved since the traumatic stressor events occurred. Consider that during the recovery process you got the chance to—or still have the chance to—reset your standards and work at building a better life for yourself.

And remember, the very fabric of your being has been altered both for good and for bad by the traumatic stressor event that you experienced. However, how you have changed, for better or for worse, and how much you have changed depends to a great extent on how you see the world around you and your place in it. Even if you cannot make complete sense out of what happened to you and how you responded to those events, even if you can't fully answer all the questions you still have about your traumatic stressor event, you are still alive. What you do with the life you have left becomes a critical element in the quality of your life. For this reason, the questions you need to address in this category of the NOW traumatic stress recovery process revolve around what you believe about the nature of the universe and human existence and how you act in the world. They ask you to script the meaning of your life and to incorporate the events of your day-to-day life into that meaning, a very human activity that everyone does to some degree.

Working Your Life Choices

In most cases, traumatic stressor events don't radically change a person's beliefs, but do not be surprised if your values and beliefs are shaken by such events and your responses to them. After a traumatic event, many people ask specific questions about how they have been changed by the powerful experiences they have had. It matters little if you had a positive or a negative experience, if it affected you deeply on an emotional, mental, or physical level, you intuitively know it has created internal change, and you've probably wondered about those changes. When it comes to traumatic experiences, maybe you've asked yourself these questions:

- **What changed in your relationships to yourself, your loved ones, and your higher powers?**
- **What was lost and what was found by living though the healing and recovery processes?**

Recognizing what has happened to you and to your reactions and response is critical to fully living your life after a traumatic stressor event. But, at this point of recovery, recognizing the choices before you now — with no open wounds and with the knowledge you gained in coming to a total understanding of the event — represents the more important task.

Helping yourself in this part of the recovery process often involves just knowing what questions to ask yourself and trying to stay out of the way while you answer them. In other words, you have to refrain from judging your own answers. This means that without judgments, you bring to awareness your personal values, beliefs, or ways of expressing what is important to you. As you consider beliefs, values, and actions, look at the choices before you. You can continue moving in the direction you are going currently by continuing to make the same choices you have been making, or you can change your direction by changing them. The possibilities for change are represented by your choices. Living in the now means accepting responsibility for the choices you make and working towards the creation of a life lived with and within your values.

If you are having difficulty recognizing what you valued and believed prior to the traumatic event you experienced, or if you cannot determine your current values and beliefs, you might want to search through your personal history to find them. Sometimes your family of origin, the family into which you were born, or your family of choice, the persons with whom you have chosen to spend your life, hold clues to your values. Sometimes your religious background can provide answers as well. You can talk to family members and ask them about their beliefs and values; then decide if they are also your own. Or ask them if they have a sense of your values and beliefs both before and after your traumatic stressor event. Ask someone within your religious organization to outline for you the basic beliefs and values of the religion. Then decide if these fit your way of thinking before of after the traumatic event or now that you have healed your open wounds from that event.

Turning to books on religion and philosophy or talking to philosophy teachers or religious leaders can help you get a grasp on some of these more esoteric questions. Many people throughout human history have expended considerable time and thought on how to answer the eternal questions: "What does *it* all mean?" and "How do I fit into *it*?" What is this *it* to which they refer? The big picture. The really big picture. The total picture of the cosmos. Why do we all ask these questions at some time in our lives? Because it constitutes a normal mental process; we want to understand. Why do we tend to ask these questions after traumatic stressor events? Because doing so represents a normal part of the recovery process. The traumatic event causes change within us, and that change causes us to rethink our view of the world and of humanity. It causes us to question our beliefs and values in general.

Therefore, those great philosophers and spiritual seekers who have gone before you and who wrote those books or are teaching philosophy and religion classes have learned some things they can share that might help you find the answers you seek. They can give you some tips about what you will have to consider in your effort to work meaning into your life. Remember the books you have read, the teachers you have valued, the people you have loved, and the conversations you have had about these kinds of questions before your traumatic stressor event occurred. They will provide you with good resources for understanding what is important to you, both then and now.

Justice in the World Before and After the Event

People who have experienced a traumatic stressor event most commonly struggle with one question in particular: "Why did this happen to me?" You might be asking yourself similar and related questions, such as: "What did I do to deserve this in my life?" or "How do I now find any justice in a world in which this can happen?" In a moment of trauma, your expectations for the world to function in a just or fair manner and to be a just and fair place can be reinforced or radically damaged. The degree to which you believe that you live in a just world is based upon the amount of congruency between your belief about what should be and what has happened. These beliefs can become incompatible after a traumatic stressor event.

For this reason, the issue of justice becomes a large one for many people who have suffered a traumatic stressor event. To discover if you are struggling with whether you live in a just world, answer the following questions:

- **To what degree do you believe the world is fair?**
- **Do you think people always get what they deserve?**
- **Do you believe that bad things happen only to those who act in bad ways?**
- **Do you think the prosperity a person has is related directly to their goodness or hard work?**

Social science gives us tools for answering these questions, such as the Just World Theory, a psycho/social system of thinking about the nature of the world in which we find ourselves and how we understand the events that happen to us and to others. Social scientists asked people of different ages, genders, races, nationalities, and social status to answer a series of questions related to their beliefs about fairness and justice. They compared the ratings of those who had had a wide range of personal experiences. This produced some clear results about how life experiences shape the way we perceive justice in the world.

Those who had lived a protected life with few traumatic stressors tended to the see the world as a just place. In their minds, bad things happen to bad people, and good things happen to good people. They tended to believe that as long as they followed the rules and were good, nothing bad would happen to them; bad things happen to those who do not follow the rules and do bad things. This outlook provides a great way to make sense out of the world and to maintain a sense of safety and security.

However, if you have this perspective on justice, when something bad happens to you or to someone you love, this way of seeing the world falls apart pretty quickly, especially if you know the person you love is good and follows the rules. When you base the foundation of your world view on the world being a just place and your experience in surviving a traumatic event proves this wrong, you lose the protective shield provided by your belief about justice. Your whole world can fall apart when you realize that the world does not operate in the manner that you had believed, and finding a way to rebuild your world and your sense of security means changing your essential beliefs.

The bad things that happen to us do not always come at the hands of other human beings, although we may assume that they do. Sometimes they come from nature. In the course of a lifetime, these "acts of God" show up in many forms ranging from hurricanes to unexplained illnesses. No matter the source of the event, you can be changed by having to face the reality that elements exist in the world that you cannot control or avoid. In the next story, consider how powerful naturally occurring events can impact us. This person's experience falls within what is considered the realm of traumatic stressor events, because it involves a life-and-death circumstance and accompanying feelings of horror and helplessness.

Sometimes I Just Wonder, "What Was God Thinking?"

A retired minister attended a training workshop to learn how to do Thought Field Therapy. When we began doing the practice exercises, he experienced a problem finding something he felt upset about that could be helped with tapping. You learn Thought Field Therapy by doing it. No role-playing or pretending. After a few probing questions, it became quite clear that he had resolved most of his issues as they had arisen in his life, and we could not arouse any upset to treat with tapping. Almost as an afterthought, however, he shared that he was having some anger issues with God. In fact, his anger was strong enough that he could feel it in his body and measure it by his increased heart rate.

He told me what was going on. A few years ago, as he had moved into his late 70s, he began having some trouble accepting what he perceived God to be doing to his body. He felt it was unfair that someone who lived a good life committed to service should have to suffer the pains of aging. When he tried to address this in ways that had worked in the past, he just got angry and upset and then stopped trying. Based on his beliefs and values, he knew what he was feeling made no intellectual sense.

We tried tapping while he thought about his anger towards God, and this proved helpful for him. With the anger eased, he focused on the reality of his aging and of his own death. I affirmed the he was not the only person who had ever struggled with this issue. When troubled in the past, this minister would turn to God for help, but most recently his anger had been getting in the way of doing so. When we had completed the tapping, he was pleased to tell me he was looking forward to prayers and meditations without the limits that came with his past upset.

<hr/>

Seeing the reality of aging and dying was easier once this minister had dealt with his anger over the unfairness of a good man aging, suffering poor health, and dying. And coming to grips with reality allowed him to return to a sense of the justness of the world, which, in turn, moved him along on his life's journey. Sometimes integrating the events in your life are not so straightforward and involve coming to a new and better sense of self and of the day-to-day world you inhabit. Once you do so, however, you will find yourself moving forward with your life as well.

In this next story, a woman becomes aware of the new choices she will have to make to complete her recovery.

Making a New Life After a Series of Traumatic Events

"Congratulations! You just passed the NOW test for Post Traumatic Stress Syndrome. You can tell me the story of your childhood and the abuse in your marriage with appropriate affect. You have been working on this for a long time, and it has been worth every minute. You have completed your treatment for the traumatic stressor events you experienced."

I said this to Sarah who had been in treatment with me for an abusive marriage and the effects of an extremely-violent physically, sexually, and emotionally abusive childhood. I hadn't known about the childhood traumas when we started working together, but Thought Field Therapy brought the rest of her story out quickly. After many sessions, things had changed for her. We had finished this part of her healing process, but she thought I had said we were done completely.

Sarah asked, "What do you mean?"

"Now you need to get on with your life without the fear," I explained.

She asked, "What do you mean?"

"It's time for you to get on with your life," I told her again.

Sarah repeated her question, "What do you mean?"

I responded, "You know, go out and find the work you love, find the life that brings you joy, find some people to love, and...."

She interrupted me with a new query: "What do you mean love someone?"

"Find some people you like and, when it feels right, open your heart to share the wonderful women you are," I suggested.

"And how am I supposed to do that?" she asked.

Not quite sure where she was going with this question, I replied, "You know...find someone you are attracted to and you trust and connect with." This seemed to be the straw that broke the camel's back.

Suddenly, Sarah started ranting about how she would never trust anyone ever again, and I was the crazy one if I thought she would ever make that mistake again and give herself to anyone. When she said, "How can I trust any man enough to love him?" it became apparent to both of us that while her Post Traumatic Stress Syndrome symptoms were gone, her treatment and our work together was not yet over.

Since she had had few opportunities in life to this point to make choices about trusting others, I explained my thoughts about trust. As *a younger man, I believed I should trust people until they gave me a reason not to trust them. This approach came out of my experience in a loving family—both nuclear and extended—and in a safe community. This experience also fostered within me a firm belief in the goodness of all people. As I, grew, aged, and got "burned" a few times, my beliefs changed. Having been hurt in different ways by several different people, I decided a more prudent approach was safer for me. I began trusting people to the extent to which they proved themselves to be trustworthy. Now, I give only to others based on what I know about them in reality, not based on what I want to believe or what they want me to believe about them.*

Then, I asked her if she trusted me. "Yes," Sarah replied, "because you have always been there for me."

"In the ways I promised to be there," I added. Sarah and I had good boundaries and she knew she was my client rather than part of my family. "So, if you can trust me, maybe you can find a way to trust others," I suggested. I then asked, "Do you love me?"

"You know I do," she replied. We had talked about this many times. She knew love comes in many forms, and the feelings she had for me were based on care, respect, and joy in our relationship.

"So, if you can love me, maybe you can love someone else and in other, fuller ways," I concluded. I then turned the conversation to setting some objectives for her life and to offering some ways I would help her achieve them.

⟡

Sometime you only need to get the symptoms out of the way to get on with your journey down the road to health, joy, and love. Thought Field Therapy provides a great way to accomplish this. But sometimes people need help finding the map or directions to proceed safely down the road of their life after Thought Field Therapy has removed the symptoms that served as obstacles to their forward movement. When you find yourself symptom-free, when the impediments to continuing down the road have all been removed, you may discover the choices before you that you could not see previously. However, if you can't see those choices—the opportunities to navigate to the left or to the right or to go straight ahead—then you might still need some help figuring out how to open your eyes to what lies before you. In other words, you might need to stop reacting and start choosing.

If you do need help beyond what you can provide for yourself or what your loved ones can provide for you, healers in all their different roles and forms are waiting for the opportunity to support you, just as I did in the story above.

Navigating Life's Forces

Understanding the world and finding your way while staying grounded in reality rather than in your beliefs and expectations about justice and fairness never becomes a simple task. You may, however, find this next tool useful in coming to grips with understanding why bad things happen to good people and grappling with the issues of fairness and justice. Before we begin, it might be helpful to spend a little time thinking about water and currents.

If you have ever gone swimming in the ocean and gotten caught in a riptide or a tidal current, you understand the force of nature. When the forces of the sun, Earth, and moon come together with the shape of the land, huge amounts of water are pulled and pushed in one direction and then another. Try to swim against a riptide directly toward the beach, and you will likely become exhausted from your efforts and drown. No mere mortal human being is a match for such a current. You only can hope you will recognize that you are caught in a riptide, have the knowledge not to fight it, and have the strength to swim across its length and then safely to shore.

However, powerful currents are not always bad. Anyone who has spent any time at a water park has experienced the fun of riding the currents on the slides and rides. If you've ridden down a "lazy river" on an inner tube, for example, you know the joy that comes from relaxing and "going with the flow."

Yet, sometimes we find ourselves caught in currents we do not expect or like. What happens when the gentle flow of a river becomes a flash flood with raging rapids without any warning? This happens to the best of people. They are floating along and everything seems just fine, and then suddenly their inner tube capsizes, and they find themselves floundering in deep white water at risk of drowning.

Anyone who says you can prepare for any force that may impact you is foolish. This person also might say you are to blame for being unprepared for the last hurricane, earthquake, flood, wildfire, or tornado. However, if you live in a floodplain or an earthquake zone and have experienced any of these overpowering acts of nature, you know death and destruction can happen to anyone despite the best pre-planning.

Now let's take this information and apply it to traumatic stressor events and your beliefs about justice and fairness in the world. Almost all traumatic stressor events that serve as the source of dysfunction, pain, fear, or ongoing upset come unexpectedly upon us—just like a riptide, a flash flood, a tornado, or an earthquake. Yet, the currents of your life are more than just the forces of nature. They also include the forces of families, communities, economics, politics, and history. Poverty, racism, sexism, family violence, war, genocide, famine, greed, dogma, or just plain human meanness they all power the negative currents that surround you all the time.

Sometimes you are standing on the riverbank and can see the river's power, but nothing can remove you from your safe place. Sometimes you are swept into the river, but you have a boat or flotation device to make it to safety. Maybe you are even able to help others not as lucky as yourself who find themselves in the water without a way to stay afloat or without a paddle to get to shore. At other times, the bank simply gives way under your feet without warning, and you are swept away without the knowledge or strength to stay safe or to help others.

Often the most innocent become the victims of these forces. In these cases, we see clearly that the world is not a just place. Surely justice is done when a person gets what is due to him or her. I believe human beings deserve concern, care, and love. Justice is not found in the forces that make up the currents of life. Why? Because justice symbolizes a human concept.

Justice exists when a person is given the care, concern, and love of another person or group of people. We treat each other justly, because we know how to do so. The forces of nature do what they do without reason, because nature has no reason. We, as humans, can reason, and, therefore, can treat each other justly. We also can expect to be treated justly. When we expect the world around us to treat us justly, though, we aren't being realistic. If you believe the universe is strictly ordered and controlled by a higher force, you still have to accept the fact that humans have limited influences on those forces.

When you find yourself caught in a powerful river current you cannot resist, a water safety instructor will tell you, "Don't panic, keep your head above water as much as you can, get your feet pointed downstream to fend off any obstacles. If you are not alone, hold on tight to whose with you, and keep looking for the safe place to get out. Do not swim directly against the current but work your way across it, and never give up." Once you find yourself caught in a life current, these same instructions can prove very helpful.

Awareness of being in an out of control situation can cause panic, so calm yourself with Thought Field Therapy. Keep your wits about you. Being able to think, to use your mind, is as important as breathing when you are being carried in a direction against your will. As best you can, protect yourself and those you love from further harm. Isolation breeds hopelessness, so stay connected to those you hold dear. Don't pull away; ask for help if you need it.

Making Choices That Help You Live with Integrity

Once you have put the past in the past, you can look forward. Running away from the events that have shaped your life requires that you keep your eyes and your focus on what lies behind you. When you worry about what has happened previously and that it might show up in your life again keeps you from seeing clearly the choices in front of you now. Looking forward serves as a much less-painful process than looking backward. Life is more enjoyable if you are running towards something you desire rather than running away from something painful.

As a traumatic stress recovery specialist, I am often asked by my clients, "Why did this happen to me?" and "Why did this happen to other innocent people?" As discussed above, these questions represent deep spiritual and philosophical concerns for which no one answer exists. My best response to these questions is found in my belief that we do not live in a just world, and the currents that drive our lives care little for our innocence. I encourage you, like my clients, to find your own answers to these questions and to answer a more productive question: *How* do you live through the traumatic stressor events in your life and create health, love, and joy? Knowing *why* the event happened only proves useful if it informs the choices we make.

Consider the questions that started this chapter again with attention on life's currents influencing you choices:

As you live your life are you:
- **Choosing your job or career?**
- **Choosing the people with whom you live?**
- **Choosing the individuals you love?**
- **Choosing how you spend your precious time and energy?**
- **Choosing your words and actions in all aspects of your life to satisfy your values?**

Remember to use Thought Field Therapy to help you with any upset. Remember to reflect on the events in your life that have led you to this point. Most importantly, choose carefully among all the choices before you and make them in accordance with your values so you move forward with integrity. Being healed NOW gives you so many choices.

The next part of the book which begins after the NOW Model Summary prepares you for dealing some of the life's strongest currents, such as the grief that comes with the death of loved ones and other losses, addictions and self-destructive behaviors, and violent childhoods. You may find the stories in this section helpful as you continue to recover. If you are feeling complete in your recovery, you may find the information useful in helping others. Or, you may find this knowledge provides you a good measure of prevention against and strategies to handle future traumatic stressor events. The following summary is an overview of this part of the book and a quick reference to finding your focus and useful questions as you move through the layers of your recovery.

NOW Traumatic Stress Recovery Model Summary

Key Elements:

- Healing is an active process in which you must participate.

- Terrifying and horrifying events require extraordinary human responses and set in motion powerful protective mechanisms throughout the whole person

- Extreme or prolonged reactions to traumatic events can cause you to deal with ordinary life in a dysfunctional manner.

- The inability of the mind, body, and soul to discern the difference between the past (the unsafe *there and then* of the traumatic event) and the safety of current moment (*the here and now*) represents the source of continuing pains and fears.

- Thought Field Therapy closes open traumatic stress wounds, thus ending the overwhelming pain and fear you feel and allowing your natural healing systems to repair the injury and regain function.

- Individual identity, history, and values must be included in addressing issues arising from how you chose to adapt to traumatic events.

- The normal way of functioning for human beings necessitates making sense of themselves and the world around them.

- A calm mind and a relaxed body are indications of good health.
- Conscious choices that line up with your values and beliefs leads to a life lived with integrity.

Recovery requires the knowledge and skills necessary to:

Navigate the common symptoms of traumatic stress that stop you.

Observe and understand what has happened to you.

Work your life choices with integrity.

Navigating thoughts or behaviors that interfere with your daily functioning and block your progress towards fulfilling your life plan requires identifying, avoiding, or eliminating inappropriate reactions to traumatic stress triggers. Answers to the following questions assess your current ability to stay in the safe *here and now* and no longer be triggered into the *there and then*.

- **Can you see in all directions around yourself?**
- **Can you hear subtle and beautiful sounds as well as loud and scary ones?**
- **Can you be patient and let things in the moment unfold as they will, or do you have to force some action?**
- **Are you engaged with the people around you or are you just keeping an eye on them?**
- **Are you involved in risky behaviors just to avoid feeling anything but the rush necessary to know you are alive?**
- **In this moment are you avoiding people, places, or things, because they set off negative sensations, feelings, memories, or thoughts?**

Being able to complete the NOW test offers a way in which to challenge your readiness to go deeper into the recovery process. Thought Field Therapy is used whenever overwhelming emotional responses interfere with being present and being able to face the past.

Observing and Understanding involves making sense out of your past traumatic experience. Once in the *here and now,* you can incorporate your past experience as part of your overall body of knowledge and wisdom. You can embrace it, learn from it, and use it to help you move forward safely, joyfully, and successfully. Answering the following questions demands that you make sense of your experience.

- Are you able to describe to your satisfaction what happened around you during the traumatic event you experienced?

- Can you recall your responses to the event in a step-by-step manner?

- Were these responses reactions or decisions?

- Can you see the difference between making choices and reacting in this situation?

- Are you able to understand your reasons for each action?

- Do you know what others say represents "reasonable expected behavior" in this situation?

If in your heart and mind you have complete and satisfactory answers to these questions, then you are well on your way through the Observing and Understanding part of the recovery process. As you search for additional relevant information to make sense of your past traumatic history and experiences, use Thought Field Therapy to resolve pains and fears if new aspects of the events surface and, subsequently, bring up emotional, psychological, or physical responses.

Working your life choices with integrity means you have stop reacting to symptoms created by your traumatic experiences and, instead, begin making conscious choices and taking positive steps forward. The final test of your recovery is measured by the degree to which you have stopped running away from your past pains and fears of the future and now are moving forward by consciously choosing your actions in a manner congruent with your values and beliefs.

As you live your life, are you:
- choosing your job or career?
- choosing the people with whom you live?

- choosing the individuals you love?

- choosing how you spend your precious time and energy?

- choosing your words and actions in all aspects of your life to satisfy your values?

You may have more choices and you may make them more in line with your individual nature after recovery than you did before the traumatic stressor events. You can get rid of troubles with your physical or emotional health and any remaining trigger responses by using Thought Field Therapy.

At the end of your life, you own:

- your memories from the traumatic event(s) you have experienced and its aftermath and the choices about how you use them to serve your values.

- the life's lesson this event taught you, which you can share as you like with your loved ones, those who will experience this type of event, or children who may someday face a similar event. Or you may choose not to share what you have learned with anyone at all.

- the choices you make that change the world in which you live and which you pass on.

PART FOUR

Frequent Concerns
in Traumatic Stress Recovery

CHAPTER NINE

Healing Traumatic Loss of Loved Ones and Grief

Traumatic stressor events almost always result in some kind of loss, and when we lose something, we most often feel a sense of grief. Your traumatic experience may have resulted in the loss of a loved one, regardless of the nature of that love. Maybe you lost your way of being in the world, because the traumatic stressor event changed your body or how you relate to yourself, to others, or to the world. Possibly what you went through caused you to lose a dream for the future or a sense of control over your day-to-day life. When you lose that which you value, appreciate, or love, you naturally feel emotional pain. You also may feel diminished by what is gone, as if you as a person are less than you were before.

While you may grieve over any of these losses, the loss of a loved one represents one of the most difficult to overcome and the most universally painful human response. Although ,our nature compels us to keep moving forward on our journey, to keep living beyond a loss of human life, doing so may seem excruciatingly hard.

Of course, Thought Field Therapy can help you reduce your truly overpowering grief, but you still will have to grieve. Feeling your sadness and the loss itself cannot be avoided when someone you love dies. However, the NOW recovery process can help you work through your grief. Using the Now process, you can navigate through the overwhelming feelings that stop you from moving forward with your life or that drive you to unreasonable actions after the loss. Then, you must observe the relationship you have (or had) to what or who you lost and understand what it meant to you and what part it played in your life. Until you can do so, you cannot know the full impact the loss has had on you and your life. Last, but most important to the grief process, you have to find ways to work wisely toward choices that allow you to move forward with integrity despite the loss.

If you get stuck in your grief, Thought Field Therapy will help you feel less controlled by your emotions and assist you in moving to a place of emotional safety. From that more secure place, you can gain knowledge about your experience and understand the direction in which your life is moving.

If you have suffered a loss, the answers to the following questions provide you with a way to begin assessing your level of emotional upset and your ability to actively engage in grieving.

- **Does the pain of your loss keep you from remembering and enjoying the joy of what you had?**

- **Does the fear of experiencing your feelings of sadness, hopelessness, isolation, rage, guilt, stop you from remembering the joy and love that you once shared with the loved one who died?**

- **Has out of control behavior interfered with your remembering the joy and love that you once shared with the loved one who died?**

- **Have your efforts to cope with your loss of a loved one involved such mechanisms as denial, avoidance, or anger and, therefore, stopped you from honoring or commemorating their life and death?**

Stay Engaged in the Grief Process

Becoming focused solely on looking backwards—remembering—after the loss of a loved one prevents you from seeing what is around or ahead of you. Additionally, the pain of what you have lost can leave you in a state of confusion and uncertainty, which can make you feel disoriented and unsure about who and what remains with you. When either of these conditions occurs, you may find yourself suffering your grief in isolation and feeling as if you have no purpose or direction. You may spend much of your time living in the past, dwelling on times when your loved one was still alive, or rehashing what happened to them and how it could have turned out differently. You may be doing this alone rather than with the people who are alive and willing to support you in your grief process.

As we previously discussed, the hallmark symptoms of Post Traumatic Stress Disorder are related to the inability of the body, mind, and spirit to see the difference between the *there and then* (an unsafe time and a place) and the *here and now* (a safe time and place). The description above contains these symptoms in a variety of forms. The reason for this is simple: The death of a loved one often represents a traumatic event, especially if the death comes unexpectedly, as in a random car crash. We almost always experience the untimely death of a loved one as a traumatic stressor event, and the death of a child, no matter what our relationship with that child, never feels right or seems to fit into any sense of universal order or justice.

No matter how much you might want to dwell on the past or linger in what could have or might have been, becoming functional after such a loss requires that you come to accept the reality of the event. Do not get stuck in the *there and then* and its overwhelming feelings of pain and loss. You must not let this misery or your attempts to avoid reminders of your anguish shut down your grieving. Throughout this book, the principles of the NOW recovery process emphasize the critical role of your participation in healing. Thought Field Therapy removes the overwhelming upset that accompanies the loss of a loved one and allows you a connection to the actual grieving process, which has a huge curative energy with your active engagement.

This next story, one of my own, illustrates how dealing with traumatic stress with Thought Field Therapy allows us to get on with the business of being human even in the face of tremendous loss.

Staying Available to Heal Ourselves and to Help Others

As long as the correct sequence is tapped, Thought Field Therapy relieves traumatic stress symptoms at impressive speed under any conditions, and the role of the interventionist or helper remains minimal. I had a chance to remember this fact at the worst moment of my life when I offered Thought Field Therapy to someone in need.

I was attending a memorial service for Trey, an 11-year-old boy, who had died a week earlier. This boy had held a special place in my life, since my wife and I considered his parents our oldest and dearest friends. Trey had died unexpectedly at a friend's birthday party when a strong wind caused a large redwood tree branch to break off and fall on him just as he happened to be running underneath the tree. The branch hit him in the head, knocking him unconscious.

As his mother put it, Trey's death represented a "blameless event." Emergency Medical Services arrived in a timely manner; Trey was air-lifted to an emergency room at the best hospital. There the doctors and nurses did more than the standard protocols required to try and revive him before declaring him dead.

Seven days later, about 500 people attended Trey's memorial service at a junior high school. Before the service, his mother greeted friends and family. I was standing nearby as she hugged one woman in particular. She mouthed the words "help her" to me over the woman's shoulder.

I was an emotional wreck myself. When the woman stepped back, however, I saw she was in uniform and realized she was the first emergency medical technician on the scene after Trey had been hurt. I could see she was having a very hard time coping. So, I identified myself as an International Critical Incident Stress Foundation-approved instructor for critical incident stress debriefing and a Certified Trauma Specialist. The woman explained that although she had been to a critical incident stress debriefing, for the last week she had been unable to get the picture of Trey out of her mind.

Using the Thought Field Therapy protocol, I asked her to rate her upset. On a 1-10 scale, the picture in her mind was so vivid and disturbing that she rated herself a level 10. In the middle of this very crowded room, I led her through one extended trauma tapping pattern. When we had finished, she reported the picture of Trey had disappeared.

I had treated myself with Thought Field Therapy many times throughout the week. Without having done so, I know I would not have been available for that emergency medical technician or for other friends who needed help coping with Trey's death. Trey's loss would continue to be painful no matter what and all who knew him would grieve his death, but tapping gave me a way to remain functional and available for my own healing and for helping others.

Thought Field Therapy offers a great gift at times of loss, because it does not change reality or interfere with grieving. Tapping offers a way through the pain so we can grieve and keep the loved one part of our life through our memories. Without Thought Field Therapy, for instance, it might have been too painful for me to tell this story or to remember Trey. Because of Thought Field Therapy I was able to share this story with you, and Trey's memory joins me at every workshop when I tell this story to attendees.

Knowing You Are Alive to Feel the Loss

The most common problem associated with grief arises when people don't grieve. When a person comes looking for help with their grief, the first question I ask is, "How are you grieving?" Most commonly I receive the following response: "It hurts too much to grieve. I cry every time I remember that he or she is gone, so I try not to think about it."

Even the toughest person will manage the pain of their grief by avoiding memories of a loved one who has died, the parts of their current life that trigger such memories, or situations in which they will feel forced to share such memories with others. In fact, many people employ avoidance, a common coping mechanism, when they are grief stricken. However, to restructure and reclaim your life after such a loss, it is necessary for you to take the time to be with your feelings of love for the one who has died and to integrating the fact that the person no longer is with you physically.

Grieving constitutes an active process requiring your engagement. Time passively passed without your conscious awareness helps you little in this process, and time spent locked in overwhelming emotion that freezes your thinking and prevents you from taking action helps even less. Integrating loss into your being requires living with the reality of having been given the gift of your loved one for whatever length of time and now being without his or her physical presence.

While Thought Field Therapy provides a means of getting unstuck and using your feelings in this change process, it does not change the reality of your situation. Thought Field Therapy does not divorce you from fundamental human processes, such as grieving. You will experience loss and integrate it into your being in a manner befitting your nature. Just like most people, you will grieve and experience periods of bereavement even when you have eliminated the overwhelming emotions or recurrent intrusive images or memories. However, you can honor your lost loved one only when you move beyond your overwhelming pain so that you are able to remember them with love and a deep sense of the gratitude for all they brought to your life. Take a moment and sense what you are feeling and experiencing as we discuss grief. If you have fresh losses now may be the time to tap before going on.

Getting Through the Pains to the Memory

A woman in her late 40s approached me after a presentation at a conference and asked for help dealing with the loss of her son, who had died three years earlier. A young man in his early 20s, he had been killed in an industrial accident. She was an experienced mental health professional and was able to describe to me her sense of being stuck in her grief. She said she was unable to move beyond the overwhelming pain she felt whenever she started to think of her son.

"How may I help?" I asked. As soon as she began to respond to my question, her tears started flowing and a look of pain spread across her face.

Without further prompting, I led her through a Thought Field Therapy treatment sequence, and calm returned to her face and the tears slowed. I then asked, "What happened to your son?" and immediately the look of pain returned. After another treatment sequence, she was able to describe for me the emotions that had overcome her when I asked the question. She said my question reminded her that he was gone and she was without him, and this caused her to feel generally overwhelmed. Each time she became conscious of her loss, her focus of attention then led her to imagine how he died. She wondered about the moments before his death, the pain he may have felt, the thoughts he probably had, and the feelings he experienced dying alone.

As she talked about her understanding of how he died while doing the work he loved, the pain returned to her face and she started to cry again, this time very hard. Her upset now was associated with the fact that she had encouraged her son to pursue this work that he loved and also was good at doing. After an additional tapping treatment, she was able to talk about her guilt as irrational and put these feeling in a manageable place.

As we talked more about her son and their relationship, we had to tap for the anger she felt about some relationship choices he had made. With the anger and guilt gone, she was able to speak about her love for her son, and this again started her tears flowing, this time accompanied by deep powerful sobs. I offered immediately to do another Thought Field Therapy treatment, but she refused any further help. Instead she said, "This is where I have been trying to get to for three years. I am remembering the last time I saw him at the airport, and I hugged my baby good-bye."

Grieving is painful, and suffering through a loss is hard work. Not even Thought Field Therapy can alter this reality. Tapping can manage the overwhelming pain and, by so doing, allow you to consciously engage in the process of integrating your loss. That's what it accomplished for this woman.

I received a post card about six months later from this mother reporting that she was doing much better. She was grieving, but no longer felt stuck in the process, and had finished a couple of projects done in her son's name. These projects had been started right after his death; previously she had been unable to complete them, because *thinking about her son had been too painful at that time. She was able to do the work of grieving, and to honor her son by finishing the projects, because Thought Field Therapy provided her with a way to manage her pain when it became too great. To fully integrate her loss, she had to be able to feel her love for her son and accept her life as changed now that he was physically absent from it—something all survivors of loss must do.*

To say her grieving was done at that point, or that she would no longer suffer the loss of her child, would be wrong in many ways. However, to think that after the loss of a loved one we are required to suffer to such a degree that our pain stops us from living in the way we value and shared with our dead loved one is even more wrong. Our lives go on even after theirs have ended, and we must find a way to continue living fully.

The struggle to stay alive and to go on after a loss can make us try some extreme things. The next story shows how one person's efforts to get unstuck from their grief led down the wrong road.

"I get it now" — Sharing to Be Understood

"I want to come in with my husband to talk about his affair," said the woman on the other end of the phone call.

"Is this marriage counseling or divorce counseling?" I asked, since I needed to know how to approach their session. I didn't receive a clear-cut response. After she answered a few more questions, however, it became clear that the woman's husband had agreed to come to counseling—and anything else she wanted—in the hope the marriage could be fixed. She explained to me that her husband told her about his affair when it became obvious that the secret would be out soon. His said he revealed the truth at that time in an attempt to protect her from hearing about it from someone else. So, we planned an appointment.

Two nice people in their mid 50s showed up in my office. They had been married for over 25 years and, judging by their interactions, they seemed very much married in all the good ways. By this I mean, their communication with one another appeared excellent, they were respectful of and caring for one another and both talked openly about how much they loved one another. Their problem lay in the fact that she felt so terribly angry and hurt by her husband's several-month long affair with a past employee. In fact, she was so, hurt that she did not know how she could stay with him.

As she talked about her concerns, the wife stressed that she was at a loss when it came to understanding how her husband could have done what he had done, especially with this particular employee. The other women, who was known to both of them, was older than the wife, by the husband's judgment was less attractive than his wife, and had a long history of emotional and financial problems. While the wife recognized her husband's courage in being honest with her and believed the affair was over, she could not stand the thought of what he had done to her and to their marriage.

As I talked with them, I had to admit I shared her confusion about what was going on here. The husband's behavior seemed out of character and not in line with what he said was important to him, what he wanted, and how he had lived his life previously. So, doing what therapists do, I started asking some probing questions about their history. In response to questions about when they thought things in the marriage started changing, I found out that about five years earlier their 19-year- old son had died in an automobile crash. The father and son had been best friends and had shared lots of sporting and outdoor activities. The mother and son had been very close also.

The moment their son's death was mentioned, both the husband and the wife became overcome with their grief. They cried openly and appeared to sink into depression. I stopped them from retelling the story and led them both through a Thought Field Therapy process. They used traumatic stress patterns that included both guilt and anger. At this point, the session's focus turned from the couple's marriage to helping them to grieve for the loss of their son and to share the story of his death. We tapped each time they sank back into a depressed state, until finally they could tell me the whole story without overwhelming upset or depression.

As they talked about their marriage after their son's death, it became clear that the joy had left their relationship along with their son, and since then they had simply been getting by day-to-day. Additionally, this wife and mother had gone into a deep depression that had lasted for about three years. While talking about what they had done to live through the loss, the husband talked about how his affair began. He explained that at the time the other women had made herself available to him, he was feeling so dead inside and hopeless that he lost sight of what mattered to him. As he said these words, a visible change occurred in his wife's affect and demeanor. She reached out to him and cried with him and told him, "It will be okay." After some more tapping, she told her husband she wanted to find a way to stay with him and make the marriage work. She admitted that she would need help learning to trust him again, but she said she really wanted to try.

When I asked her how she had come to her decision, her response was very clear. When she heard her husband talking about how dead and hopeless he had felt at the loss of their son, she had related to his words, because she had felt the same way. She knew how crazy that feeling made her feel and what she herself was capable of doing to try to rid herself of that emotion. She got it. She had found a way to understand how her husband could have had the affair. With this explanation, she could go on with the marriage.

The couple worked hard to do what had to be done to reestablish trust in their marriage. They worked out a system where he had a dedicated cell phone that only she used. He would answer this phone under any and all condition, at work or play, in the middle of conversation, or racing a car. He was always available and accountable to her. They had a few more sessions with me but did not need any long-term work once they found a way to keep talking. The course of their marriage counseling was shortened considerably, because Thought Field Therapy helped them get unstuck from the place where they had gotten stuck in the grieving process. Thought Field Therapy helped them bring the pain of their loss down to a level where they could feel alive and have hope again. From that place, they could also feel their love for one another and continue their marriage. Additionally, they could focus upon their daughter while keeping the memory of their son alive. When her older brother had died, she often was ignored by her parents, because she too would easily become overwhelmed, triggering all three of them. This would cause a shutdown in communications and grieving. Now, they all had a way to share their loss and to move forward in their lives.

With Thought Field Therapy, this couple was able to get to the real problem in their marriage quickly. Without Thought Field Therapy, a high likelihood exists that this couple's marriage counseling would have taken a long time and might have ended unsuccessfully. In either case, both the husband and the wife in this story provide perfect examples of the fact that when you shutdown your capacity to feel as a way of shielding yourself from the pain of loss you also shutdown your capacity to feel the love you need to recover from that loss. You do not have to lock yourself in the frozen pain of loneliness and hopelessness when someone close to you dies. You can open yourself to allow others in, to share hope, and to heal.

Shared Values and Beliefs Provide Power to Go On

The powerful feelings you carry from living through loss can become a source of strength for carrying on with your life's purpose and direction. Couple this strength with a desire to make right the injustices you or those you love suffered and which led to their death and you turn your loss into the power you need to demand that justice be done.

If your purpose in life includes making changes in your culture or society, then you might find this next story of my own grief useful. Strong emotional expressions can provide the best tool for connecting with others to create change. I use Thought Field Therapy only when these strong emotions become overwhelming and stop me or others from growing and going on to create change.

171

Using the Feelings From My Father's Death

I have used Thought Field Therapy many times to help myself deal with my own grief and to come to grips with the reality of life. My father died over 30 years ago at the age of 51 as a result of an industrial-related cancer. I feel sadness when I think of him and miss him in my life. I also miss his presence in my mother's life. I don't always feel a need to tap when I think of him. Sometimes my memories bring up positive and joyful feelings, and sometimes the sadness of his loss keeps me grounded in the reality of my life. However, I can find no sense of justice in my father's death. No matter how I think about it, I cannot say that he deserved a painful, early death.

My father's illness resulted from his efforts to support and care for his wife and children. He had performed many labor and blue collar jobs, including cleaning plating tanks, maintaining electrical transformers, and working in a magnet factory. He found the best jobs he could, given the fact that he left high school before graduating to work his family's farm when his step-father became sick. He did finish high school the same year as my older brother, but by then he had suffered extensive occupational exposure to carcinogens.

More often than not, our culture and society does not treat hardworking men and women fairly. Often many are put in harm's way to serve the financial and power interests of a few. My father did not choose cancer nor was it fated. He was not treated fairly by life. Do I sound sad and bothered? Do I sound angry? I am, but not so angry as to keep me from my memories. And I tap when the feelings overwhelm me, and I cannot function. I also tap when the overwhelming feelings interfere with my commitment to making the world better for men like my father.

Justice does not exist in the nature of the world or in the institutions of our society. Justice exists in only in the relationships between people. When we treat one another with love, care, and concern justice exists. Only when rules and laws support our love, care, and concern for one another does justice go beyond individual relationships. This is my belief and a guiding principle in my life. My father was not shown the basic concern for safety and well-being in his workplace that I think is right. So, I take my sense of loss and injustice — and my anger — and I channel it into doing something to change this for other men like my father.

I chose to become a social worker because of the explicit role this profession has in making change in the larger systems that impact individuals. I tell this story about my father to teach others about the importance of the environment that forms the context of our daily lives. I support all efforts to improve regulations and laws so they protect us in the workplace and in our homes. Even as a psychotherapist working with individuals who struggle to take more control of their lives, I encourage them to act with care and concern for all who share their world. I encourage individuals to act in ways that demand attention to injustice, as part of a community to change standards of care, and as a voting participant of a representative form of government. In this way, my emotions become a source of power when I am not overwhelmed by them.

Despite my feelings about the injustice of my father's death, the action steps I've taken and the way I have chosen to make my response to my father's death a positive force in my life keep me from becoming frozen in loneliness and hopelessness. I feel all my feelings and their full force fuels my actions. I will grieve for my father in this way forever, and I know this is a good thing.

I had to tap several times for several different feelings as I wrote this story for you. The loss of some one you love and who is important in your life always constitutes a powerful experience that can take your emotions over the top. I encourage you to spend a few minutes now thinking about and feeling your emotions concerning your deceased loved ones, and considering what is important to you personally in relationship to them. Tap whenever overwhelming feelings interfere with honoring them as you enjoy the memory of them.

The grief story that began this chapter and the story above are both from my own life and are offered as a further invitation to try Thought Field Therapy for yourself. I have found tapping, both personally and professionally, to be the best way to deal with loss and to get to a place where my clients and I are able to honor those we love — living and dead. In this way we can fully engage in the grief process and move further on our journey of traumatic stress recovery.

The Loss of a Child's Pet

The next story will give you some insight into the experience of grief in two areas often unrecognized or underrated in the lives of those who experience the loss. Children working through loss may appear and act differently in many ways from adults going through the same experience, but the loss and the pain they feel are just as real. Depending on the type of loss, the experience may even seem more intense for a child.

For both adults and children, the loss of a pet can provoke responses as powerful as the loss of a human loved one. Any animal in your life that is not thought of or treated as an object represents a pet. That said, sometimes animals are seen as objects, such as in business, or as a food source, entertainment, or something used to fill our needs. However, once viewed as a being worthy of your love and care, regardless of its species, you will grieve its loss.

The following story provides an example of how simply Thought Field Therapy can be introduced to children and how important it is to address the traumatic events in children's lives. Written as a children's story, it is intended to be read to children dealing with loss and for any one who has grieved the loss of a pet. The characters and the events are fictitious, but the responses in the work are based on real-life people and events.

Cinnamon and Sierra — Getting to the Good Feelings

This is a story about a hard time in my family's life, and how we got through it. I hope what we learned will help you and your family get through your hard times.

My name is Bobby, and I live with my Mom and Dad, my older brother Johnny, and our cat, Cinnamon. We have a beautiful house and a big yard. Johnny and I have a great room, which we share. We all love and take care of each other and are always there to help each other. We have time every day to talk and play. And when I need it, my parents or my brother help me with my homework and other stuff.

In our room, Johnny and I each have a bookcase. On mine, the bottom shelf holds all my sport stuff. I keep my safety pads and my helmet for my scooter and bike there. My baseball glove and my basketball are there, too. The next shelf holds my collection of space crafts and my favorite toys. On the next shelf, I have all my favorite books, videos, games, and papers from school that I have saved. Sometimes I find fun things from the Internet that I like to have, so I print them out and keep them there. I keep my most special things on the top shelf of my bookshelf. I have pictures of my friends and the places we have been together. I have pictures of my family. But, my most special picture is one we can never take again. It's a picture of Mom, Dad, Johnny, and me by the fireplace with our cats, Cinnamon and Sierra. Johnny is holding Cinnamon, the big calico with all those colors. I am holding Sierra, the big tabby.

I miss Sierra. She died after she was hit by a car. Sometimes it seems like a long time ago, and sometimes it seems like it just happened. Our cats came from Friends of Cats, a place where homeless cats go until they find a home. Sierra was with us for as long as I can remember. She was always here. In our house, we have one rule for the cats: Cats stay inside, because we live on a busy street and near a big canyon with cat-eating coyotes. But sometimes Sierra would find her way out of the house. We don't know why she liked to go out, but she did. Cinnamon never likes to go outside.

One day in the fall, we came home after school and Cinnamon was sitting on the sofa waiting for her afternoon pet, just like every day, but Sierra was nowhere to be found. She was not in the bedroom or in the kitchen. She had not gotten locked in a closet or shut in the laundry room. So, we did what we always do when she gets out. We all went outside to bring her back inside.

We looked in the backyard. We looked under the porch. We look over the neighbor's fence. I was looking up in the tree in the front yard. (Once we found her climbing around up there.) I looked out in

175

the street, and I saw her. She was lying in the street and did not move when I yelled at her to get up and back to the house. Then, I yelled for my mother. When she arrived, she went into the street when no cars were coming and picked Sierra up. When she laid Sierra down on the porch steps, she didn't move. Her eyes were open, but she didn't move. Her month was open, but she wasn't breathing. I wanted to hear her purr, but when I touched her she was stiff and cold.

"Is she dead?" Johnny asked Mom.

"Yes," said Mom and then told us to go in the house while she took Sierra to the garage. Then she called Dad.

Dad looked very sad when we all went to the backyard to bury Sierra. She was in a box in a deep hole Dad had dug. Dad said we all should tell a story about Sierra. He remembered when Johnny and I were still very little and Sierra was new to our house. He said the three of us would fight over the best spot on the sofa, but Sierra always won. Johnny talked about one time when he was really sick, and every time he woke up during the day Sierra was looking right at him and purred until he fell back to sleep. Mom laughed as she told the story of Sierra bringing a mouse into the house, and how everyone got so crazy chasing the mouse to get it out of the house again. I wanted to tell everyone that whenever I would have a problem at school Sierra was always there when I got home and would make me play with her until I forgot about whatever had happened earlier that day, but I just couldn't talk. So, Dad said I could tell my story later.

Then Dad covered Sierra in the box with dirt and put up a wood marker. He said after we have time to think about what we want to use, we will find a permanent marker instead — maybe a tree or a statue.

That night Johnny woke me up. I was breathing hard and felt all sweaty. Johnny said I was yelling out loud, "Get out of the street!" I was dreaming that Sierra was in the road with a car going by her. I couldn't get back to sleep, and I just lay there. The next day at school, I fell asleep with my head on my desk. It felt like a hard day to get through, and that night at home Johnny had to be told to get off the computer about 20 times by my parents.

As the days went by after Sierra's death, things got worse for me. Every time I remembered Sierra or saw a picture of her, I would just see a picture in my mind of how she looked lying in the road when I found her. I took down the picture of the family with Sierra in it, so I wouldn't be reminded of her. I pushed Cinnamon away when she would try to come into our room, because she reminded me of Sierra. My heart felt like a balloon with no air in it.

Mom and Dad kept telling my brother and I to go school and practices and to be with our friends. All I wanted to do was forget about Sierra lying in the road and figure out why this had happened and where she was now. I kept asking questions about death. All my friends and teammates had something different to say about what happens after you die. One day, Dad and I had a long private talk about death as we worked in the garden. He told me what is known and what people believe about death. He told me what our family has believed since his great-grandfather's time. I liked having some idea about where Sierra was now, but it didn't make my bad dreams go away.

Sometimes I thought it must have been my fault that we didn't find Sierra in time to keep her out of the street. Other times I would think that it was Johnny's fault that she got out of the house. Mom had warned him to be careful when going in and out of the house. I remembered lots of times when Mom had told him to not be so careless in leaving the door open. Thinking about this made me start worrying about what I was doing or what others were doing, because I didn't want anything else bad to happen. And that made me unhappy and not much fun to be with. I started getting into arguments with every-one over little stuff that didn't really matter.

Things changed when Uncle Roger came to dinner, though. Uncle Roger has seen animals and people die a lot in his job. He works as a firefighter, and he understood exactly what I was talking about when I explained to him about the picture of Sierra in my head. He told me that even grown-ups sometimes get a picture or memory of an ugly thing stuck in their heads. When that happens, we do all kinds of things to make the picture and the terrible feelings that *come along with it go away. Then he told me that the best way to get rid of those "in-your face pictures, feelings, and memories" is to tap them away. I didn't know what he was talking about, but Uncle Roger showed me how he did it. Then I followed what he did right there in the dining room.*

Thinking of the ugly picture of Sierra, I felt the bad feelings inside and showed Uncle Roger how big the bad feelings were by spreading out my arms to show the size of the hurt I was feeling. Then we tapped together, Uncle Roger on himself and me on myself, with our fingertips on the side of our hand, under our nose, at the beginning of our eyebrow in the middle of our head, under our eyes, under our arms on our ribs, under our collarbone, on our little finger, under the collarbone, on our index finger, and under our collarbone. This took about a minute, and then when Uncle Roger asked me to show him how big the bad feeling was, I showed him that it was smaller than before. So, he showed me the next part. We tapped the back of our hand and did nine different things: closed our eyes, opened our eyes, looked down to the left, looked down to the right, whirled our eyes in a big circle, whirled our eyes in big circle in the other directions, hummed a tune, counted to five, and hummed a tune again. After this we tapped just like we did when we started: at the beginning of our eyebrow in the middle of our head, under our eyes, under our arms, under our collarbone, on our little finger, under the collarbone, on our index finger, and under our collarbone.

Afterwards, Uncle Roger asked me to think about Sierra again, and the hurt was so much smaller that I wanted to tell him and the rest of the family what I had not been able to say when we buried Sierra. So I did. Everybody cried, including me. And I realized that everybody missed Sierra, including Cinnamon. I decided the next time Cinnamon curled up next to me, I would not push her away. That night when I went to my room I wanted to put back the family picture with Sierra in it. When I looked at it the hurt started again, but Mom reminded me to tap. We went through the tapping routine that Uncle Roger had written down for me. After we tapped, I felt happy to look at the picture of all of us on my shelf.

I still miss Sierra, but the ugly picture in my mind is gone, and I just think about our good times together now. It's so good to remember her purr and the feel of her furry tail brushing against me when I would read with her lying against me.

This story demonstrates the importance of getting your overwhelming emotions under control and eliminating any intrusive images you might have related to such the loss of any loved one — human or animal. This family's response was appropriate and supportive, but Bobby needed Thought Field Therapy to go forward with his grieving. We tend to underplay the importance of events like the loss of a pet in children's lives. Whether we think about a loss like the one described in Bobby's story as a traumatic event with a lower case t or one with an upper case T, dealing with the death of a pet for the first time represents a big deal for every child. Thought Field Therapy, however, gives us a way to help them stay in touch with and work through their strong emotions so the wound does not remain open but instead heals naturally.

The loss of innocence that comes from confronting death constitutes a developmental task every human being must complete as part of growing up. Sometimes, however, children experience more than just one or two losses in their early years. If losses come relentlessly, these traumatic stressor events become part of children's every-day lives, and the hurt they feel as the traumatic stress builds becomes a way of life for them and remains that way into adulthood.

Understanding the NOW process — No Open Wounds — serves as a critical step toward allowing children to grow on their life journeys with health, love, and joy. If they get stuck in their grief, they may not complete developmental phases of growing up and may carry overwhelming emotions from traumatic stress forward into adult years. As you move from one developmental set of tasks to the next, your success often is determined by how well you have healed traumatic stress responses in earlier stages. When you are out of control with traumatic stress responses then you become unable to attend to the developmental task in front of you. Chapter 11 discusses how Thought Field Therapy helps you regain control and move towards complete recovery and a better life no matter at what age you address the issues that may have thwarted your development.

CHAPTER TEN

Ending Addictions
and Other Unhealthy Habits

We can't control many of the things that happen in life. In particular, most traumatic stressor events will appear unmanageable, because many of them, indeed, are beyond our control. For example, you cannot have any influence over the car crashing into you at the intersection, being trapped inside a building during an earthquake, or walking into the bank at the same time as a bank robber. If you had the ability to choose whether to have these thing happen to you, you would not choose the experience or the pain and suffering that would accompany it.

You lack control of a situation when you possess little or no power to stop things from happening or to change events or conditions once set in motion. If you do not have the power to change to an event, then you cannot control the event; therefore, it follows that you also have no responsibility for its occurrence. When it comes to most traumatic stressor events, you can let yourself off the hook. You likely bear no responsibility for many things that happened to you in your life. Using that same line of reasoning, when you are reacting without awareness, thought, or the power to do otherwise in a state of traumatic stress you are not responsible for your actions.

That said, you are responsible for the choices you make. When several possible courses of action exist and it is within your control to pick among them, you are responsible for the outcome of that decision. If you opt for self-destructive behavior in response to a traumatic stressor event when you could make another selection, you bear the responsibility not only for this choice but for all the ramifications of it. This means that if your choices hurt yourself, someone you love, or someone you don't even know, you remain responsible for both your choices and your actions—and the results of your actions. You posses control over the situation to the extent that you have options available from which to choose.

Fortunately, you now have more options than you did before you picked up this book. Reading this book, understanding and following the NOW recovery process, and tapping to end overwhelming emotions gives you more possible ways to respond to events and choices before you. You now have more control in your life. With this control, however, comes responsibility for the outcome of the decisions you make.

When you experience a traumatic stressor event, it's common to react to the lack of control you feel by trying to make choices that give you a sense that you are in charge. Sometimes the only options you can see for regaining control are found in negative or self-destructive behaviors—out of control behaviors, such as substance abuse, because these behaviors appear to offer you ways to relieve your pain or overwhelming feelings. The choice to behave in an out of control or self-destructive manner seems illogical to those who have not experienced traumatic stressor events. Those experiences, however, often produce the kinds of intense pain and fear that drive people to do anything to find relief.

If you have experienced these strong feelings after your traumatic stressor event, you may have made your decisions about how to gain control using a criteria based on what would stop the pain or give you some rest from the overwhelming negative feelings. The better choice is to use criteria grounded in what was best, healthiest, most healing, or would move you towards recovery. It's common for people who feel they must take action to do things like self medicate with alcohol or drugs, put themselves in danger, even cut or self-mutilate to gain a sense of control. Even though it might seem like a good choice at the time, selecting a self-destructive behavior or doing something injurious to others never constitutes the best choice.

Confronting the Current Negative Patterns

Possibly your pain and fear have made it difficult for you to know if the choices you have made to date have been healthy or unhealthy ones. Therefore, the first step in evaluating whether you are selecting self-destructive behaviors involves understanding if you are behaving in an out of control manner. You are out of control if you are doing something obviously unhealthy and unsafe. That said, you will find it very difficult, if not impossible, to look at your own behavior and see the dangers and problems that stem from your actions. You most always will have a good reason for choosing them. So, judge your own behavior and decisions based upon a standard you would set for someone you love. Ask yourself if you would want them to choose the behaviors you have picked. Or ask yourself what your parent, grandparent, child, Chaplin, therapist, spouse, or anyone who really knows you and cares about you would think about what you are doing. If your answer sounds like, "They wouldn't approve," "They wouldn't like it," "They'd tell me to stop before I get hurt or in trouble," or "They'd tell me it was bad for me financially or was illegal," you are probably out of control and behaving in a self-destructive manner.

Here are some more questions to ask yourself as you evaluate if you are out of control and acting in self-destructive ways.

Is your eating out of control?

Are you gaining or losing weight unintentionally?

Are you eating when you are not hungry?

Are you using eating as an activity to fill up the empty feeling inside?

Is your drinking alcohol or taking drugs out of control?

Compared to how much you used before the traumatic stressor events, are you using these substances more often or in larger amounts?

Are you numbing out the bad feelings with alcohol or other drugs?

Do the calories from alcohol make up one third or more of your daily energy source?

Is your sexual activity out of control?

Are you engaging in unsafe sex, risking disease, or pregnancy?

Are you using sex as a way to avoid emotional intimacy?

Are you unable or unwilling to perform sexually as fits your values?

Are you unable to have sex?

Is your sleep and rest out of control?

Do you get less than a good seven to eight hours of sleep every 24 hours?

Do you avoid going bed for fear of bad dreams?

Do you wake up feeling as tired as when you went to bed?

Is your driving out of control?

Do you ever drive after having used alcohol or other drugs?

Do you every drive faster than law enforcement says is safe?

Do feel like you are pushing the limits on the road in anyway?

Is your anger set off by other drivers?

Does your driving scare the people who care about you?

Can you balance your work and home life?

Do you use work to avoid being home?

Do you use your home life to avoid pursuing meaningful work?

Do you use relationships at home or work as excuses for your failures?

Do you act in any ways that are unhealthy or self-destructive?

Are you afraid to seek help for a physical, mental, or spiritual problem, because you will have to confront the reality of your out of control behaviors?

If you answered "Yes" to one or more of these questions, you need to make some new, healthier, safer choices about your actions and behaviors. If you don't know how to do that—and you probably don't or you would have made better choices already—don't worry. Tap for any upset around approaching these issues if you need to do so and engage in the processes of complete traumatic stress recovery.

Be honest with yourself in answering the questions above. Remember, you want to achieve a life with integrity. You want to heal the wounds from your traumatic stressor event completely and finish the NOW process so you function each day without impairments and with an adherence to a set of values. If you are out of control in one part of your life, you are likely attempting to regain control in some other part of your life. That means something hasn't healed; this causes you to make choices that aren't based on your true values and to move forward in an impaired fashion. When you do so, you also remain out of touch with yourself, and, therefore, remain incomplete as a person. The goal of NOW involves not only helping you make choices with integrity and move forward unimpaired but also to help you feel complete.

Searching for What Works

If you've chosen to abuse drugs or alcohol or to engage in harmful behaviors since your traumatic experience, you are not alone. As mentioned earlier, many people trying to cope with a traumatic stres-

sor event do so with self-destructive behaviors. These can include addictive use of alcohol or drugs or by engaging in repetitive behaviors,
such as excessive shopping, sex, fighting, eating, exercising, or cleaning.
No matter the traumatic stress responses from which you suffer, these
choices rarely manage the responses well or ultimately help anyone
heal from a traumatic stressor event. In fact, these behaviors simply
avoid the healing process altogether, leaving the wound not only open
but allowing it to fester. The self-destructive behaviors simply add new
symptoms, or problems, into the mix of symptoms with which you are
already struggling.

Yet, if you are so distraught by your traumatic stress responses
that you find yourself choosing between these types of self-destructive
behaviors, or worse choices like suicide, directly hurting others, or living in terror of flashback, hyper vigilance, or numb isolation. When
that happens, the self-destructive choices may not seem so bad. In such
a case, your biggest problem comes down to the limited options available due to your traumatic stress response.

Traumatic stress responses sometimes overwhelm us to such a
degree that we will do anything—safe or not—to stop our pain and
fear. This next story demonstrates the desperation some people feel
after a traumatic stressor event and how bad choices lead to bad habits and self-destructive behaviors. Additionally, it shows the extent to
which people will go in an effort to help themselves.

When Alcohol Does Not Work

*Linda called me late at night asking for help. When I asked
for a description of her problem, she said she had not slept for three
nights.*

*When I asked her what had caused her sleeplessness, Linda
explained that her son had died in her home of an accidental drug
overdose two days ago. He had just finished a plumber apprentice-
ship program after years of struggles to overcome childhood and adult
problems. He had gone out with friends to celebrate the beginning of
his new life, and when he returned home very late, he went directly*

to bed and fell asleep. But as she was heading to bed Linda checked on him and noticed that something about his breathing seemed off. So, Linda had stayed awake most of the night to periodically check on him. Early the next morning, after dozing off briefly, Linda went in and found her son had stopped breathing completely. She called 911 and the dispatcher instructed her in rescue breathing, but, despite her efforts, her son never revived even after paramedics arrived. Now, she told me, whenever she closed her eyes to rest she found herself confronted with a vivid image of her son's dead eyes looking at her as she gave him CPR. If she did fall asleep for even an instant, she would awaken with a jolt to find his eyes staring at her.

Linda was beside herself. Sleep deprivation provides a sure path to complete dysfunction. Linda said she had tried everything to get some sleep but couldn't get any relief. "What's the last thing you tried," I asked.

"Vodka," she responded. Many people commonly use alcohol to medicate themselves, and, in most cases, enough alcohol will cause you to fall asleep. If you sleep in an alcohol-induced slumber, though, you will not rest well. In this situation, even large quantities were failing to do the job for Linda. Occasionally she would fall asleep only to awaken moments later with a sudden start and that image in her mind.

Linda knew she needed to sleep, so when I suggested she try Thought Field Therapy, she tapped as instructed without hesitation. After just two rounds of tapping, I could hear her becoming sleepy, and when I asked her what she saw when she closed her eyes, she replied, "Nothing but blackness." Linda was asleep by the time I put the phone down.

Imagine if you could not sleep because of the images that came to mind when you closed your eyes — or maybe you have had this experience. Intrusive thoughts and pictures, like the ones Linda saw when she tried to sleep, constitute common responses in the aftermath of traumatic stressor events. The reason for this actually is quite simple and involves the sympathetic part of the nervous system. When it is activated in the flight or fight mode, changes in the way you take in and hold information keep you seeing the most important information at the time of the event; in Linda's case, she saw her son's lifeless eyes. Activation of the para-sympathetic nervous system creates a relaxation response that helps calm the mind and relax the body. This cannot happen, when you are constantly re-stimulated by the pictures in your mind. So when the normal system isn't getting basic needs met—when you can't sleep—you must do something extra to help distract yourself from the pictures and help yourself relax and fall asleep. Like Linda, you might turn to a depressant drug, like alcohol or sleeping pills. But an inherent problem exists in turning to alcohol or other drugs as a solution. Over time, it becomes very hard to get the right balance of alcohol or drugs into the body to calm the nervous system down so you can sleep without ending up drunk or high and thus disturbing the sleep. In other words, while you might initially only need one drink or pill, eventually you develop a resistance and need to drink much more or take multiple pills. Plus, as seen in the story above, even in the beginning, these choices may not always work.

If you try to get the right balance enough times and fail, ending up drunk or high instead, this eventually will give you another whole set of problems. These may be much worse than your other post traumatic stress symptoms. For example, if you continue getting drunk or high, you might end up dead or injured from driving drunk, get into physical fights, have sex with the wrong person, destroy your liver, lose your job, or get arrested. These represent just a few of the bad outcomes that come with choosing to cope with the traumatic stress responses by using drugs and alcohol—either as a sleep aid or a coping mechanism of any sort.

And then, of course, once you begin getting drunk or high, this behavior easily can be taken to the point of abuse, meaning that you choose to repeat it consistently. And when you repeat a behavior enough times, it becomes a habit. A habit constitutes something you do without choosing to do so consciously or even without awareness of doing it. An alcohol or drug habit is driven by your need to manage the overwhelming feelings related to the traumatic stressor event you have experienced. It also is driven by your need to relieve the withdrawal symptoms that come from stopping the negative behavior once a physical dependence has occurred. In more simple terms, when you develop a drinking or drug use habit, you become addicted to alcohol or the drug you are taking. You then stop having a choice about whether or not you continue using them to sleep or to help eliminate whatever traumatic stress response from which you suffer. Your body simply demands that you continue the behavior. And you may behave in this manner with little awareness of the fact that you are doing so.

If you find yourself in the situation where self-destructive or out of control behavior choices have caused you to become addicted, or if attempts to overcome the pain or suffering associated with your traumatic stressor events have resulted in addiction, Thought Field Therapy can help in two ways. One, it gets rid of your overwhelming traumatic stress symptoms so you can cope without the alcohol or other drugs. Two, it eliminates the withdrawal symptoms you feel when you stop using alcohol or drugs and stops the urge that drives continued use even when you are not overwhelmed by traumatic stress. Once your traumatic stressor responses and symptoms are managed and the urge to continue drinking or taking drugs has been eliminated, you can break your alcohol or drug habit.

In fact, you can change the habit easily in a few days. In most cases, depending on the drug and its half-life (the time it takes for the drug to leave your system), your physical addiction will be gone within a few days. Some conditions require a medically monitored detoxification, and you should consult an addiction specialist if you have any uncertainty about what constitutes a safe withdrawal. Central nervous system depressants, like alcohol and barbiturates, and some anti-anxiety drugs, like valium, are the most dangerous. If you drink alcohol everyday or take these kinds of pills every day, consult a medical expert before you stop usage abruptly.

In most cases, however, Thought Field Therapy allows for a comfortable withdrawal and eliminates the underlying cause of the original desire to use drugs or alcohol. Of course, there have been no reported cases of dying of withdrawal from habitual shopping, sex, or other such compulsive repetitive behaviors that don't involve substance abuse. Feel free to tap for these, and to stop them as quickly as you like.

Although Thought Field Therapy can break your addiction quickly, changing life-long habits can be difficult even with tapping. Thought Field Therapy easily gets rid of the addictive urge. Breaking a habit used to soothe yourself when you have little else to take its place poses a more difficult issue. If you have been addicted to an unhealthy relationship, albeit with food, a person, or shopping, giving up that unhealthy friend who has been there for you when times were tough can be hard indeed.

In this story you meet one of my clients, a man with all the right intentions but with limited emotional, social, and financial resources necessary to make the life altering change he desires.

This Is What It Feels Like To Be A Nonsmoker!

Robbie had been a client of mine for awhile and he fully understood Thought Field Therapy and its power. He had seen the positive influence using tapping had on his life. Yet, he had not quit smoking despite my repeated attempts to convince him of the impact doing so would have on his mental and physical well being. A man in his late 40s, Robbie had made amazing changes over the last year as he recovered from a vehicle crash that had taken his left leg, a devastating divorce, and ongoing legal and medical challenges. He knew how to use Thought Field Therapy and did so to help himself in many ways, including with pain management and with traumatic stress recovery. And tapping worked well for him every time—until he smoked again.

The fact that smoking a cigarette would cause the benefits of Thought Field Therapy to decrease or go away is not unusual. In Thought Field Therapy, conditions exist that disrupt all of a person's healing mechanisms. This disruption is corrected easily, and then you can use Thought Field Therapy or other activities to take care of yourself once again. When you are in those disrupted states, however, you don't even think about doing something to help yourself; instead you continue the disruptive activity. In Robbie's case, this meant he just kept on smoking.

Most of the time this disruption in a person's healing mechanism results from exposure to something to which they are addicted. Such a disruption also can occur from stressors in a person's life. For Robbie, each time he smoked a cigarette, the disruption would undo the previous treatment for his urge to smoke as well as his anxiety about any number of problems in his life. When anxious, he would do what he had done his whole life — smoke away his feelings. However, smoking that cigarette also reversed the benefits of his treatment to alleviate pain and affected the healing of his stump.

Robbie and I had only been able to met once or twice a month, because changes in his living situation and taking part in an out-of-town physical rehabilitation program demanded lots of his time. During our sessions, he usually avoided the issue of smoking, but we had dealt with this addiction on more than one occasion. At a previous session, we had completely eliminated any urge to smoke, and he reported that for hours after he left the session he felt no desire to pick up a cigarette. Out of habit, however, he had a smoke that evening, and for the next day or two only smoked a couple of cigarettes rather than his usual two packs a day. Over a short time, he returned to his normal smoking patterns, however. While he was honest about the events and his continued addiction, he was unwilling to make quitting smoking a priority again. Towards the end of the session, we discussed what was next in his treatment plan, and I made it clear that stopping smoking constituted the most important change he could make to improve his life.

As we talked about this, I could see Robbie's anxiety level getting higher. Since we had only a few minutes left, I asked how strong his urge was to smoke a cigarette as soon as he left the session. He reported his urge was very strong. We tapped for his urge. He was immediately relieved and sat back calmly with no urge to smoke and no anxiety apparent.

"Robbie, will you use Thought Field Therapy to stop smoking?" I asked him.

"I know that it's the right thing, and I will be a nonsmoker if I do," he said pointing to the center of his head, "but . . ." he continued while waving his hand over a large area outside and to the right of his head, "this part just keeps saying, 'No way,' and 'How long can I put him off.'"

Robbie had been smoking since age 12 when he found that a smoke relieved his upset after seeing or hearing his father beat his mother or older brother. He was always at risk for a beating himself. Smoking was the friend that was always there when things got rough. He could count on his cigarettes when he could count on nothing else.

For awhile, though, cigarettes had become a different type of friend—one that could help him end his life. For a time he considered smoking a slow way to commit suicide, but he admitted now that since his divorce and his work in therapy he had stopped thinking about smoking in that way. It was clear that he wanted to be alive for his children. Since we had worked in the previous session on his self-esteem and self-worth, he was certain he would stop smoking some time. But, right now too many other things were more important than valuing himself enough to make the time to stop. Using this lead-in, I asked him what it felt like to say, "I am a worthy human being, deserving of being a nonsmoker." This statement made Robbie feel uncomfortable, so we tapped to ease his discomfort. After less than two minutes, he could say the same statement with no distress. Again he sat back and said, "This is what I imagine it feels like to be a nonsmoker." As he left, he playfully looked over his shoulder and asked me, "Is there a monkey on my back, because I can't see or feel one, and that feels strange!"

Quitting smoking wasn't quite that simple for Robbie. He was able to reduce his cigarette consumption right away and continued to strengthen his desire to live, but he still found himself turning to his old friend—his pack of cigarettes—in times of difficulty. When his ex-wife would remind him of his lack of control regarding visiting his children or would offer an olive branch and then pull it back, the feeling of being alone and hopeless would come on. Then, the soothing touch of a cigarette in his hand, the warmth of the smoke, and the immediate rush of nicotine through his body brought a moment of feeling okay that he needed and chose at that moment.

Only when he had stopped smoking again for three full days and then started again could Robbie identify the strong feelings that brought his urge to smoke to an intolerable level. He came to see me then, and we tapped for the feeling of isolation and being out of control it brought on, and the urge went away. Robbie left my office that day with renewed hope that he could control his urge to turn to his old, destructive buddy when he felt the need for support and find a new friend to help move him out of his sense of isolation.

Traumatic stressor events, such as Linda's son dying of an overdose in her home, can drive a person's addictions. So can a life of traumatic stress, such as that brought on by Jim's accident and childhood abuse. Addictions sometimes can be driven by anxiety conditions related to a person's genetic make-up or coping style as well. However, the underlying reason that fuels the addiction does not matter if the use of Thought Field Therapy relieves the urge to continue using the drug or performing the behavior and offers the person another way to cope.

On the whole, I have had a blessed life with some traumatic stressor events scattered across the years, but I cannot find one event that drove the addiction I describe in the following story. Nor can I say I fit very well into other types of anxiety disorders, even though I know I tend to have a sensitive emotional system. Whatever the cause of my addiction, Thought Field Therapy provided the only tool to finally end my urge to smoke marijuana and give me the ability to change my life patterns. I never discovered the underlying cause of my addiction, but I am glad to be done with it.

Free at Last: Done with Marijuana

I smoked marijuana on a daily basis from my first year of college until about 12 years ago. After graduating from college, I spent 25 years as a professional mental health care worker. So, I knew a good deal about substance abuse and addictions treatment, but I was still using this one drug daily myself. I had worked with addicts and in substance abuse education and treatment programs on my professional journey, but this had not stopped me from being a user myself.

In the beginning, I felt safe and comfortable using this drug within my circle of friends ,As I began my professional career, I soon became aware of the impact getting caught smoking marijuana or being in possession of this drug would have on my life. It could ruin my career. This made me nervous. Later, I began to understand that my substance abuse caused those I respected and cared about to judge me. This made me feel uncomfortable about using in front of or around them. And I often found myself focusing on issues that arose around obtaining and using an illegal substance. This curtailed many of my activities. Thus, I discovered that I was changing both who I would spend time with and how I would spend my time—all because of my addiction.

I became aware of other problems as well, such as how the side effects of my marijuana use affected my work and leisure time in day-to-day life. But, seeing no workable alternative, I continued to use. Being a functional addict, I never used before or at work. I never used before or in class. I seldom used before or during important personal or family functions. I did, however, smoke marijuana to relax after work, on weekends, on vacations, and during most every other unstructured part of my life. I continued using for one simple reason: each time I used this drug, I found my anxiety gone. The sense of discomfort I normally felt in my own body and in my own life disappeared after a couple of tokes on the marijuana cigarette.

Since I knew it would be better to quit using, I had tried to break my addiction. Using most of the standard techniques for stopping drug use, I had on occasion stopped smoking marijuana for a few days or weeks, but my urge to use and the addiction always returned.

One day I found myself at a workshop for a new technique called Thought Field Therapy. I had just spent what I thought at the time was an absurdly huge amount of money on four-day's of training to learn this new treatment technique. I had been impressed by what a colleague had demonstrated in a short workshop previously.

However, I had no idea how powerful this technique was or how it would change my life and the lives of so many others with whom I would later share it.

I have a professional rule: I will only use techniques on my clients that I will use on myself. So, I decided this workshop provided another chance for me to deal with my marijuana addiction. I would test Thought Field Therapy by seeing how it impacted my marijuana use.

My experiment was made easier by the fact that I did not have to reveal anything about my addiction or my history to this group of strangers in order for me to use Thought Field Therapy and to get the help I needed. Plus, I perceived no risk in tapping with my fingertips on my body. To my amazement, I felt the tapping working right away. In fact, I was amazed at how quickly the technique worked. In the moment I performed the tapping sequence, I could feel my desire and need for the marijuana dissipate.

"For the first time in 25 years, I don't have to smoke," I thought after that first experience with Thought Field Therapy. "I don't have to worry about smoking. I don't have to think about smoking. I can go where I please, when I please, and stay as long as I like. I don't have to hide what I do from any one. I can be with people comfortably and confidently knowing they have nothing on me. After 25 years as a professional helper, I found something that helped me."

The four days of the workshop passed without me smoking a marijuana cigarette even once. I treated myself several times a day while at the workshop and by the time I went home I only needed to treat myself on a few other occasions. The urge to use was gone permanently. The anxiety that had plagued me for no good reason was gone as well. I was free from figuring out when, where, and how I would get to light up. I was so relieved to be done with that addiction; I have never gone back to it or replaced it with any other addiction.

The Not-So-Obvious Behavioral Addictions

You can easily apply the definition of being out of control that began this chapter to use of alcohol, tobacco, marijuana, and other drugs. Their use quickly can become self-destructive, habitual, and addictive. However, when your response to traumatic stressor events involves out of control behavior revolving around things required to sustain your body, it can become more difficult to draw the line between that and normal behavior. Eating and sexual activity, for example, constitute natural parts of living. These behaviors in and of themselves are not unsafe or unhealthy. Yet, it is possible to eat and have sex in unhealthy, self-destructive, and out of control ways. So, consider a few factors to decide if you have lost control in your eating or sexual habits.

An alcohol or drug abuser can be defined as a person unable to accurately predict when and how much he or she will consume. If you say you will only have one drink but do not—or cannot—stop at one, you are out of control. If you say you will not drink and you do, or can't stop yourself, you are out of control. If you say you will only drink at home and you leave home to drink more, you are out of control. Using drugs and alcohol in this way always leads to unsafe and unhealthy results.

The same idea can be applied to eating, sex, or any other behavior. If you say you will only run 12 miles this week and you run 28 miles, you are out of control. If you say you will only have sex with someone you have known for at least three months and you have sex on the second date, you are out of control. If you say you will drive no more than 10 miles per hour over the speed limit and you consistently drive at least 25 miles per hour over the speed limit, you are out of control. If you drive on public streets as if you are on a race track, this is always unsafe and unhealthy regardless of your driving ability, and you are out of control.

As you consider whether or not you have lost control in any area of your life, do not lose sight of your common sense. If you say you will eat healthy and balanced meals, and then you eat less than the 1,500 calories a day you know is required to do so, or conversely you eat a whole box of ice cream, you have lost restraint. If this happens once in a blue moon or fairly infrequently, don't worry, you are just on vacation or exploring or stretching or indulging or making another choice. Drawing the line for when you are out of control or not is ultimately up to you alone. Just stay honest. If you are crossing the line, you can get back in control by tapping.

When it comes to these types of unrestrained behaviors, it can be helpful to understand why you resort to them. So, why do you eat the whole box of ice cream, have sex on the first date, run until you can't run any more, or drive like a maniac? For the same reason people drink or take drugs — to manage the feelings that they cannot manage any other way. While you are eating, are you aware of the fear or loneliness in your life? No, because most people see food as a reward or as a connection to a caring relationship. In the midst of orgasm, are you aware of the terror that awaits you in the next moments of your life? Probably not, since the sensations filling your body are all-consuming. While you are driving at 100 miles per hour, can you focus on the road and on your memories of the past at the same time? Not if you want to stay alive; you must focus on driving alone.

These behaviors all serve a purpose: they help you put overwhelming feelings at bay for a few minutes. If you want to change out of control behavior into something safer, you have to address the underlining source of this behavior.

Hungry and Empty are Different Things

Susan knew it all when it came to weight loss. From nutrition to exercise physiology, she was well read and well trained. A nurse who had experience working with eating disorders, she defined herself as significantly overweight and could acknowledge her problem but could not stop her out of control, late-night eating. In the Thought Field Therapy workshop she attended, she was pleased to learn that she could use tapping to control her urges. She challenged herself to end her desire for bread at lunch. After imagining a hot bun sitting before her at the lunch table, her urge to eat that bread was a 10 on a scale of 1-10. After tapping, Susan's was able to continue imagining the bun — she could even smell it, but she did not feel the compulsion to grab it. After another round of tapping, she was able to imagine herself not even wanting the bread.

After lunch Susan, reported to the group that she had not eaten any bread with lunch and had made healthy choices. However, she was not feeling her usual self after lunch, and needed to nap. She wanted to explore how else she could use Thought Field Therapy to help herself. She was aware that the hardest time for her to control her eating came later in the evening; often she would end a good, healthy day of eating with massive amounts of sugars or other simple carbohydrates. She admitted to regularly getting dressed after having put on her pajamas so she could go out to buy a "fix." Susan wondered if Thought Field Therapy would help her with this nightly eating urge.

In the workshop, she imaged being home at night at bedtime. As she felt the urge to eat, she again tapped for the addiction and felt the urge leave her. "That's strange," Susan commented. "I don't feel the urge to eat, but I do feel emptiness in me — an emptiness that makes me want to cry."

The workshop facilitator reminded Susan that often addictive behaviors provide a way to deal with overwhelming feelings and asked her to consider what the emptiness was about. Susan remembered that growing up in her family it was not okay to talk about feelings like loneliness or sadness. In her family, she could talk about being hungry and ask for more, but she couldn't say she was upset. Focusing on her sad feeling, she used Thought Field Therapy to address several events in her younger years that resulted in big losses that had upset her. One after another, she was able to identify events in her life that caused her to feel alone and sad. Many of these also met the criteria for traumatic stressors. By the time she was done she was able to make new decisions about reaching out and establishing new relationships. The underlying upset driving the urge to eat had been addressed. At the end of the workshop, Susan was able to imagine herself alone at bedtime with no urge to eat and no bad feelings. With confidence, she said she knew how to lose weight and could now stop sabotaging her efforts to slim down.

Ending self-destructive behavior and beginning a healthy activity becomes easy once you identify the overwhelming feelings these actions are trying to cover up and resolve them. Sometimes just stopping the urge to behave in an addictive or out of control manner will leave you in a good place to do the right thing for yourself. Sometimes stopping the urge will help you understand what is occurring at an emotional level and allow you to do more Thought Field Therapy to work out those problems.

As you gain control of your life and increase awareness of what underlies your choices you may come to understand achieving a life of health, love, and joy is more complex than getting rid of your bad habits. For some people moving forward in life requires examining other ingredients that make up the whole person. The next chapter in this part looks at some other factors affecting complete traumatic stress recovery.

CHAPTER ELEVEN

Living in the NOW,
Free from the Violence of Childhood

The violence you may have experienced in childhood complicates complete traumatic stress recovery. Therefore, it is essential to take a look at past violent experiences. However, many of you will find the following information presented on this topic interesting but unnecessary for reaching your goal of recovery. Some of you will find the concepts presented here bring up unexpected trigger responses, and, therefore, useful in putting lingering feelings to rest as you tap to resolve them. A few of you will find including this piece of knowledge essential to complete recovery. By incorporating the violent traumatic stress events from your childhood into your recovery process, you can finally navigate the recurrent hazards in your day–to-day relationships and activities. You will be able to observe and understand your past experiences in a more comprehensive way; and work your life by making adult, rather than childish, choices.

If, at this point, looking backward feels easy and the past provides a source of many joys for you, you may not need to read this chapter. With that said, it will offer you some more insight into your behavior and the behavior of others. If looking backward feels difficult, it may seem hard just to remember what happened, to face the reality of those old situations and events, and to accept how those events have affected you and the way you live in the world today. Looking at the violence you faced as a child will allow you to see how it has been a part of shaping who you are today.

The Past as Part of NOW Recovery

Looking at the one event or series of events that gave you a reason to read this book may not be enough to close all your wounds. The source of them may come from other traumatic stressor events and responses in your life that you have not yet examined or brought to your consciousness. Consider the following questions:

- **Are you spending too much time tapping to relieve traumatic stress responses or otherwise navigating through your symptoms of distress?**

- **Are you unable to make sense out of your responses to past traumatic stressor events?**

- **Do you find it impossible to stop thinking about these past events and to focus on current events in your life?**

- **Does it seem like you keep getting caught in the *there and then* as opposed to the *here and now* of your life?**

- **Does it seem like there are no new choices to make in your life, so you are left making the same ones that you've made in the past?**

If you answered "Yes" to any of these questions, you may not have totally completed the NOW process and may need to examine your earlier life again and how it has affected your current life. The most recent events, or the most problematic ones, may provide a link to previous events that need addressing. Understanding what is happening to you now may require delving deeply into what you experienced and learned as you developed during your childhood, but doing so may reveal that traumatic events from childhood are currently affecting your self-esteem and the choices you make.

Traumatic stress accumulates; one event builds on another. Sometimes you have to treat an earlier traumatic event to get full recovery from the most recent event and to live fully in the now. Unlike computers, human beings cannot be manipulated by deleting a program or inputting some data. If I scrub the hard drive on my computer, it behaves as if nothing had ever previously been on it, and I can load new programs with no concern about what existed there before. Human beings, however, are the result of every experience we have had, and we cannot just erase the bad stuff from the past and start over. Your memories and experiences always will influence whatever you add to your life's programming.

Once an event has occurred, you can't remove it from your personal history. Let's look at this another way: If you put too much buttermilk in a pancake batter, you can never take it out. It's in there for good. Instead, to fix the batter, you can add more of the other ingredients to make the prefect stack of cakes. In the same way, once a traumatic stressor event has been added to the mix of your life, like the buttermilk, it's there to stay. You can, however, add other ingredients to make your life better again. At this point in the process, therefore, you want to understand what is in your mix already and what you can add to make your life work better. A good measure of Thought Field Therapy, supportive relationships, self-acceptance, and love always brings better balance to the recipe and lets you cook up a good life experience.

You cannot be in the now if you are feeling emotions from the past as though they are happening in the current moment. Plus, actions you chose in response to past experiences will not be actions appropriate for your present conditions or circumstances. The same holds true if you are choosing actions based upon predictions for the future. Being in the now means feeling what you feel at this particular moment, not what you imagine you will feel in the future. It means acting in an appropriate manner given what you know about your current circumstances, not past events you have experienced.

Yet, you might find it difficult to imagine things being different from what you experienced previously. If your past causes you to understand and to see the present, as well as the future, as being only the same as the past, you will miss the chance to have a different experience in the current moment and to enjoy the now. And while you might think it is easier to focus on a present and a future with fewer traumas than the past, this tack causes you to miss the chance to experience and be a part of the present moment as well. While you do so, you still fail to perceive your current situation with any sense of immediate reality.

To discover if your past is affecting your living fully in the *here and now* as opposed to the *there and then*, answer these questions:

- **Are you able to shut off your feelings and bodily sensations and send your consciousness to another place, and do you do this often?**

- **Are you triggered by things, people, or situations, but you don't understand why they should trigger you?**

- **Are you unable to say and believe the following statement: "I am a worthy human being—deserving of good in the world?"**

Your answers to these questions reveal important information about your early childhood environment and how you learned to cope as a child. The first question concerns disassociation, a skill sometimes learned through many years of study as part of spiritual practice but often learned without conscious intent as a coping mechanism in moments of childhood terror.

The second question revolves around your awareness of what controls you. If you seem to always be in an unconscious reactive state, it may be because your efforts to stay alive as a child in a violent environment were achieved by reacting to cues without thought or understanding. You may now be reacting to the same childhood cues that indicated an unsafe situation—even though you currently feel safe—but still doing so unconsciously.

The last question is linked directly to childhood resources and exposure to violence. Self-esteem and self-worth in children develop from being cherished and valued as unique individuals, something that does not happen in violent situations. If you can't say this statement and believe it, a high likelihood exists that something violent happened in your early past that you should explore.

Up to this point, the focus of your complete recovery efforts have been on specific events or responses to those events. A complex history of traumatic stressor events can, however, require looking at their impact on your life as a whole. If you know you have a history of abuse or violence, if these were a fact of life during any period of your childhood, this chapter offers you ways to help yourself on your journey towards further healing of these traumatic stressor events.

Be careful to monitor your responses to what you are reading, though. Take care of yourself by using Thought Field Therapy, reaching out to others, or seeking professional help if you sense the need to do so.

Violence as a Traumatic Stressor

It may seem obvious that a violent act either witnessed or experienced can become a traumatic stressor event. However, violence comes in many forms. Therefore, you must know all the faces of violence if you want to determine if violence has been a factor in your life to any degree.

Violence is defined here as one person acting in a way that violates another person's rights or the act of a group of people to violate another group of people's rights. It serves as a traumatic event stressor most of the time. In the broadest sense, you have the right to be safe in your body. This includes the right to be safe from physical harm or pain caused or allowed by another person. Other rights include being safe to feel what you feel and to express these feelings; safe to think what you think and to express these ideas; and safe to do what you choose to do as long as it does not harm another person or violate their rights. When someone applies force or threat of force to infringe on others' rights and limit their choices, that act constitutes violence. If your response to an application of force that limits your choices involves feeling a sense of horror or helplessness, then that indeed, represents both violence and a traumatic stressor event in your life.

Consider for a moment the choices you have in life: you have choices about whom and what you enjoy, when and how you care for yourself, and how you expend your energy and resources. The type of violence that limits choices can be inflicted by more than the strength of a body. It can be inflicted emotionally and mentally. For this reason, when discussing children, in particular, the definition of violence must include the withholding of all elements of nourishment, both physical and emotional, necessary for growth. A parent making a decision for a child is not committing an act of violence if the decision is made to support the growth and development of the child and honors the child's rights. If the decisions are made in a way that dishonors the child's rights and prevents normal growth and development, such a choice on the parent's part would be deemed a violent act.

Child abuse in all its forms constitutes violence. And violence experienced by children shapes the adult they become. Again, child abuse comes in many forms. If physical force is applied to a child and it causes injury, this is child abuse and is punishable under most U.S. state laws. For example, acts performed by a parent or other adult that cause a child to suffer a bruise, welt, scratch, cut, broken bone, blow to the head, shaking injury, or other impact affecting the brain are criminal acts of child abuse. These acts may leave physical as well as emotional scars on the child. Each case of physical child abuse can become a traumatic stressor event that leads to an open wound that needs healing.

Emotional, mental, and spiritual abuse leave open wounds and lasting scars as well. In an ideal world, all children would be raised by adults who love one another and love and protect the children in their charge. Since we don't live in an ideal world, many of us are faced with the job of looking at our past and trying to decipher the events of our childhood to see if we suffered any type of abuse.

If you find that your childhood contained elements of violence, you will want to process these both by tapping for any emotional upsets that come up and by going through the steps of the NOW process again with these events in mind.

Healing Childhood Injuries

A poet once shared a truth about her experience of childhood abuse. She said "the green wood of her life was split and twisted for life. " Indeed, once a sapling's outer bark is damaged, it forever bears the scars of that trauma.

When doing formal testing, sometimes the person being tested is instructed to draw a person, house, and tree. This has been done tens of thousands of times, and there are patterns that come out in these drawings that reveal a great deal about what goes on in a person's psyche. A great psychologist evaluated a picture of a tree drawn by a client as part of a set of such projective tests. With this particular drawing, the evaluator asked the referring therapist what had happened to his client at the age of eight. During the summer of that year, she had been repeatedly raped. These violent and traumatic stressor events showed up as big as life as a huge knot in the trunk of the tree she had drawn.

What happens to us at any given point in our life stays with us in some way forever. Just like a scar, sometimes we notice the differences these experiences make in our life and sometimes the affects seem to fade and become unnoticeable. And at other times, like physical injuries that require us to do physical therapy to strengthen muscles, these powerful events become a source of strength or understanding and knowledge that informs our growth and our choices.

At other times, though, abusive events mark a place in our development that we never grow beyond. When that happens, we become emotionally stuck at that developmental stage. For example, when children are hurt over and over again, they develop a world view grounded in the reality of mistrust, fear, and pain that comes out of their experience. This often means that even as adults these people continue to live with a large degree of mistrust, fear, and pain. In addition, their sense of self will forever be shaped by their early childhood experiences.

Also, if you have suffered an abusive childhood, another traumatic event experienced as an adult may do more than just trigger that specific memory from your past. It might actually simulate younger parts of yourself—the parts that are still stuck at that earlier developmental stage—and take you out of your adult grown-up self. When this happens the *inner child*, the part of you that is stuck in younger de-velopmental stages, takes over. At such times, you will find that your inner child's world view becomes the only one accessible to you. This means you understand and perceive everything as if you were a child of the age you were when you first experienced abuse. This makes it difficult to function as an adult.

The story that follows illustrates this point. Only after the original wounds were addressed did it become possible to resolve the person's current problem and for him to behave in a manner not influenced by his inner child.

Sebastian and His Boy

At age 65, Sebastian had made the decision to marry. His first wife had died four years earlier after a two-year struggle with cancer. Sebastian knew a great deal about grief. He had tried hard not to stay stuck in the depressed feeling that expressed his loss internally. After his wife's death, he had retired from his career as a case manager and gone on doing volunteer work as a therapist, social worker, and artist. A couple of years later he had found a way to open his heart to another woman, and now they wanted to share their commitment to each other in the sight of God and their community. The closer the date of the wedding came, though, the more Sebastian found himself ruminating on every possible thing that could go wrong with his decision to get married. Sebastian's greatest fear was that he would fail to love his bride as much as she loved him.

In discussions with his fiancée, Therese, during couple's ses-sions with me, she seemed clear that despite his negative thinking, struggle over his decision, and fear about the outcome of the marriage, he would not fail her. At first I thought that Sebastian's crazy thoughts and the discomfort that came from his over thinking his decision was related to unresolved grief from his wife's death. Yet, as we worked with Thought Field Therapy on his overwhelming feelings from the loss it became apparent that he had not failed his first wife in any way. They had worked together to make decisions, and he had supported her throughout their long and happy marriage. Yet, even after the grief *work he had done, he still would find himself awake at night running over every possible problem and every possible solution for every possible future eventuality with Therese. This fear of failure and anxiety obviously was based in something other than the loss of his first wife.*

So, we explored farther back into his past. There we discovered a childhood filled with severe physical and emotional abuse by his mother. For this reason, at the age of 13, when he was given an opportunity to go to boarding school, he had jumped at the chance to leave home and get away from the abuse. We again explored how this related to his upcoming marriage. When he imagined himself standing at the church altar ready to take his vows, he could feel the anxiety in his body and the racing thoughts in his mind. He felt this at level of 7 or 8 on a 1–10 point scale. His upset was so extreme, in fact, that he had discussed putting off the wedding with his best man. I asked Sebastian to focus on this feeling, and then asked, "Does this feeling seem familiar to you in any way?"

He replied, "Yes."

"When do you remember the first time you felt this feeling?" I asked. He explained that the feeling was one he remembered having on many occasions as a young child. I asked him to focus on the feeling and one time in his past when that same feeling was very strong.

He reported, "I was a nine- year-old boy. I had broken my arm in the woods and walked out of woods and back home even though I was afraid and in pain."

The reward his mother gave him for his bravery, effort, ability to keep his head, managing the pain, and getting to help was a guilt trip. "You know I have heart problem," she told him. "You are going to kill me doing these things."

No matter what he did, no matter how cautiously he planned and acted, no matter how hard he worked, in the end it was not good enough and often ended with severe physical punishment, Sebastian recalled. Although in this case he'd only suffered verbal abuse, Sebastian's mother's words were most always followed by real physical pain inflicted upon him.

When I asked Sebastian to picture himself at the church alter again, now he saw a very hyper and scared boy pulling at him and jumping all around. The boy it seems was terrified that he would not be good enough and pain and suffering would result. Repeated attempts as a child to be good enough always proved he was right to worry. We used Thought Field Therapy to treat the feeling of anxiety and the memories of disappointing his mother and his fear that came from his childhood. After a couple of tapping sequences, Sebastian reported that the picture at the altar now included a calm boy trusting that the adult Sebastian would protect him. The child, Sebastian, had become part of the wedding party — the ring bearer. At last the adult could see himself calm, relaxed, and completely present while sharing his vows with his new partner in life.

<hr/>

Healing the Inner Child's Open Wounds

In the psychotherapy business, the work Sebastian did is called Inner Child Work. It is based on awareness that there exists within us a part of ourselves that represents ourselves at different ages and in different conditions. This is the part that seems to get stuck in a development stage when overcome with traumatic stress. I say "seems to" because the inner child represents a theory, not a fact. No one can see another's inner child. However, it is true that many adults think and behave like children and that people report having an experience of the presence of some childlike consciousness that at times overwhelms their adult activities. It is a fact that an awareness of this wounded child impacts adults and that many techniques that deal with these feeling and that address the inner child have been developed and are helpful. Sometimes just imagining the inner child being supported and protected by the adult is enough to calm a person's feelings of anxiety, fear, or hopelessness that stem from childhood traumas. Using Thought Field Therapy with or for the inner child, however, represents the most effective means of calming it and allowing the adult to make decisions with out the influence of the inner child.

Will the inner child ever grow out of its fear and stop being trigged into traumatic stress responses? People who become aware of their injured inner child ask this question quite often. In my experience, I don't think so. This injured part of yourself learned one way of being at a particular time during your development and stopped developing at that specific time. It cannot suddenly begin developing again now, since you have progressed in age and cannot go back in time. Again, remember the inner child model represents just a theory and not a reality. In reality, no one knows exactly what happens to abused children's psyches.

No matter your age, your feelings are your feelings, and no one can tell you they are wrong or you are not feeling them. Therefore, I encourage relating to your inner child, or children, as you would with any child. Allow the child its feelings; do not try to convince the child what he or she feels is not real, is wrong, or is unimportant. When a child feels scared, telling it to not feel afraid constitutes an uncaring, disrespectful, and useless exercise. You can best help by telling children that they are protected and by actually protecting them. They need to be taught how to appropriately express their emotions and thoughts and to stay in control. Just telling them to, "Grow up," does no one any good. When children see the cause of pain and fear has been eliminated and their feelings aren't going to destroy them, they will do what children do—play, love, and enjoy life.

Early Wounds and Physical Pain

As you've seen, traumatic stress responses are intensified by previous responses to traumatic stressor events in childhood. It is also intensified when other sources of stress are factored into the current traumatic stress symptoms or problem. Even when the sources of the triggered feelings are unknown, though, Thought Field Therapy reduces the emotional and cognitive impairment that prevents recognizing available adult coping mechanisms.

The following story focuses on the importance of remaining aware of all stressors when looking for solutions. Strong recent research shows a relationship between many chronic physical health conditions and severe abuse as a child. For this reason, Thought Field Therapy can provide an important healing tool for both emotional and physical conditions that cause impairments to a good life. As you read this next story, look for all the sources of the traumatic stress and the interplay between all the parts (inner children) of the person.

Getting Out of the Closet

Turn your oven on to about 400 degrees, stick your arm in, and leave it there. If you can image what that burning sensation would feel like, you can start to get an idea of the kind of pain Trish dealt with every day. Imagine the pain in your arm spreading to another limb, and another, and until the burning sensation covered your whole body. Now you understand the affects of Trish's illness.

Trish has Reflective Sympatric Dystrophy (RSD), an incurable disease that eventually will continue to spread and kill her. She has lost the function of one kidney already due to Reflective Sympatric Dystrophy or to complications of her treatment. Good pain management with medication, keeping her stress level as low as possible, and Thought Field Therapy help Trish most at this point. Trish and I had worked together over the course of seven years and she still had issues to work on. When you are physically depleted by such a disease, day-to-day life can easily overcome you.

On this day, we were discussing Trish's first appointment the day before with a new primary care physician. The doctor she had had for the previous six years had moved to a hospital practice and could no longer treat her. This new doctor was the second in an attempt to find someone who knew something about her condition. The first doctor had flat out refused to accept the fact that she could possibly need the levels of pain medications she currently required and made it clear Trish should move on to a different doctor. This caused a problem, because this clinic had not forwarded her records to the next doctor. So, when she got to Doctor Number Two, Trish received little assurance that she would be helped. The doctor said that even people with cancer don't get the level of pain medication she requested and referred her to a pain clinic. Trish and I thought the pain clinic was a good idea, but the doctor had only given her enough medication for two weeks, and the first pain clinic appointment was five weeks away.

Trish's day-to-day struggles were similar to that of many chronic pain sufferers with public insurance and providers who relate little to traumatic stress. She had Medicare, because she was disabled, and she had Medicaid, because she is poor and without financial resources to pay for cost of meds, home health help, rent, and food on her own. Overall, though, her choices of medical services were limited. Underlying these issues, however, lay the traumatic stress elements of her story.

On this day, Trish felt a great deal of pain and upset. We used Thought Field Therapy to help lessen the pain. The biggest immediate problem revolved around her fear that she would run out of medication and be in unbearable pain. She could not stand the thought of having uncontrollable pain, and the possibility of this reality brought on thoughts of suicide, which scared her and set off a higher degree of stress response in her body. This stress response triggered increased pain, and the cycle spiraled downward.

At home alone, sometimes Trish felt overwhelmed by her feelings of being out of control and would cut herself. Technically, she was not suicidal; hurting herself in this manner drew her back to the present moment and a sense of being in control. The action of hurting herself, whether because she would see the blood and realizes the reality of her actions or because the action actually activated healing mechanisms within her, effectively worked to stop her from doing more damage to herself. In the office, Thought Field Therapy decreased the pain and diminished the fear, but she was stuck at about a 4 or 5 on a 1–10 rating scale.

At this point, I asked Trish to focus on her out of control feeling and to notice how old she felt. When a person's rating of their upset won't move down the scale and the person is having trouble clearly identifying the trigger, I always ask how old he or she feels. This helps identify if a trauma that occurred at an earlier age pertains to the cur-

rent upset. Trish responded that she felt she was about eight or nine years old. I then asked her if she had a sense of what she might be doing or what might have gone on at that age. She replied, "I feel like I'm back in the closet again hiding with my brothers and hoping my mother's drunken rage won't be directed at us."

She reminded me that when her father would go out of town, her mother would often drink until she was lost control. When she was drunk, she would blame Trish for anything and everything, shouting at her and beating her as well. At age nine, her only hope of remaining safe was found in trying to keep her brothers quiet and safe in the closet.

This violent personal history represented the traumatic stressor currently affecting Trish. Her fear of being out of control with her pain and with her doctor related to her mother's behavior when she drank. In addition, it played into Trish, as a child, feeling she had no control over the situation when her mother became drunk and angry. In other words, Trish's inner child was influencing her current state of fear and stress. Rather than responding from an adult consciousness, she was responding, at least in part, from a childish consciousness that felt fearful and had issues about lack of control.

Trish and I tapped for the little girl part of her activated by being out of control with her doctor and the fear left her. This also reduced her current level of pain. With the pain lessened and the fear gone, the adult Trish and I could do the strategizing and problem solving she needed to get some thing done to help her. At home, if she could keep the little girl from being activated she would be less likely now to cut herself and more likely to keep making the calls to get the help she needed.

***

This story represents only a small piece of the amazing example Trish's life offers of surviving many terrible traumatic stressor events in childhood and in adult life. Despite the severity of her childhood abuse, other traumatic stressor events, Individual Energy Toxins sensitivities (discussed in Part Five), physical illness, and lack of resources, she does have a better quality of life because as she struggles she grows. If you ask her if Thought Field Therapy helps her, she will provide example after example of how it does, indeed, help her not only heal but also grow and live her life more fully even given the limitations with which she is faced. Working with her also challenged me to find more and new ways to use Thought Field Therapy to assist her in improving a very complex life.

Thought Field Therapy has been successful many times in eliminating completely or greatly reducing the physical pain associated with some chronic pain conditions. Have no fear: trying the pain algorithm in the basic steps, which is included in the next chapter, will not make a chronic pain condition worse. It will likely make it better. Additionally, Thought Field Therapy does not end pain that serves an important role in protecting the body from further injury. I have successfully used Thought Field Therapy for migraine headaches, menstrual pains, phantom pain after amputations, muscle strains, and many other conditions.

Traumatic stressor events often result in physical trauma and physical pain. Reducing the physical pain reduces stress on the whole person bringing traumatic stress recovery closer to a reality. Chronic pain can complicate recovery from severe childhood abuse as well, so reducing or eliminating it remains an important step in healing open wounds.

Physical illnesses, such as lupus, arthritis, fibromyalgia, Crohn's, and irritable bowl disease, can cause people to wake up every day feeling as though the torture of their childhood has continued into the present. A neurological disease, like Reflective Sympatric Dystrophy, provides a good example of how illness becomes an ever-expanding source of pain that influences more than just the physical realm of a person's life. A life limited by chronic illness contains numerous stressors. Getting and maintaining adequate heath care in and of itself requires a great effort. It is hard finding doctors who understand these complicated conditions and treatments The need for help with daily living activities, overcoming the social and psychological pressures of being on large quantities of pain and other medications, and not being able to make a living and, therefore, having to subsist on a limited income all add to the incredible difficulties. These stressors cause stress responses; these stress responses become additional stressors, which, in turn, cause more stress. All that stress leads to more pain—physical as well as emotional.

Extreme Coping Mechanisms

When children are exposed to on-going violence, pain, and injury, they learn to cope with the trauma in many ways. They will please and soothe the older person causing the pain. They will do what they can to avoid to the situation. They will try to control themselves and others to reduce the harm caused or received. Children will hide in closets, care for their younger siblings and control them in hopes of helping them evade the pain. They will even lie to protect those who harm them, because to do otherwise means getting hurt more severely at a later time. When they cannot escape the pain of abuse, children even learn to leave their bodies and move their consciousness to a place without pain. This skill, called disassociation, which we've mentioned before, can save their lives, because it allows them to endure in silence when protesting, or even giving voice to their pain, could result in more pain or even death.

Depending on the intensity and duration of the abuse experienced, a child will develop the ability to totally ignore their bodily sensations and pain messages and focus on something else instead. This ability becomes second nature to them as abused children, and they carry the skill into their adult lives. This disregard for their own bodily sensations, along with the caregiver's disregard for their welfare, form the foundation of the child's self-worth and value. Thus, abused children only posses a sense of being of value when they satisfy the demands of the older, more-powerful person controlling them. The will of the child is replaced with subservience to the whims of the abuser. If all this rings true to you through your own experiences, you were abused as a child and open wounds from then may be affecting your healing now.

Those children, whose childhoods were filled with extreme, prolonged, ongoing violence but lacked love, care, or concern from or by others, may grow up with impairments in their ability to create positive relationships to self and to others. If the violence starts at a time before the child has developed any sense of themselves as an independent person, they may develop a rare form of coping mechanism called multiple personalities. Not the same as sensing your inner child or acting from the inner child, this constitutes a consciousness problem. People with multiple personalities have an issue with the way they know and recognize themselves. Each personality represents a separate consciousness

The symptoms of multiple personalities, or Dissociative Identity Disorder (DID), include a sense of losing time — not knowing what you have been doing or how you arrived in the location you find yourself. This loss of time is different from an alcoholic blackout, which happens only under very specific and knowable conditions. People with Dissociative Identity Disorder may also have unaccounted for activities, behaviors, relationships, expenditures, or other unexplained events or situations. The explanation for this is that they cannot access memories created while in a disassociated state. They simply don't remember what they did while the other personality was in control of their body. In most cases of Dissociative Identity Disorder, a person has some awareness of at least some of the other personalities, but some personalities remain unknown to all the others.

The treatment goal of Dissociative Identity Disorder differs for each person and each personality but the vision remains the same: to create a more healthy, loving, joyful life for the person. This area of traumatic stress recovery represents a very complex one requiring skill and knowledge far beyond what is needed to heal most traumatic stress conditions. If you think you have Dissociative Identity Disorder, please seek professional help.

Traumatic stressors that we felt as children almost always affect our development, but most of the time we still manage to function and enjoy life. The following story revolves around my work with a wonderful woman who taught me a great deal about the nature of consciousness. I tell it to illustrate that change and improvement and finding health, love, and joy always remain possible. One of her personalities was 14 years old, and the story is about teaching her to tap and giving her a place to feel safe. She learned how to stop her self-destructive behavior and to do the work of any 14 year old – to begin to find an independent identity.

Being Safe Enough to be Yourself

The first time this 40-something women came into my office, I explained Thought Field Therapy to her and how it feels and works. She had called me for the first time over a year earlier and had told me she had multiple personalities and wanted to know what I could do to help. I explained my approach and how Thought Field Therapy worked, but at that time she decided not to make the more than one hour drive to start seeing me. We talked again after her last therapist made a sudden change in their work together. He stopped wanting to work with any of the other "alters," or alternate personalities that make up the parts of the personality system that inhabits her body, and refused to talk to any part not using her legal name. It seemed he had changed supervisors, and his new supervisor did not believe multiple personality disorders existed. So, what had been a supportive relationship had turned into another relationship requiring she deny the truth about herself and act like someone else wanted her to act. She called me this time, because she thought she would give me a try as a therapist.

The women who sat front of me, and who called herself Theresa, looked and acted like a 40-year old women, except she told me she had no memories of her own before seven or eight years ago when she came in to consciousness. She knew the history of the "system," meaning all the other personalities, through other parts of the system, or other specific personalities, but her role in it revolved around finding help for the total system. Theresa was impressed with Thought Field Therapy and my approach to therapy. We set some goals and started developing the trust to allow the others to become present as they needed help.

After a few sessions with Theresa, I met another personality named Melissa. While residing in the same body, she presented, acted and was very different from Theresa. A 14 year old rather than a 40-year old (but still in the same body), Melissa had a tendency towards self-mutilation and felt a great deal of emotional pain. Later, I found out that Melissa came into being when the body was 14 and the rest of the system felt too overwhelmed to go to school or to do other jobs. Melissa knew she was one of several multiple personalities within the whole system and was aware of many other younger alters who were always afraid and in pain. She believed the physical and emotional pain she felt actually represented their pain, and that the way to end it was to let it out by hurting herself. After years of carrying this overwhelming pain for everyone else in the system, she just wanted to die.

Melissa did not know me or anything about Thought Field Therapy when she first came forward in this session, so I had to start with her as I would with any teenager. I had to teach her Thought Field Therapy to help her manage her pain. And we had to begin to sort out her life and find the way in which she wanted to live. She shared with me her art and tried to help me understand her desperate situation. I knew that over time, when we could use tapping to bring Melissa's level of pain far enough down to interact more easily and get to know one another better, we could start trying to help her make sense out of her experience. She had a good sense of visual art and could express herself well using pictures and ideas. The biggest problem we encountered lay in helping her understand that she could be more than just the pain she experienced.

The following is a short dialogue during one of our sessions between Melissa (M) and myself (B). It will give you a taste of the ongoing struggle that occurs as I try to help an abused 14 year old—who is really just one personality in a system of personalities within a 40 year old woman—come to grips with her identity and better cope with life.

    M: I cannot stand to be this pain any more. You promised you would help me die! You said you would help me kill myself.

B: *I promised to help you end the pain. So if your job is to hold the pain of the younger parts inside of you, then you must be something other than pain.*

M: *No, all I am is pain, and that's all I feel.*

B: *How is that possible? Think about it this way. If the water in a bottle is pain, then the bottle that holds the pain — or water — must be something other than water. If you try to put water in a bottle made of water what happens?*

M: *That can't happen. You can't have a bottle made of water.*

B: *Exactly. For you to hold the pain, you must be something other than pain. What is that?*

M: *I don't know.*

B: *Pain is a feeling. You are something that holds feelings. If you can feel pain, you can feel other feelings also. Can you feel me touching your hand?*

M: *Yes.*

B: *How does that feel to you? Painful? Should I stop holding your hand?*

M: *No, I like it! It feels good. I don't feel so alone.*

B: *Okay. So let's figure out how to have you feel good feelings and hold and manage the painful feeling better.*

M: *If I die, the pain will be gone. I just want to end the pain.*

B: *If you die physically, you will kill those other parts of you that you agreed to help. If you, Melissa, die — cease to allow the body to continue — those younger parts will have lost your help with their pain. We have to find a better way to help manage your pain and for you to be stronger. Do you think those younger parts of yourself should be left to suffer alone without help or die because of you?*

M: No, that's not right.

B: Ok, so next time you start to feel the pain, figure out if it is your pain or the little ones' pain, and tap for yourself or for them. Let's tap now.

Very soon after this conversation, Melissa's habit of self-mutilation started to diminish and later stopped. Her suicidal thinking continued for a long time and still comes up now and then, however. We are still in regular contact, and I have learned from my relationship with this teenager about how we each can find our way to our true self even when everything that brought us into being was violent and painful.

Theresa and Melissa presented as very different people and I easily could see their differences when they felt safe enough to show themselves. Many other personalities existed in the woman's whole system, and each required a separate relationship with me and another round of demonstrating and teaching Thought Field Therapy just for them. It resembled having numerous clients but all in one person's body.

Theresa felt proud that the system of personalities was able to get off all medications and not become hospitalized for over three years after we began Thought Field Therapy. For the first time in her life, she is living by herself and establishing work that will get her off Social Security disability. Theresa is certain that Thought Field Therapy represents the major difference between the work she has done with me and previous therapies used to help the alters cope and her whole self's ability ultimately to be free to find her way to joy, love, and health.

❦

The last two stories in this book represent worst cases scenarios and are presented to you as encouragement to keep going no matter what you have experienced in the past or face currently. The concepts and stories in this chapter will resonate and feel different to each of you depending upon your childhood history. You may feel as I do when I think of my childhood—truly blessed. Or you may be aware of many unresolved pains from the past driving your anxiety about the future. Please take from this book a message of hope. If years of physical and emotional mistreatment and, at times, torture can be survived by those whose stories have been told in this book, and they can continue the struggle for complete traumatic stress recovery, then anyone can heal their open wounds and learn to live now, including you.

Conclusion

Congratulations. By reading to this point you accomplished a great deal. You learned more about traumatic stress responses: the variety of normal and healing reactions you can have to traumatic events; the ranges of dysfunctions and problems that develop as a result of your reactions to traumatic events; and the impact that open wounds have on living your life. You also learned about the healing power of Thought Field Therapy, which offers you easy-to-use steps that immediately end your overwhelming suffering. These lessons included ways to use tapping for achieving complete traumatic stress recovery and for creating a life of your choosing. Additionally, you have discovered the NOW traumatic stress recovery model, which gives you a way to understand your own processes for moving forward. Gaining this knowledge is no small thing; rather it is a huge accomplishment.

An even bigger achievement comes in having engaged in your own healing. While reading the stories included in this book and the discussions around them, no doubt your own wounds have been touched. This awareness of your wounds has informed both your actions and decisions. The scars left after the wounds have healed bring an appreciation of what you have suffered and worked to repair. Now you better understand the still-healing wounds, and you can speedily complete their recovery. You have become acutely aware of the open wounds that cause your pain from the past and the fear of the future, and you have used Thought Field Therapy to close them. You have demonstrated your concern for your condition and that of others, as well as your commitment to care for yourself and others. And in doing so, you have shared your love.

To me, this means you are acting in a just way to make your life, the life of your family, and the lives of all those in your community more joyous. We all benefit from these healing actions. You have stepped out of your old ways of understanding and acting by learning and using Thought Field Therapy and the Now recovery model. This kind of change requires courage.

Thank you for your courage and efforts in making our shared world a more just place.

PART FIVE

Doing Thought Field Therapy

Introduction

This section offers you a simple, easy-to-follow and comprehensive approach to doing Callahan Techniques® Thought Field Therapy for a limited range of traumatic stress recovery issues. Please remember that this book is intended to help you recover from traumatic stress. It is not a course in Callahan Techniques®Thought Field Therapy Algorithms or Causal Diagnosis. Association for Thought Field Therapy (ATFT)-approved training is available through Dr. Callahan's office or a certified trainer, and, if you want more information on this method, you can find his books through his office as well. The tapping patterns offered here consist of standard Callahan Techniques® Thought Field Therapy algorithms with some additions. These additions make using and learning the patterns simpler and are designed to help you accomplish the changes you need to heal traumatic stress as quickly as possible.

Contents of Part Five:

- List of Problems
- Location of Tapping Points
- The Basic Tapping Patterns
- The Next Steps
- Collarbone Breathing Exercise and Discussion
- Tips on Focusing on Your Problem
- Tips on Rating the Level of Upset
- Psychological Reversal Discussion
- Understanding and Identifying Individual Energy Toxins
- Thought Field Therapy for Other Conditions

List of Problems

Pick one of the following that best describes your current problem. (If you feel uncertain about which one to choose, start with the traumatic stress pattern.) Find the Basic Step for your choice below, and follow those instructions. If the pattern of tapping you choose works to relieve your upset, learn it, and us it as often as needed. If you do not experience significant relief after doing the pattern you selected three or four times, go on to the The Next Steps section on page 247 and follow those instructions.

- **Traumatic Stress** (if it happened in the past)

- **Simple Anxiety and Stress** (if you are worried about what will happen in the future)

- **Phobias and Fears** (except for those involving spiders, air turbulence, or claustrophobia)

- **Addictive Urges** (feeling a strong desire or a sense you must do something)

- **Fear of Spiders**

- **Claustrophobia** (fear of closed in or small places)

- **Air Turbulence in Flight**

- **Addictions** (if the first pattern did not work)

- **Depression**

- **Physical Pain**

- **Rage**

- **Shame and Embarrassment**

- **Anger**

- **Guilt**

Where to Tap

Location of Tapping Points

Under Arm	On the ribcage about four inches down from the arm pit (at the bra line for women)
Collarbone	One inch down from the V of the neck and 1 inch over, either left or right
Chin	In the cleft between the chin and lower lip
Under Eye	In line with the pupil, just below the rim of the eye socket bone)
Eyebrow	Inside eyebrow (where the eyebrow begins above the bridge of the nose)
Gamut Spot	Between the knuckles of the little and ring fingers, and about 1/2 inch toward the wrist
Index Finger	Between the bed of the fingernail and the first knuckle towards the thumb
Little Finger	Between the bed of the fingernail and the first knuckle towards the thumb
Outside of eye	About 1/2 inch from the corner of the eye, on the edge of the eye socket bone
Side of Hand	About 1 inch below the little finger
Under Nose	Midway between the bottom of the nose and the upper lip

LOCATION OF POINTS

THE CALLAHAN TECHNIQUES®

Treatment Points
© 1994 by Roger T. Callahan

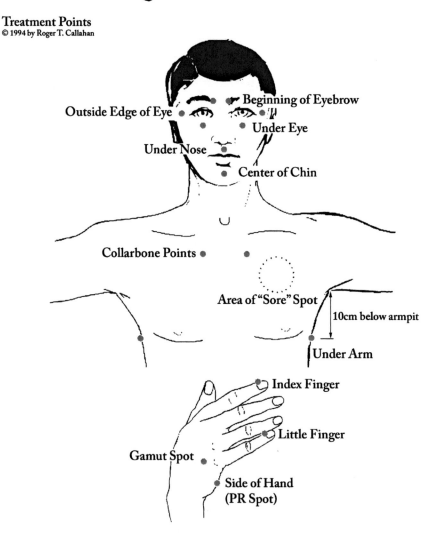

Outside Edge of Eye

Beginning of Eyebrow

Under Eye

Under Nose

Center of Chin

Collarbone Points

Area of "Sore" Spot

10cm below armpit

Under Arm

Index Finger

Little Finger

Gamut Spot

Side of Hand
(PR Spot)

Basic Steps for Traumatic Stress

Step One. As you focus on the problem, determine your Subjective Units of Distress (SUD) by rating the upset on a 1 to 10 Scale (1= no upset, 10=worst).

Step Two. Using your fingertips tap about ten times each:

> Side of Hand,
> Under Nose,
> Beginning of Eyebrow,
> Under Eye,
> Under Arm,
> Under Collarbone,
> Little Finger,
> Under Collarbone,
> Index Finger,
> Under Collarbone.

Step Three. Do the *9 Gamut Series*. While continuously tapping the gamut spot:

1. Close eyes
2. Open eyes
3. With your eyes look down and left
4. With your eyes look down and right
5. Whirl your eyes in a complete circle in one direction
6. Whirl your eyes in a complete circle in the other direction
7. Hum a couple bars of any tune
8. Count to five
9. Hum again.

Step Four. Using your fingertips tap about 10 times each:

> Side of Hand,
> Under Nose,
> Beginning of Eyebrow,
> Under Eye,

Under Arm,
Under Collarbone,
Little Finger,
Under Collarbone,
Index Finger,
Under Collarbone.

Step Five. Think about the problem in the same way again, rate your upset 1-10 as in step one.

Repeat steps Two through Five until:
Your SUD rating is a 1or 2, then go to Step Six.

Or your SUD rating stops changing then go to NEXT STEPS on page 247.

Step Six: The floor to ceiling eye roll.

While continuously tapping the gamut spot and holding your head level, roll your eyes on a vertical line from the floor to the ceiling over 6–7 seconds.

The BASIC STEPS for:

- **Simple Anxiety and Stress**
- **Phobias and Fears** (except for those involving spiders, air turbulence, or claustrophobia)
- **Addictive Urges**

Step One.   As you focus on the problem, determine your Subjective Units of Distress (SUD) by rating the upset on a 1 to 10 Scale (1= no upset, 10=worst).

Step Two.   Using your fingertips tap about ten times each:

> Side of Hand,
> Under Nose,
> Under Eye,
> Under Arm,
> Under Collarbone,

Step Three.   Do the *9 Gamut Series*. While continuously tapping gamut spot:

> 1. Close eyes
> 2. Open eyes
> 3. With your eyes look down and left
> 4. With your eyes look down and right
> 5. Whirl your eyes in a complete circle in one direction
> 6. Whirl your eyes in a complete circle in the other direction
> 7. Hum a couple bars of any tune
> 8. Count to five
> 9. Hum again.

Step Four.   Using your fingertips tap about 10 times each:

> Side of Hand,
> Under Nose,
> Under Eye,
> Under Arm,
> Under Collarbone,

Step Five.   Think about the problem in the same way again, rate your upset 1-10 as in step one.

Repeat steps Two through Five until:
Your SUD rating is a 1or 2, then go to Step Six.

Or your SUD rating stops changing then go to NEXT STEPS on page 247.

Step Six: The floor to ceiling eye roll.

While continuously tapping the gamut spot and holding your head level, roll your eyes on a vertical line from the floor to the ceiling over 6–7 seconds.

The BASIC STEPS for:

- **Spiders**
- **Claustrophobia (closed in or small places)**
- **Air turbulence while Flying**
- **Addictive Urges (if the first pattern did not work)**

Step One. As you focus on the problem, determine your Subjective Units of Distress (SUD) by rating the upset on a 1 to 10 Scale (1= no upset, 10=worst).

Step Two. Using your fingertips tap about ten times each:

> Side of Hand,
> Under Nose,
> Under Arm,
> Under Eye,
> Under Collarbone,

Step Three. Do the *9 Gamut Series*. While continuously tapping gamut spot:

1. Close eyes
2. Open eyes
3. With your eyes look down and left
4. With your eyes look down and right
5. Whirl your eyes in a complete circle in one direction
6. Whirl your eyes in a complete circle in the other direction
7. Hum a couple bars of any tune
8. Count to five
9. Hum again.

Step Four. Using your fingertips tap about 10 times each:

> Side of Hand,
> Under Nose,
> Under Arm,
> Under Eye,
> Under Collarbone,

Step Five.   Think about the problem in the same way again, rate your upset 1-10 as in step one.

Repeat steps Two through Five until:
Your SUD rating is a 1or 2, then go to Step Six.

Or your SUD rating stops changing then go to NEXT STEPS on page 247.

Step Six: The floor to ceiling eye roll.

While continuously tapping the gamut spot and holding your head level, roll your eyes on a vertical line from the floor to the ceiling over 6–7 seconds.

The BASIC STEPS for:

- **Depression**
- **Physical Pain**

Step One.   As you focus on the problem, determine your Subjective Units of Distress (SUD) by rating the upset on a 1 to 10 Scale (1= no upset, 10=worst).

Step Two.   Using your fingertips tap:

>   Side of Hand 10 times
>   Under Nose 10 times
>   Tap Gamut Spot 50 times
>   Under Collarbone 10 times

Step Three.   Do the *9 Gamut Series*. While continuously tapping gamut spot:

1.   Close eyes
2.   Open eyes
3.   With your eyes look down and left
4.   With your eyes look down and right
5.   Whirl your eyes in a complete circle in one direction
6.   Whirl your eyes in a complete circle in the other direction
7.   Hum a couple bars of any tune
8.   Count to five
9.   Hum again.

Step Four.   Using your fingertips tap:

>   Side of Hand 10 times
>   Under Nose 10 times
>   Tap Gamut Spot 50 times
>   Under Collarbone 10 times

Step Five.   Think about the problem in the same way again, rate your upset 1-10 as in step one.

Repeat steps Two through Five until:

Your SUD rating is a 1or 2, then go to Step Six.

Or your SUD rating stops changing then go to NEXT STEPS on page 247.

Step Six: The floor to ceiling eye roll.

While continuously tapping the gamut spot and holding your head level, roll your eyes on a vertical line from the floor to the ceiling over 6–7 seconds.

The Basic Steps for Rage

Step One.   As you focus on the problem, determine your Subjective Units of Distress (SUD) by rating the upset on a 1 to 10 Scale (1= no upset, 10=worst).

Step Two.   Using your fingertips tap about ten times each:

> Side of Hand,
> Under Nose
> Outside of Eye,
> Under Collarbone,

Step Three.   Do the *9 Gamut Series*. While continuously tapping gamut spot:

1. Close eyes
2. Open eyes
3. With your eyes look down and left
4. With your eyes look down and right
5. Whirl your eyes in a complete circle in one direction
6. Whirl your eyes in a complete circle in the other direction
7. Hum a couple bars of any tune
8. Count to five
9. Hum again.

Step Four.   Using your fingertips tap about ten times each:

> Side of Hand,
> Under Nose,
> Outside of Eye,
> Under Collarbone,

Step Five.   Think about the problem in the same way again, rate your upset 1-10 as in step one.

> Repeat steps Two through Five until:
> Your SUD rating is a 1or 2, then go to Step Six.
>
> Or your SUD rating stops changing then go to

NEXT STEPS on page 247.

Step Six: The floor to ceiling eye roll.

While continuously tapping the gamut spot and holding your head level, roll your eyes on a vertical line from the floor to the ceiling over 6–7 seconds.

The Basic Steps for Shame and Embarrassment

Step One. As you focus on the problem, determine your Subjective Units of Distress (SUD) by rating the upset on a 1 to 10 Scale (1= no upset, 10=worst).

Step Two. Using your fingertips tap about ten times each:

>Side of Hand,
>Under Nose,
>Chin
>Under Collarbone,

Step Three. Do the *9 Gamut Series*. While continuously tapping gamut spot:

1. Close eyes
2. Open eyes
3. With your eyes look down and left
4. With your eyes look down and right
5. Whirl your eyes in a complete circle in one direction
6. Whirl your eyes in a complete circle in the other direction
7. Hum a couple bars of any tune
8. Count to five
9. Hum again.

Step Four. Using your fingertips tap about 10 times each:

>Side of Hand,
>Under Nose,
>Chin
>Under Collarbone,

Step Five. Think about the problem in the same way again, rate your upset 1-10 as in step one.

>Repeat steps Two through Five until:
>Your SUD rating is a 1or 2, then go to Step Six.

>Or your SUD rating stops changing then go to

NEXT STEPS on page 247.

Step Six: The floor to ceiling eye roll.

While continuously tapping the gamut spot and holding your head level, roll your eyes on a vertical line from the floor to the ceiling over 6–7 seconds.

The Basic Steps for Anger

Step One. As you focus on the problem, determine your Subjective Units of Distress (SUD) by rating the upset on a 1 to 10 Scale (1= no upset, 10=worst).

Step Two. Using your fingertips tap about ten times each:

> Side of Hand,
> Under Nose
> Little Finger
> Under Collarbone,

Step Three. Do the *9 Gamut Series*. While continuously tapping gamut spot:

1. Close eyes
2. Open eyes
3. With your eyes look down and left
4. With your eyes look down and right
5. Whirl your eyes in a complete circle in one direction
6. Whirl your eyes in a complete circle in the other direction
7. Hum a couple bars of any tune
8. Count to five
9. Hum again.

Step Four. Using your fingertips tap about ten times each:

> Side of Hand,
> Under Nose,
> Little Finger
> Under Collarbone,

Step Five. Think about the problem in the same way again, rate your upset 1-10 as in step one.

> Repeat steps Two through Five until:
> Your SUD rating is a 1or 2, then go to Step Six.
>
> Or your SUD rating stops changing then go to

NEXT STEPS on page 247.

Step Six: The floor to ceiling eye roll.

While continuously tapping the gamut spot and holding your head level, roll your eyes on a vertical line from the floor to the ceiling over 6–7 seconds.

The Basic Steps for Guilt

Step One.   As you focus on the problem, determine your Subjective Units of Distress (SUD) by rating the upset on a 1 to 10 Scale (1= no upset, 10=worst).

Step Two.   Using your fingertips tap about ten times each:

> Side of Hand,
> Under Nose
> Index Finger,
> Under Collarbone,

Step Three.   Do the *9 Gamut Series*. While continuously tapping gamut spot:

1. Close eyes
2. Open eyes
3. With your eyes look down and left
4. With your eyes look down and right
5. Whirl your eyes in a complete circle in one direction
6. Whirl your eyes in a complete circle in the other direction
7. Hum a couple bars of any tune
8. Count to five
9. Hum again.

Step Four.   Using your fingertips tap about ten times each:

> Side of Hand,
> Under Nose,
> Index Finger,
> Under Collarbone,

Step Five.   Think about the problem in the same way again, rate your upset 1-10 as in step one.

> Repeat steps Two through Five until:
> Your SUD rating is a 1or 2, then go to Step Six.
>
> Or your SUD rating stops changing then go to

NEXT STEPS on the following page.

Step Six: The floor to ceiling eye roll.

While continuously tapping the gamut spot and holding your head level, roll your eyes on a vertical line from the floor to the ceiling over 6–7 seconds.

Next Steps

If the Basic Steps have not helped you at all or have not brought down your Subjective Units of Distress to a 1 on the 1–10 scale, then do the following steps one at a time. After completing each of these steps, repeat the Basic Step for your problem. If this works continue with the Basic Steps until your distress is gone. If the Subjective Units of Distress stops going down again return to Next Steps and try more of the Next Steps.

Next Step #1:

Tap your index finger 15 times. Then rub the sore spot with the flat of your hand as you think of the problem and the upset it causes overall in your life. Repeat the Basic Step for your problem. The sore spot is located on the upper chest and you can find it on one or both sides of the body. You will notice as you rub the area it feels a little more sensitive than rest of the chest. One side may be sorer than the other. Gently work this area for 10–20 seconds.

Next Step #2:

Do the collarbone breathing (see instructions below), and then repeat the Basic Step for the problem.

Next Step #3:

Try a different one of the other Basic Steps. For example, you might need to tap for rage when tapping for anger does not help.

Next Step #4:

Reduce the impact of Individual Energy Toxins by getting some fresh air, drinking a large glass of water, cleaning or rinsing off anything with a scent, such as makeup, perfume, or lotions, change your clothes, or try tapping again on another day or another location. Individual Energy Toxins are discussed later in this part of the book

Next Step #5:

Learn more advanced Thought Field Therapy techniques from other books or training materials, or seek assistance from a peer or professional with more training and experience with Thought Field Therapy. Referrals are available by contacting Dr. Callahan's office: **http://www.tftrx.com**

Next Step #6:

This represents the most important step: Do not give up. You can get better and be healed. Reach out for more help and support. Do not let yourself become isolated and hopeless. Always remember that the world contains many good, caring people who want to help you. Just as you would offer aid to someone reaching out to you, let someone else do what they can to help you. Be prepared to ask for it, though. Don't expect others to know you need help.

Collarbone Breathing Exercise

There are five breathing position that you will use during this exercise:

- Breathe normally.

- Take a full deep breath in, and hold it.

- Let half of that breath out, and hold it.

- Let it all out, and hold it.

- Take a half breath in, and hold it.

The Touching Positions:

1. Take two *fingertips* and touch one of the collarbone points and, with your opposite hand, tap the gamut spot on the back of that hand while going through the five breathing positions. Tap rapidly about five good taps for each of the breathing positions.

2. Now bend the same two fingers towards your palm and touch your *knuckles* on the collarbone point while tapping on your gamut spot with the opposite hand and going through the five breathing positions.

3. Move your *knuckles* to other collarbone point, and tap while going through the five breathing positions again.

4. Now touch the same two *fingertips* to this collarbone point while going through the five breathing positions.

5. Now take *other hand* and repeat steps 1-4 as described above.

When you have finished, you will have completed 40 breathing and tapping exercises, 20 with the fingertips and 20 with the knuckles and five breathing positions on eight touching positions.

Collarbone Breathing Discussion

Occasionally, you may find that your Thought Field Therapy sessions don't work or work very slowly. This happens when the current condition of your psychological and biological system do not allow for normal processing of thought fields. This condition is referred to as *neurological disorganization*.

If you find that your tapping yields no results or that the results seem slow in coming, this may indicate that you need to try something called *Collarbone Breathing*, a fairly simply breathing technique that helps balance the body in such a way that tapping becomes effective once again. You need to try Collarbone Breathing if :

- Thought Field Therapy and/or Psychological Reversal Corrections won't work or won't hold.

- Your Subjective Units of Distress are going down very slowly, i.e., 8, 7, 6, 5, 4, etc.

- You are uncoordinated and awkward.

- You have an unbalanced gait—your arms don't swing evenly and smoothly when you walk. (Four percent of people walk with restricted movement in one arm, and two percent of people walk with both arms restricted, that is with no or limited swing).

- You chronically reverse your actions, concepts, and thoughts.

- Your performance and/or competence are declining.

- Your timing is off and you feel confused.

- Reading makes you yawn or feel sleepy even when rested.

- You are hyperactive.

After you complete the Collarbone Breathing exercise, return to the Basic Steps and start again. As with all Thought Field Therapy, you cannot harm yourself by doing this exercise even if you actually do not need it. So, when in doubt, simply try it and see if your condition improves and if your tapping becomes more successful.

Tips on focusing your work

To begin using the Thought Field Therapy process, you identify your upset. What is the picture in your mind, the idea in your head, the memory you are recalling, the sensations in you body, or the emotions you are feeling? As you focus your attention on this, you tune in to what you will address with your tapping and the change you want. You do not have to spend a lot of time on this. As soon as you become aware of the triggered sensation or your overwhelming upset, you can go on to rate the level of upset you feel.

Sometimes you will not find the focus in a mental picture or memory but rather in a feeling you cannot shake. Feeling depressed, afraid, angry, or uneasy in some way without a conscious link to any incident from the past or present interactions can provide a way to tune your focus for a Thought Field Therapy session as well. Just focus on the feeling or sensation. After you tap for that emotion you may make sense out of what you are experiencing or find it easier to do so.

Some people have difficulty experiencing or feeling the upset when they are not in the presence of the problem or trigger situation. Just thinking about it may not cause a difficulty until they are directly reminded of it in some organic way—a sight, a smell, a sound, an action, or event around them. These people know they have a problem but only can experience it when presented with it directly. You can see this condition in small children who have limited language and cognitive skills. Asking them to think about their trigger may not set off the overwhelming feelings that can be rated. Sometimes we have expended a lot of energy learning to separate ourselves from overwhelming feelings. We learn to do it so well that we cannot experience the upset even when we choose to do so.

To solve this problem, place yourself in the situation that brings up your overwhelming feelings. Be careful and gentle with yourself. As soon as you begin to feel upset, begin tapping. No need exists for you to become overwhelmed to get the help you need. You can also consider exposing yourself to related experiences and conditions and rating your upset in those situations. For example, if you know from experience that you become upset in a certain location but do not feel the same upset when you remember being in that place, imagine that you are going to travel to that place and notice how reluctant you are to going there. You can rate your degree of reluctance or trepidation, and use that to guide your tapping.

When you have pinpointed a focus for your Thought Field Therapy session, do not worry about staying concentrated on the initial subject during your tapping. Once you have placed your attention there, it will stay there. If you could easily slip off the subject and not feel the upset, you would not need to read this book. That said, it can be helpful to note in your mind or in a journal the source of your upset as you begin tapping so you will be aware afterwards of what changes. For example, if you retain the same mental focus, sometimes after tapping the pictures in your mind will change. Sometimes the pictures will be of a different scene or viewed from different angle. The change you experience may be in the intensity or location of sensation in your body. You may notice a change in the focus of your thinking, and that indicates positive change as well. However, as long as you see positive change occurring of any type as you tap, keep using Though Field Therapy as necessary.

Tips on Rating Your Level of Upset

The next step in performing Thought Field Therapy involves rating your level of upset. Using the Subjective Units of Distress, sometimes referred to as the SUD rating, offers a simple and direct means of tracking and sharing what is going on or changing in your reality as you move through the tapping procedure. In the end, it only matters how you feel. For this reason, when doing Thought Field Therapy you must track your emotional or physical progress so you know if you are feeling better or not. You do this using a 10 point rating scale.

The second step you will take when using Thought Field Therapy, therefore, requires rating your emotional or physical starting point. When you think of the problem or situation you have decided to focus upon for your Thought Field Therapy session, then rate how much distress you feel *with 1 representing no distress and 10 representing the worst distress possible.* Your rating should be based upon what you are experiencing in this moment. Of course, the last time you experienced this feeling or when the traumatic event actually occurred you probably felt differently than you do now. In Thought Field Therapy, we concern ourselves only with what is happening now, how you feel in this current moment.

Here are some ideas about how to find and rate your Subjective Units of Distress. As you think about the problem:

- Focus on how heavy or light you feel.

- Notice how tight or relaxed your body feels.

- Rate how restricted vs. how easy breathing feels.

- Focus on the location of the distress in your body

- If rating with numbers feels too difficult, try showing the size of the problem by spreading you arms apart or bringing your hands together.

- If the rating scale doesn't work for you, use a smiley-face/sad-face chart.

Remember the 1 to 10 scale simply provides a way to measure change that occurred during tapping and to direct you to the next Thought Field Therapy action you need to take. You cannot rate your feelings or sensations incorrectly, and only you can determine your Subjective Units of Distress rating. Find a way to rate your Subjective Units of Distress that works for you. The more you use the Subjective Units of Distress scale, the easier it will become to recognize and rate your feeling and sensations.

If you are still having difficulty finding a way to gauge how you feel, try rating how well your mind works while focused on the problem. Some people find it easier to rate how well they perceive what is around them than how they actually feel. They may rate their clarity of vision or sharpness of hearing. Ask yourself how well you are able to concentrate or do problem solving while focused on the upset. Then rate this ability. How well your mind is working is an indicator of the level of impact focusing on the problem is having on you overall. For example, a 1 would equate to: "My perceptions are clear and my analysis of the situation is precise." A 10 would equate to: "My perceptions are blurry and muddy and my analysis of the situation cannot even begin." Each person will develop a sense of what elements are important to rate in their change efforts.

After each tapping sequence, once again rate your Subjective Units of Distress. Find a way to measure the change occurring that works for you. For one man it was how well his eyes focused. When he started tapping, he could barely make out some writing on a poster, but by the time he finished he could easily read even the small text on the wall. For one woman, it was how well she could write. When she began tapping, her cursive writing was weak and barely understandable even to her. When she finished, everyone was able read her writing. Another person's ability to concentrate on or analyze a cognitive problem was the standard used. For other people, they simply use their emotions as a indicator.

You are done tapping when you are no longer overwhelmed by the upset or when you get to 1 on the Subjective Units of Distress. You may never get to a place where you feel good about the focus of the tapping. For example, if you were tapping to relieve a snake phobia, do not expect when you are done you that you will like or enjoy snakes. Thought Field Therapy will eliminate your overwhelming upset, but it will not change reality.

Understanding Psychological Reversal

Psychological Reversal literally is a state of reversed direction of energy flow in the body. This state or condition blocks natural healing and prevents otherwise effective treatment from working. It also causes a person to reverse concepts, number, or words. For example, you may say north when you mean south, or you may be talking about something on your left and point to your right. Psychological Reversal can impact your mood and behavior in negative ways as well.

Psychological Reversal in the physical body sometimes can be measured by using a voltmeter. A voltmeter is used to measure the electrical energy in people. If you use it to measure a person enjoying good health with no psychological reversal, the direct current of the body will be measured in positive numbers. However, when people have a health condition, such as a specific pain or wound, they often also will suffer from a psychological reversal. The direct current of that person's body will flow in the opposite direction and be measured by the voltmeter in negative numbers.

Psychological Reversal is *not* something you can choose or control. One does not intend to be reversed; it just happens without conscious thought. Until the psychological reversal is corrected, however, no healing technique will work. Psychological Reversal represents a common occurrence, and making the correction for it is an important element in Thought Field Therapy procedures. Psychological Reversal is corrected by tapping on the side of the hand and tapping under the nose in the Basic Steps. Rubbing the sore spot is recommended in Next Steps if the corrections are not working or holding. This basically means that your Thought Field Therapy sessions, or the tapping procedures, are not working, then you may be experiencing a neurological disorganization, as discussed earlier. In such a case, you may need to do the Collarbone Breathing exercise. Additionally, if you cannot correct a psychological reversal with the mechanisms built into the tapping procedures in this book, you may have an Individual Energy Toxin interfering with your Thought Field Therapy.

Understanding and Identifying Individual Energy Toxins

When Thought Field Therapy works and the emotional upset or problem being addressed is resolved, then you have healed your open wound, at least to some degree. You have found a cure. In most cases, this cure will last, but, in some, the cure will be temporary and the disturbances and symptoms will show up again. The wound will reopen

However, as mentioned earlier, sometimes Thought Field Therapy will not work at all. After working with many clients, Dr. Callahan determined that the cause of this difficulty lay not with the tapping procedure itself but a person's negative reaction to exposure to certain substances. These substances may be found in everyday life situations. Many people may not have a reaction to them or not be bothered to a point of awareness by them, but for some people they cause serious problems. Since the reactions these substances cause are unique to each individual and affect the person's energy systems in specific ways, they are called Individual Energy Toxins. Individual Energy Toxins come in many forms, and these substances can be ingested, inhaled, or enter your system simply by contact.

Common Individual Energy Toxins include tobacco, alcohol, pesticides, and various chemicals found in clothing, carpets, upholstery, paint, etc. However, many Individual Energy Toxins are found in unexpected products and places, such as in wheat, corn, eggs, milk and other dairy products, perfume, laundry soap, scented tissue, or deodorants.

Allergies and Toxic Sensitivities are not the same thing. You can have a toxic sensitivity to a substance and not be allergic to it. However, if you have an allergy to a substance, you often will have a toxic sensitivity to it as well. For this reason, it becomes important to recognize your allergies and to avoid exposure to those allergens as much as possible. For the same reason, one should avoid exposure to Individual Energy Toxins once you have identified a toxic sensitivity. The general stress and specific-system demands of such exposure drain you both physically and energetically. In the case of allergies, exposure to an allergen can cause disruption of the whole bodily system. In the case of Toxic Sensitivity, Individual Energy Toxins can cause disturbances energetically, which results in upset and sometimes in chronic conditions.

Allergies are a medical condition and can be diagnosed by blood and skin tests given by a physician. Toxic Sensitivities can be identified in several ways, which are discussed in the next section. Once you have identified your Individual Energy Toxins, stay away from them as much as possible. This will help maintain positive results from your Though Field Therapy work or allow Thought Field Therapy to work initially. Plus, you will remain healthier and more balanced in general.

Methods for Identifying Individual Energy Toxins

Method 1: Find the Patterns

When a Thought Field Therapy cure has been undone or has not held and your level of distress goes back up after the distress had been eliminated while focused on the it, you have been exposed to an Individual Energy Toxin. Notice what you have eaten or inhaled prior to the return of the problem, and look for patterns in your psychological and physical responses to exposure to certain things with which you have come into contact. Think about everything you did—what you ate, when you put on perfume or lotion, if you noticed a strong smell in the elevator—and then think about how you felt afterwards. Also, outside of your Thought Field Therapy sessions, notice when you are having a bad day or moment. Then track what you have eaten, inhaled, etc. Your family and friends may have already noticed some patterns, so ask them for input. It also can be a great help to keep a journal to record your daily exposures.

Method 2: Use a Pulse Test

Dr. Arthur F. Coca, author of *The Pulse Test*, provides extensive background and instruction in his book for using your pulse to help identify Individual Energy Toxins. To do so, find your baseline pulse when at rest and compare this to your pulse immediately after and up to an hour after exposures to something you think might be an Individual Energy Toxin. A heart rate of more than 84 beats per minute usually indicates ongoing exposure to an Individual Energy Toxin. An increase of pulse rate of more than a few beats after exposure will also identify sensitivity.

Method 3: A Significant Drop in Heart Rate Variability

This method, unfortunately, requires special equipment and special training, but it represents one of the best objective measures of the impact of Individual Energy Toxins on the body. Heart Rate Variability is defined as the difference in time between heart beats measured in milliseconds. By looking at how your heart rate varies when you are exposed to certain possible toxins, you can identify if these actually constitute your Individual Energy Toxins. (For more information on this method, read Chapter 18 in *Stop the Nightmares of Trauma* by Dr. Callahan.)

Method 4: Thought Field Therapy Causal Diagnosis

Thought Field Therapy causal diagnosis using kinesiology muscle testing can quickly identify Individual Energy Toxins. Callahan Techniques® Thought Field Therapy also has a procedure for neutralizing the effects of symptoms of these toxins called the Seven Second Treatment. This treatment will be of great help when you are not able to avoid the cause of the problem or have a great many individual energy sensitivities. Anyone can learn the skills of causal diagnosis from books, home study programs, or taking Thought Field Therapy approved training. A video home study package with instructions for identifying and neutralizing Individual Energy Toxins may be purchased from Dr. Callahan's Website WWW.TFTRX.COM

Thought Field Therapy for Other Conditions

Callahan Techniques® Thought Field Therapy has been used successfully to treat many other conditions besides traumatic stress. The focus of this book has been on traumatic stress recovery. As such, the stories told, the examples provided, and the general information has been limited to wounds incurred from traumatic stressor events and how to heal them. Beyond the emotional and psychological states and conditions discussed in this book, Thought Field Therapy is used to treat and manage the full range of psychological problems. These include schizophrenia, eating disorders, obsessive/compulsive disorders, panic attacks not related to traumatic stress, depression, post-partum depression, bipolar disorders, somatoform disorders, and sexual disorders. If you have been labeled with a psychiatric disorder, or if you know some one who has been labeled with one, then Thought Field Therapy may help. Psychological factors affecting medical conditions and treatments also respond to Thought Field Therapy.

Many medical conditions respond to Thought Field Therapy as well. Thought Field Therapy can and should be used with any and all other effective treatments for serious illnesses. Cancer, phantom pain, and chronic pain of many types, for instance, often are responsive to Thought Field Therapy techniques. In most serious illnesses, complete recovery involves more advanced knowledge and skill with tapping than presented in this book. They may also require treatment by a medical doctor as well. Thought Field Therapy cannot necessarily cure cancer, but it provides a treatment aid in correction for Psychological Reversal and is effective with reducing many symptoms of the illness and the repercussions of its medical treatment. For example, Thought Field Therapy can be used to eliminate the side effects of chemotherapy. For those patients with heart disease and diabetes, Thought Field Therapy treatments improve heart rate variability. Thought Field Therapy can help speed up physical therapy. You do not have to stop your current medications or therapies to use Thought Field Therapy. In fact, you should not stop your current medications or therapies until you know you it is safe to do so. Just add some Thought Field Therapy into your treatment plan, and check with your doctor about your medications and therapies as you begin to feel better.

Just as with traumatic stress recovery, no matter the issue you choose to address with Thought Field Therapy, you must actively engage in the healing process regardless of the injury or illness impacting your life. The responsibility to be aware of your condition, to make healthy choices, to seek assistance when you are not progressing, and to find health love, joy, is yours alone.

Thought Field Therapy and the NOW approach to full recovery have been presented in this book to help you heal the wounds of your traumatic past. I hope that you use them, but also that you share both methods with others, as well as the body of evidence you created as you went through this book.

Resources

Comments and Questions about this book:
www.NoOpenWounds.com

Thought Field Therapy Center of San Diego:
www.RLBray.com

Association for Thought Field Therapy:
www.atft.org

Callahan Techniques® Thought Field Therapy:
www.tftrx.com

Bray, R L, 2006. Thought Field Therapy:Working Through Traumatic Stress Without the Overwhelming Responses. In J.Garrick & MB Willams (Eds.) *Trauma Treatment Techniques: Innovative Trends.* NY, The Haworth Maltreatment & Trauma Press

Callahan, R., & Callahan, J. (1997). Thought Field Therapy: Aiding the bereavement process. In C. Figley, B. E. Bride, & N. Mazza (Eds.), *Death and Trauma: The traumatology of grieving* (pp. 246-266). Washington: Taylor and Francis

Callahan, R. & Callahan, J. (2000). *Stop the nightmares of trauma.* Chapel Hill, NC: Professional Press

Callahan, R. & Trubo, R. (2001) *Tapping the healer within.* New York: Contemporary/McGraw-Hill

Carbonell, J. L., & Figley, C. (1999). A systematic clinical demonstration of promising PTSD treatment approaches. *Electronic Journal of Traumatology,* 5(1), Article 4 [On-Line].

Connolly, S. (2004) *Thought Field Therapy Clinical Applications Integrating TFT in Psychotherapy.* George Tyrrell Press

Cooper, J. (2001). Thought Field Therapy. *Complementary Therapies in Nursing and Midwifery,* 7(3), 162-165.

Folkes, C. (2002). Thought Field Therapy in Trauma Recovery. *International Journal of Emergency Mental Health*, 4(2), 99-103.

Johnson, C., Shala, M., Sejdijaj, X., Odell, R., & Dabishevci, D. (2001). Thought Field Therapy – Soothing the bad moments of Kosovo. *Journal of Clinical Psychology*, 57, 1237-1240.

Schaefer, J. (2002). *The pretzel man: A true story of phobias and & back problems*. Bloomington IN. 1st Books.

Index

A

action
- action processes of recovery, 123–24
- action steps for healing can get in the way, 117
- choosing actions that match beliefs and values, 137

active engagement, 104

acts of nature, unexpectedness of, 151

Acute Stress Disorder, 19, 75

addictions, overcoming, 21–23, 181–99
- alcohol, 22, 34, 111, 182, 196
  - determining if you are out of control, 183–84
  - using alcohol to get to sleep, 186–89
  - withdrawal from, 189–90
- Basic Steps
  - for Addictions (if other doesn't work), 228, 235–36
  - for Addictive Urges, 228, 233–34
- behavioral addictions, 196–99
  - determining if you are out of control, 184
  - fighting as an addiction, 22
  - high-risk behavior as an addiction, 22, 105, 184, 196
  - sex as an addiction, 22, 196
  - story of dealing with control of weight (Susan), 197–98
  - weight gain or loss, 22, 105, 183, 196–97
- drugs, 22, 111, 182
  - determining if you are out of control, 183
  - failing to find a balance in use of, 187–89
  - story of dealing with smoking marijuana (author's story), 193–95
  - withdrawal from, 189–90
- smoking as an addiction [story dealing with (Robbie)], 190–93
- traumatic stressors driving people's addictions, 193

aging process, anger at, 146–47

Air Turbulence in Flight, Basic Steps for, 228, 235–36

alcohol as an addiction. See under addictions, overcoming

algorithms, Thought Field Therapy, 32–33, 227. See also Basic Steps

Alice [story about dealing with childhood sexual and physical abuse], 83–84

allergies vs. Toxic Sensitivities, 256–57. See also Individual Energy Sensitivities to Toxins

American Psychiatric Association, 64, 81
- *Diagnostic and Statistical Manual of Mental Disorders* , 64, 68, 85, 87

analogies used
- blue print analogy, 29–30
- car's electrical system analogy, 73–74
- computer analogy, 46–47
- currents and water analogy, 150–52, 153–54

Collarbone Breathing Exercise, 255
computer analogy, 46–47
control
    determining what controls you, 204
    lack of control, 181, 182, 192, 214
    out of control, 5, 13, 68, 77, 113, 114, 150–52, 162, 179–80, 182, 189, 199
        determining if you are, 89, 131, 165, 183–85, 204, 211
coping mechanisms, 67–68, 69–70, 89, 125, 131, 165, 204, 211
    extreme coping mechanisms, 216–18
    numbness, 110–11
    self-destructive [dysfunctional] coping mechanisms, 33, 36, 68, 87, 141,
        182, 185, 186, 188
courage for change, 223
CTTFT. See Callahan Techniques® Thought Field Therapy
current moment, staying in the. See now, being in the
current position, identifying, 106–08
currents and water analogy, 150–52, 153–54

D

Dan [story about shooting in a high school], 27–28
danger
    creating a safe environment, 106–08
    dangerous behaviors, 22, 182, 184. See also addictions, overcoming;
        high-risk behavior as an addiction
    story about fear of danger, 43–44
day-to-day stressors. See everyday stressors vs. traumatic stressors
death. See also grief
    of a child, 66
    healing traumatic loss of loved ones and handling grief, 161–80
    stories as examples
        dealing with anger at God about aging (minister), 146–47
        dealing with father's death (author's story), 172–73
        dealing with helping self while helping others handle child's
            death (author's story), 163–65
        dealing with loss of a child's pet (Bobby and Sierra), 174–79
        dealing with violent death of son (Bea), 130–31
        death of innocent people (chaplain), 52–53
        learning to understand death of fiancé, 122–23
    what you own at life's end, 157
decision making, 33, 72, 95, 104, 112, 119, 130, 139, 182, 206, 210
    purpose-driven decisions, 103–04
    reactions vs. decisions, 120, 156
depression, 2, 32, 34
    Basic Steps for Depression, 228, 237–38
    linked to a past traumatic event, 251
DESNOS. See Disorder Of Extreme Stress Not Otherwise Specified
destination, 112–13

fears, 10, 14, 16, 19, 37, 38, 56, 87, 154, 156. *See also* phobias
    Basic Steps
        for Air Turbulence in Flight, 228, 235–36
        for Claustrophobia, 228, 235–36
        for Phobias and Fears, 228, 233–34
        for Spiders, 228, 235–36
    fear and pain, 15, 16, 17, 19, 49, 56, 186, 211
    of the future, 1, 5, 20, 45, 58, 90, 156
    irrational fears. *See* phobias
    linked to a past traumatic event, 251
    and pain, 9, 10, 57, 105, 154, 182, 183
field, definition of, 29–30
fighting as an addiction, 22
fight-or-flight response, 72, 188
flashbacks, 37, 69, 124, 128, 186
flying, fear of, 228, 235–36
focus, 84, 126, 129, 154
    on changes in your reality. *See* Subjective Units of Distress
    focusing on traumatic events, 13, 45, 46, 72, 105, 128, 153, 162, 197, 202
        tips for focusing on your work, 251–52
    improving focus, 36, 96, 104
Fred [story about dealing with anger and rage after of 9/11], 131–35
future fears, 1, 5, 20, 45, 58, 90, 156

G

gait, unbalanced, 250
Gamut Series, 30, 58
    location of gamut spot, iii, iv, 229, 230
    use of in Basic Steps, i–ii, 231–32, 233–34, 235–36, 237–38, 239–40,
        241–42, 243–44, 245–46
    use of in Collarbone Breathing Exercise, 250
Grace [story about inability to sleep], 25–27
grief, 66, 161–80
    death of a child, 66
    grief process, 162–63
    importance of grieving, 161, 165–66
    stories as examples
        allowing self to grieve after son's death, 166–68
        dealing with father's death (author's story), 172–73
        dealing with grief by not sleeping (Linda), 186–87
        dealing with helping self while helping others handle child's
          death (author's story), 163–65
        dealing with loss of a child's pet (Bobby and Sierra), 174–79
        dealing with violent death of son (Bea), 130–31
        grief leading to an affair, 168–71
        learning to understand death of fiancé, 122–23

M

N

CPSIA information can be obtained at www.ICGtesting.com
Printed in the USA
LVOW121352250312

274429LV00004B/2/P